EMERGE
Be You!

HUGHES SUFFREN

Copyright © 2023 by Hughes Suffren

All rights reserved. No part of this book may be reproduced or used in any manner without written permission of the copyright owner except for the use of quotations in a book review. For more information, address: hughes@hughessuffren.com.

First edition: June 2023

Cover art by Andrew Ostrovsky
Cover design by Steve Kuhn

ISBN 979-8-9894363-0-9 (paperback)
ISBN 979-8-9894363-1-6 (ebook)

www.hughessuffren.com

For more information on how we may serve you, visit www.hughessuffren.com

To read Hughes' latest thoughts on self-discovery and authenticity, visit www.hughessuffren.com/blog

CONTENTS

Author's Note 9
Introduction 11

Section One: Transcending Boundaries 16
   The Takeover 18
   Chapter One: The Weight of Our Fears 19
      Nature and Self-Empowerment 23
      When Others Answer Your Questions of Purpose 25
      Falling and Getting Up 31
   Chapter Two: Events Do Not Define Us 34
      Engineering Your Will 36
   Chapter Three: We Are What We Are 41
   Chapter Four: People-Pleasing Is Self-Sacrifice, Not Leadership 54
      Fear of Failure 55

Section Two: Achieving Through Dreaming 60
   Surrender to Your Dreams 62
   Chapter Five: Take Your Thoughts and Dreams Captive 63
   Chapter Six: Dreams Offer Pathways to Achievement 68
   Chapter Seven: Dream of the World You Want to Live In 74
      Manifest Your Dreams 78
   Chapter Eight: Living the Dream 81
   Chapter Nine: Carl Taylor's Dream 86

Section Three: Being in the Zone 94
   I Got This 96
   Chapter Ten: Slow Motion, Part 1 97
   Chapter Eleven: Slow Motion, Part 2 102

    The Flow State 106

    Chapter Twelve: Motorcycle Days 108

Section Four: Perspective, Progress, and Strategies 112

    Fascinating, Isn't It? 114

    Chapter Thirteen: The Story of Mary Ann, Part 1 115

    Chapter Fourteen: Life Is a Journey 124

        Learning From Mistakes 128

        We're All on Different Paths 130

        Progress May Be a Stone Thrown Away 131

        Coping Strategies 135

        Coping Strategy 1: Withdrawal 135

        Coping Strategy 2: Separation 136

        Coping Strategy 3: Assimilation 138

        Jill 138

        Marisha 139

        Sarah 140

        Rachel 141

        Coping Strategy 4: Self-Affirmation 142

    Chapter Fifteen: The Story of Mary Ann, Part 2 147

Section Five: Transformative Insights 154

    Uplift! 156

    Chapter Sixteen: Emerging 157

    Chapter Seventeen: Valuable Perspectives 159

        My Father's Practical Wisdom for Powerful Living 168

Section 6: Control What You Can 174

    Trouble Won't Last 176

    Chapter Eighteen: Control What You Can 177

    Chapter Nineteen: My Video Won't Go Viral 186

        Merging Schooling and Education 191

        Breaking Point 192

Chapter Twenty: Cross-Country Trip 200
Chapter Twenty-One: Conflicting Impulses 207
Chapter Twenty-Two: Accepting Does Not Mean Giving Up 216
Chapter Twenty-Three: What Is Your Legacy? 228
    Stone 1: Self-Acceptance 230
    Stone 2: Self-Help 231
    Stone 3: Self-Preservation 237
    Stone 4: Self-Discovery 239

Acknowledgments 243

AUTHOR'S NOTE

Overcoming Insanity

In abject secrecy,
We deliberately walk the plank.
Anxiety-filled, still willing to leap,
Trading our brilliance for shiny fragments
Others portray as their whole.

Betrayers dance among us
Without integrity, beat or poise.
Like sheep, we flock,
Conned and cloned,
Ambitions within destroyed.

Click-type friends only follow
To record you at your worst.
Pay no mind to your trauma.
There's only whether they posted first.

If what makes you, you, were currency,
Would you value their nature more?
Vain appetites covet stranger's dreams.
Our dreams we just ignore.

Self-discovery unleashes power
Kept tightly locked inside.
We have the key but seek elsewhere first.
Lust for our truth and our worth
In material and external guides.

Meanwhile, some of us discovered
Vast power in us all along.
We found that overcoming elevates
God's spirit in our song.

My brain summons champion's thoughts.
Through life's ebbs and flows, I pray.
Then defining myself to the world, courageously,
Living life my way.

Overcoming insanity!

Hughes Suffren

INTRODUCTION

My target was one thousand revolutions as I mimicked boxers in training, hard-core fitness enthusiasts, or anyone skilled at jumping rope. Borrowing the state-of-the-art jump rope had much to say about my confidence, or maybe I was showing off by taking it. Indeed, all eyes were on me as memories of my jump rope prowess as an adolescent were vivid. Yet, maxing out at six jumps before a failed turn was present and why was unclear. Over and over again, the rope wrapped around my shins or slapped me on the back. "This crap is stupid!" I shouted. It looked like other people skipped rope effortlessly. I contained the f-bomb that also wanted to move freely. Then, I vowed, out loud again: "Time to try something different." I reimagined the form of advanced jumpers and their tricks. For example, I tried running in place while jumping. I failed. I tried jumping higher to keep the momentum going. That didn't work. Searching for a quick fix, I repositioned my hands when I felt a miss was imminent. I bombed. You precisely know my frustration; its nature thrives on eating away people's confidence.

I couldn't give up. I was determined to reach one thousand. Numb from attempts and failures, I paused for two deep breaths and relaxed momentarily after my second exhalation. When I started jumping again, I silently counted revolutions and no longer barked numbers out loud. Then, as I was experiencing success, I stopped counting altogether. Technically, I didn't need to track my jumps. Instead, the rope's Bluetooth technology synced the running tally to my phone, which I had carefully placed in my line of sight. Less noise allowed me to focus on the rhythm of my jumps. It was my rhythm and nobody else's to copy. Soon afterward, I increased my rate of successful jumps to an occasional miss. Then, I mainly stopped to recover from fatigue.

It was clear that mediocrity was my destination had I continued to follow someone else's pattern. What other people considered their natural movement was awkward for me, no matter how hard I tried. Among other lessons, I learned that stops and starts were much more demanding than fluid motion. Figuratively, one was the herky-jerky jabs of stop-and-roll traffic, and the other was a smooth-flowing drive along the coast with the top down. Efficiency, then, wasn't born out of effort. Instead, my limbs and jumps moved in unison once I connected to what I already had inside of me. Ultimately, it was up to me to let "me" come out.

Emerge: Be You! means actualizing your untapped power for optimal living. You may picture a phoenix rising, Hercules breaking his chains, or Nelson Mandela leaving prison after 27 years and becoming president of South Africa. All are visual depictions of what it means to emerge. Yet, all the power you need to achieve is being yourself.

Unfortunately, the dance between seeking to live outside of self and forcibly returning out of necessity is commonplace. For example, for differentiation, we release radical representations of ourselves while "likes" and "follows" herd us into a copycat's world that thirsts for the following trifecta: approval, connection, and importance. Through our devices, we will solve our need to communicate something that will capture all three; if we're lucky, our message will circle the earth. Does no sacrifice seem too great for the chance to go viral? What natural utility will we ignore for the sake of being different, which ultimately makes us all the same? Soon, if not already, you may discover that the chase brings only the noise of newer, more substantial hurdles, constraints, or ceilings. However, this book will detail ways to access your power to improve your future through a series of true stories. Each one reveals various methods you can use to walk your way. The most challenging part is deciding to emerge despite dissatisfaction, frustration, or failure. Fortunately, you can do this at any time and any age.

Emerge: Be You! is a call, a command, a challenge, and a philosophy to embrace. For example, two boxers sat exhausted in their respective corners before the final round of their fight. Each fighter had beaten the other to a pulp. Yet, simultaneously, each boxer wanted to throw in the towel—quit. Rumors circulated that at that moment, each boxer told his cornerman that the other guy was too crazy. However, one cornerman famously called out his fighter for all the fighter's big talk while promoting the fight. He said, "I thought you said you are the greatest." With that, Muhamad Ali got up at the sound of the bell. He defeated Joe Frazier, who did not get up. And by simply standing, Ali emerged again as the World's Heavyweight Champion.

I understand we do not all have a cornerman as Ali did in Angelo Dundee, who knew where to find Ali's hot button and when to press it. Thankfully, our pivotal moments are not always born in battle. Still, like Ali, our uplift requires serious individual critique followed by action. *Emerge: Be You!* provides a way to move with such intention.

The cover of *Emerge: Be You!* is a powerful and inspiring image of a person rising, metaphorically embodying the book's message that we all have the power within us to create the life we want if we believe in ourselves and tap into our inherent resources. On this premise, the first of *Emerge*'s six sections will expound on personal impressions concerning fear and how it holds us back. These chapters examine our responsibility for digging deep to discover who we are, affirming our true selves, and moving with purpose. Like the Ali story, if living with intention and purpose are worthwhile goals, so must our appetite for introspection. Then, the ability to muster individual strength and attract resources for progress follows. In discussing these and other topics, I reveal moral dilemmas that will encourage side discussions rather than wholehearted agreement. I hope you insert yourself into the stories and keep the conversations going by saying, "I agree, or I would have done this instead." One way to address deep-seated issues is by making them relatable. I have done that by emphasizing the need to answer critical life questions. The first and most important question is, "Who am I?"

Section 2 will focus more precisely on our dreams' role in overcoming challenges and reaching peak performance in all areas of our lives. The ability to control your dreams will offer a broader perspective on our untapped power. Section 3 relies on personal stories to drive home dreams coming to life and how your body can switch to autopilot once you've done the work of mental and physical preparation. Athletes call it "being in the zone." Reaching this level of behavior or performance is life changing.

Section 4 introduces Mary Ann, a woman who understands what it means to chase something elusive. In her case, it is weight loss. For change to come, she must be open to removing things and even people that work against her interests. That we must place a greater emphasis on who we let into our inner circle is revealing. For one thing, those who start with you may not finish with you. This section also includes a chapter that shares a strategy for becoming your best "you." Overall, this section addresses the importance of knowing what you must give up and what you must surrender to.

Since we all have imperfect knowledge, I offer many perspectives in Section 5. Here, I ask that you examine traditions that lead us to think as we do. For example, we weren't made feeble, hateful, or fearful. Therefore, changing perspectives may require shifting what you give energy or power. Let's agree that everything must change. That would also lead to conceding that we can change what we've been. Finally, Section 6 discusses the impact of trauma on our decisions, emerging, and helping others emerge. If you carefully read this chapter, you will consider ways your traumas repeat and might consume you if you don't give them the attention they need.

Rather than cite many other works, I use personal stories fraught with challenges to drive home my conclusions. Where I can, I also use two approaches to provide clarity: biblical scripture and nature. Both guide us to truth and harmony differently; the former explains, and the latter offers living examples. All the stories in this book are true, although I have changed most of the names.

Finally, my early training in higher education administration taught me that we must strive for consensus. Sometimes we scheduled meetings just to schedule more meetings to get on one accord, literally meeting to meet. At the same time, my daily experiences proved that people disagree on facts and that no amount of discussion will find agreement for everyone. Therefore, people will debate *Emerge: Be You!* as well. Thus, I hope that you will approach this information willing to take what you find helpful. Ask questions about things that spark your curiosity. Create a persuasive argument supporting my viewpoint for all you oppose. Then, see where you land. Emerge. Be you!

Section One

TRANSCENDING BOUNDARIES

The Takeover

When doubt, exhaustion, and fear converge,
Scattered thinking and crippling thoughts emerge,
Unforced, unwelcomed, and relentless.

This takeover happens with your permission(s).
You're both destroyer and the victim.
Fitting in is dying, not livin'.

Hughes Suffren

CHAPTER ONE
THE WEIGHT OF OUR FEARS

It was chilling to see mom too far away to grasp the pool's edge; a couple of strokes and kicks might have propelled her close enough to reach. Instead, she thrashed the water with her palms and coughed up some. Onlookers refused to go near her. They seemed to heed a warning we know all too well: stay away from a person drowning because a panicking victim may take you down with them. Everyone watched in horror and distress as she screamed. She gurgled and spat and continued to splash the water heavy-handedly. Even the lifeguards watched with concern and still chose not to intervene when she needed them. How could they refuse to extend their long lifesaving pole for mom to grab?

We all knew mom couldn't swim when dad pushed her into the public pool. Maybe he hadn't noticed that she wasn't wearing wrist and ankle floaties or a bright orange life jacket. Not likely. Those items were personal luxuries owned by rich people and not complimentary at the city park's public pool. The staggering reality was that personal floatation devices would have saved her. Likewise, a strong swimmer, like my dad, could have rescued mom if he had taken her panic seriously. Instead, dad never talked about why he pushed her or whether he regrets ignoring her desperate gasps that would rush into our nightmares. He frowned and dismissed us with a wave when we questioned him about his role as the perpetrator. Sometimes, he would make a "chups" sound by sucking spit behind his teeth. Caribbean people make that noise when they hear something they have deemed absurd.

Dad was unfazed in the moments following his homicidal shove. He just walked quickly in the opposite direction toward the high dive without looking back, no doubt overselling that he did nothing wrong. My eyes followed the beginning of dad's brutal act to him standing, arms outstretched, overwhelmed at the end. I also saw regret behind his tough exterior, as if he could not look away quickly enough when we asked about it. Of course, he would demonstratively deny that too. As time passed, I stopped asking.

Instinctively, I would have done anything to help my mom. Paralysis stole any well-intentioned heroics instead. After all, experiencing shock could happen to any kid who witnesses the demise of two people in this world they thought were invincible. I might remember one as a cold-hearted killer and the other as one who allowed something as familiar as water to overcome her. Then, as quickly as it started, it ended. She was no longer screaming at a fever pitch. The retching sound of her coughing spit, which pooled at the back of her throat, was gone. Absent also were her strong flailing arms and lurching panic. Instead, mom popped up and stood in the waist-high water, embarrassed and laughing.

Everybody got a big laugh that day, and we still do every time mom retells the story. She's a great storyteller who is not afraid to laugh at herself. Our family is chock-full of storytellers who can deliver daily encounters or our family history with punchline endings and laugh hysterically at each authentic account. Tragically, of course, mom's screams were also genuine. Her quick guttural gasps and throaty, broken words and sentences were hard to forget.

Nonetheless, I learned an essential lesson from that moment in the pool. Mom nearly drowned by the weight of her fears. I suspect that everyone can apply that lesson metaphorically. Think about it. Because of fear, real or imagined, someone may not introduce themselves to a crush, ask for a raise, speak on stage, seek additional education, change jobs, or start a business. Thus, one further aspect of fear is its paradox—that when opportunities pass, and they will pass, people have allowed their obsession with feeling safe and secure to sabotage their futures.

However, as demonstrated in the pool example, my father favored total immersion against fear, reasoning that to be scared was weak and silly. Now, I am not suggesting that we take fear lightly. On the contrary, fear can be a paralyzing emotion that may resurface if not adequately challenged. Therefore, my interpretation of dad's push is that we must address our fears head-on or fall victim to them. We can't afford to give away our power, which is the same as not using it. Both tendencies will impede our growth.

The apparent irony is that while fear played a critical role in mom's panic, she could have changed her circumstances at any time. Consider this apt biblical reference: "Therefore put on the full armor of God, so that when the day of evil comes, you may be able to stand your ground, and after you have done everything, to stand" (Ephesians 6:13 NIV). I am not a Bible scholar. Nevertheless, my interpretation of that scripture is that we are more than enough even when we feel trapped by the relentless cycle of life's circumstances. We have at our command strength, agility, creative thought, and all sorts of skills and tools to produce our desired outcomes, and in every instance, the first thing we must do is stand. You don't win battles lying on the ground. Again metaphorizing, we may also glean that most "able-bodied adults" do not need to be rescued.

Wait! This should not raise questions about my father and our relationship. He was cool as a fan and the life of any party. He is a playful prankster who pulled a fast one at the pool that went wrong. That's all. Careful of what you think of my mother, too. Mom faced a spontaneous moment, bushwhacked. We have all been there, so she gets a pass. No person in our natural world is more driven, spiritual, or well-balanced than my mother. Therefore, her pool incident expresses the significance of fear when it can momentarily creep in and impact us, even someone like my mom.

Something fearful can loom over you, menacingly . . . or booyah! Fear may come unexpectedly, like a sneaky push. Whatever form fear comes in, we must deal with it. First, individuals decide whether to rally or wane. Then, they may find new ways or settle for old habits, choose creativity or unproductivity, employ wisdom or foolishness, seek a lifeline, or exercise their power. My mom opted for her power. For me, there has never been an option. I favor the sufficiency of the individual power placed in me, which I have learned to access through failures and victories.

In my experience as a former university dean and later as an entrepreneur in health and fitness, I have examined the questionable acceptances of students and adults and witnessed psychological withdrawals that followed. Their half-hearted attempts at reaching goals collided with misfortune, as do most self-fulfilling prophesies and other acts of self-sabotage. So many had quickly forgotten their power to contribute to the positive and be thankful when life went their way. Instead, they embraced the negative as inevitable—their lot in life—only giving thought when the momentum shifted.

For instance, the typical type of pessimism—assuming doom and gloom—is the repressive practice of anticipating adversities. Here are three examples:

- A well-performing student who expects a crisis of difficulty will torpedo final grades.

- The couple, blissfully in love, jump to relationship-ending conclusions because things are going too well or the catastrophe that must have happened because one did not return the other's text fast enough.
- The qualified job candidate who may not interview because, in their minds, they've already failed.

One might wonder why people in this group fall into self-inflicted traps. Of course, they experience the good; many have reached the status of role model or influencer; still, most need to learn to handle a minor setback. Thus, they find comfort in predicting bad times to minimize the personal sting of disappointment and the judgment of others.

There's a smaller minority of pessimists who may have experienced something hard to miss and find moving on complicated. Unfortunately, there are an infinite number of circumstances that cultivate this complex mindset. Some patterns, like the ones listed below, may skew the difference between what is real and what is imaginary:

- A person who's experienced a termination or eviction may live in fear of it happening again.
- The person who must divulge their felony conviction, knowing that employers routinely deny employment to applicants with a criminal history, may give up on seeking gainful employment.
- An individual may classify their bankruptcy as a human failing, thinking that others view them as irresponsible.

People in this group tend to embrace the victim role and spew paranoia. As if everyone knows of their setback or someone is holding their past against them. These are all examples of living passively or worse, in fear. Meanwhile, no shining moment or negative one will last forever. In other words, there is an essential fact about life. All highs are fleeting. So are disappointments if we choose to let them go. Holding on to fear and dismay is like a small, dark storm cloud that follows and only rains on you. At first glance, everything you encounter reminds you of your issue, conversations you have, or overhear. Television shows' storylines have subliminal meanings. Newsflash: Most of this is in your head.

Nevertheless, people in both groups create a small world for themselves to live in, reducing themselves to insignificant if that's what the world dictates;

instead of emerging by being themselves, they shrink and become a fraction of their potential. I recall an extreme example when a referee mentor-turned-friend shared with me that he had an older brother living on Los Angeles' skid row, an area of severe homelessness.

"How can you live with abundant wealth and have a brother who is homeless?" I asked.

"I tried to help. For my brother's reasons, he won't accept more than bottled water every now and then, if I'm able to find him, which could take days or sometimes weeks. It breaks my heart, man. I offered him a place to live, a job. Still, he wants to live on the streets. My brother has had some hard knocks trying to make something of himself and decided it's better not to fight anymore. It scares the crap out of me, knowing that one day, I will get a phone call and he will be gone."

Seeing people fall off the rails is heartbreaking, allowing doubt to consume them and convince them to give in to fear. In other words, those confined by barriers—real or self-imposed—grow abnormally.

Nature and Self-Empowerment

As you will discover, I like to look at nature and scriptures to make sense of hard-to-explain phenomena. Therefore, this time we will look at how the relationship between the growth of an alligator might parallel human development. In college, I owned a baby alligator whom I named Coach, after the leather designer. If I had a pet, something that matched part of my personality would be best. Like me, it would mind its business; only heaven could help you if provoked. Perfect. A salesperson named Mike at the pet shop, puzzled by the increased frequency of my visits, made a valid point:

"I think your alligator is getting too big to eat goldfish. Would you mind if I came over to look at it?" Mike asked.

"Come anytime."

When Mike arrived later that day, he said, "Dude, your alligator is deformed because your tank is too small. He is growing wide instead of long because he is adapting to his surroundings." Then, Mike left and returned with a larger tank, approximately 12 feet long, 2 feet wide, and 2 feet deep. He also had a small, brown paper bag containing two mice. Mike tossed each mouse, one after the other with seconds in between. In the rhythm of Mike's toss, Coach caught, crunched, and swallowed the mice headfirst before they could splash into the water from their flight. The following week, Mike tossed twenty mice into my tank in succession. Coach ate all twenty mice in twenty-one seconds. No chewing. Just "cut and swallow," as my father said when I ate too fast. Coach regained his natural form weeks after we changed his habitat and diet—he finally grew long. That was my perspective. However, from Coach's standpoint, he was wholly dependent. He lived confined to the tank I approved. Sure, Coach could get out, just not on his own, of course, and only when I decided it was good for him. Thus, he couldn't do anything without the approval of others. All of whom determined how he would grow.

Meanwhile, human beings are no different. Our constrictions could be our surroundings, negative self-talk, or not trying. It could be our willingness to jump into the boxes other people assigned us. There are endless possibilities, producing a distorted version of us. In other words, fear, doubt, and the inability to self-define create underachievers by stunting and disrupting their growth. They become what other people think of them. Sometimes they answer by any name people are willing to call them, like Coach. I reminded myself and Coach that he could be my next belt or briefcase if he ever challenged me by wanting to be himself. In other words, it is not easy emerging and being you when you must expend so much of your energy resisting all who might oppose your ascension, even yourself.

Suppose you stopped searching for legitimacy and began to see yourself as more than enough, not inferior, ill-fated, or jinxed—also capable of making life-changing decisions. The visceral reaction would cause the following. First, you'd reimagine your aspirations instead of taking on other people's aspirations as yours. Second, you'd stem the best efforts of your most prominent haters. Third, it would brighten your light. In other words, the influences that devalued you in the past would no longer be relevant. There's no doubt about it. Your revised thoughts would bring about new dreams, beliefs, and behaviors.

Additionally, removing dependency and unlearning "I can't" takes practice. It means diving deep into your core and addressing the pile of unpleasantness that may scare the crap out of you. Even so, the awakening is worth it. Then, soon every unsolicited layer you remove will increase self-esteem and self-confidence. Therefore, dignity, self-respect, and morale are reasons we must make defining and redefining ourselves a ubiquitous part of our lives—the same way we think of learning. Most simply, life teaches us that we will face the following unanswered questions: Who am I, what is my essence, what contributions will I make, what am I capable of achieving, what is important to me, what do I need to improve, and what is my power? Your answers may be verbal or nonverbal, involving action or inaction. However, if you do not answer them, someone will answer them for you, which we can all agree is dangerous.

When Others Answer Your Questions of Purpose

Summer break had ended, and it was the first day of the first class of my senior year in college. The professor walked in from the back of the room, and as he walked by, I said,

"Hey Dr. Collin, how was your summer?"

"It was marvelous, and it's good to see you again in my class," he said.

We chopped it up a few seconds more. We relied on superficial talk about our summers that would allow enough ammo for one-liners, not to learn or remember much about one another. Seriousness between us would have been unusual. Playful banter was more our thing. And interacting with my teachers was part of my blueprint for academic success. Dr. Collin was a jolly man known for witty comebacks. I would practice my zingers on him as well. Most often, I got the last laugh.

Dr. Collin was easy to talk to, and his clean-shaven face always bore a smile. If you can picture the typical cartoon Santa Claus without a beard and suit, you would see Dr. Collin. He even held his shaking belly when he laughed, like how television shows portray Santa. However, he walked with an unnatural forward lean and quickly like someone tall chasing something small and elusive that is getting away, also found in television cartoons.

He usually lumbered into his classroom at a reckless pace, too fast for indoors, scanning the room for recognizable faces. He had favorites, and his playful bants signaled that I was one of them. The class knew he was coming because the most pungent coffee smell preceded his arrival. A conversation at arms-length or closer made most students nauseous, even the heavy coffee drinkers. Moreover, his drink was far from a sweet caramel macchiato popular for students—no cinnamon dolce latte for him. Instead, Dr. Collin's robust blend of black coffee could clear a room when it escaped through his pores. Understandably, Dr. Collin's was the only class I've attended where students arrived early to secure seats in the back of the classroom.

An elder told me years ago of a comparative analysis of student performance based on where students sat in the classroom. He said they found that teachers awarded eighty percent of A's and B's to students seated in the T-zone—the first few rows in front of the class and a row down the middle. This is because teachers subconsciously direct their attention to those students, whether lecturing or fielding questions. Students too far on the edges or seated in the back traditionally received lesser scores. So, while Dr. Collin's caffeinated funkiness crushed my desire for a front-row seat, I still chose a seat within the T-zone.

I sat between two friends who were also African American. Big Rick sat to my left. He was one of my best friends and a football teammate. The student on my right was Alicia, a senior like Rick and me; she was a theater major from Chicago. I had planned to go to the athletic facility after class. So I wore my athletic department-issued gray sweatsuit, not jeans, and a button-down shirt I would typically wear to class. I was not fond of advertising that I was an athlete. To do so was the risk of bringing about unwanted attention. No doubt, not standing out because of a difference, in this case, is different from trying to be invisible.

As Dr. Collin walked toward the front of the room, I asked, "Dr. Collin, what will it take to get an A in your class? I plan to do whatever it takes."

Dr. Collin turned around to face me. His happy-to-see-me face turned into a scowl. His voice dropped a full octave as if he were trying to speak in a demonic bass tone, haunting echo effect included.

Finally, he said, "You know a C is good enough for you." He held his glare for a second or two. Again, our seriousness was unusual. Then, to ensure I understood, he said, "A C is good enough for you."

He tilted his head as if seeing me over his glasses would punctuate his point—that I had no business aspiring to academic excellence. Then, he proceeded to the front of the class to teach.

In such instances, I would respond the way my mother taught my siblings when we hear something stupid: "Exactly what do you mean by that?" It is our familial response when someone says something stupid enough to perplex us. It would have told Dr. Collin that I knew what he said was ridiculous and that he must explain his ridiculousness. Instead, I just sat there. I pondered which of my identities he attacked. I was unsure whether he was attacking my Blackness or my identity as an athlete. It was only clear that I wasn't welcome in his class, or better yet, he would not fairly reward my efforts. The fix was in.

His remarks made me question everything about him. First, I wondered whether his greeting was genuine. I overcomplicated that point. Anyone who could publicly demean and marginalize someone could not be glad to see them. Second, I pondered whether he was a bigot or did not like football players. However, a more pressing concern was whether I had earned a C from him in a class I had taken earlier. It could be that he had just confessed.

After class, I met with the athletic advisor for the football team, who called one of my coaches to meet with us.

"This is BS. What can we do?" I asked.

"Bite the bullet and move on," the coach said as the advisor nodded, waiting to chime in.

"I agree," she said. "You need this class to graduate. Just go in there and—"

"And work like a dog for a C? Maybe I need to introduce you to me. I'm not going for that."

"He can make it difficult and affect your eligibility if you make a stink out of it," the coach fired back. "My advice is to tread lightly. Besides, you would need proof."

"First of all, I'm gonna' go to class and verbally drag his ass like he did me. I refuse to walk on eggshells when I did nothing wrong, and it's his turn to feel uncomfortable. Second of all, I do have proof. I kept all my work from his previous class. Can't I file a grievance or call the newspapers, something?"

"You did what?" The advisor perked up.

"I have my work."

"Pull it all together and I'll make a call."

"You did good son," my coach muttered with a smile.

Dr. Collin taught two courses that met the subject requirements for my degree. Just in case I needed the information in the future, I archived the work I completed in my major courses. Filing coursework was my fail-safe, a way to cover my ass. Better to have it and not need it than need it and not have it, as the saying goes. So I gathered the paperwork from the first class, which included the syllabus, course materials, and graded work, at the request of my academic advisor. We hoped to have a higher authority review it.

Fortunately, the College's academic dean agreed to meet before my next class. When I told the dean about the incident in class with Dr. Collin, he decided to regrade my past work. When I arrived to drop off my work, the dean exhaled loudly, breathing heavily into his hand, partially covering his face.

"Make sure that your name is on everything inside the folder. Leave it here in the tray, and give me a few days, a week, tops," he muttered, shifting his eyes up to acknowledge my presence. "By the way, do not attend Dr. Collin's class until I have completed my review."

Then, he let out another big breath. I have heard such an exhale in the past. It was not annoyance; it was exasperation. I got the impression that the dean had addressed Dr. Collin's indiscretions before, and he was over it. I gave him a thumbs-up and left.

In the meantime, I asked Rick and Alicia about previous grades from Dr. Collin. Sure enough, Rick previously got a C. Alicia, who was not an athlete, gasped and swallowed hard, which was her way of holding back choice words. Then, she explained how she received her C.

"I thought I earned an A," Alicia said. "I received my final grade during summer break, I assumed I bombed the final exam and decided not to question it."

"I also thought I did well in the first class, until he submitted my C grade," I shared.

Like most students, I gave blind trust to my teachers concerning final grades. Going along with their calculations was a widespread practice. I thought, "Would this re-examination of my work reveal a discriminatory act? Did Dr. Collin profile me based on stereotypes?" To him, I may have been a less advantaged, poorly prepared ghetto kid, a dumb jock, or just Black. Either way, he has communicated that I should be grateful for college admission and lucky to earn Cs. I wrestled with whether he'd come to the university each year determined not to see athletes or Black students perform above his predetermined ceiling and which group it might be.

Well, I didn't have to wait long for answers. The dean pushed through and finished regrading my work in two days. Then, he summoned me back to his office. Unfortunately, I did not meet with him as I expected when I arrived. Instead, his administrative assistant returned my work. She extended one hand, holding the file. She repeatedly pointed at my skin with the index finger of her other hand in a jabbing motion. The assistant did not release her grip on the file until I acknowledged with a nod what she was saying inaudibly. Later, the dean retroactively changed my grade from a C to an A-.

I understood all too well what happened, and the vile character of Dr. Collin rushed to the front of my mind. With the dean's permission, I dropped Dr. Collin's class. In its place, I enrolled in an independent study course supervised by the dean to meet my graduation requirements.

Over the following years, the dean and I became solid acquaintances. We maintained our relationship while I pursued a graduate degree. He later confided that tenure protected Dr. Collin from any discipline for his apparent biases. He was already part-time, and the university could not fire him. "There you have it," I thought. "He is a bigot."

Dr. Collin's words echoed strongly for months after he said them: "A C is good enough for you." Thinking about them still stings as sharply and deeply as hearing them the first time. It is easier to stomach a racist cop who profiles Black men by hiding behind a badge or politicians who advance policies that favor their interests, which simultaneously diminishes yours. However, it is entirely different when someone looks you in the eye and tells you publicly that you don't matter and that if you must exist, you should be grateful for scraps.

My presence was irritating to him, deeper-rooted than stepping on chewing gum or waving at an elusive gnat that follows and buzzes in your face at the cookout. Those are things to remove. Instead, I was something to tolerate, such as speed bumps, noisy neighbors, or having to keep a hated job. Worse yet, hurting me made sense. His disingenuous banter was his way of "just laughing with them," as mothers taught their children when their peers poked fun. But his hidden agenda was far more insidious. He knew he would laugh last with one discriminatory stroke of his grading pen.

Everybody knows that recipients of lower scores are less competitive for graduate schools and professional school programs. Thus, average scores in your degree program cause underrepresentation at prestigious graduate schools and professional schools such as law, engineering, and medicine. Indeed, Dr. Collin knew this. Still, he stood in the way of countless students like Rick and Alicia.

Of course, Dr. Collin's issue was race. However, biases of any kind are an affront to human decency. A person who knows themselves will not accept limits from other people. You demonstrate self-knowledge by answering the recommended questions of purpose for yourself: Who am I, what is my essence, what contributions will I make, what am I capable of achieving, what is important to me, what do I need to improve, and what is my power?

Dr. Collin tried to define me and my capabilities. However, those questions of purpose were mine to answer, not his. At times, everybody has their Dr. Collin to face: that person, thing, or thought betrays and undermines your advancement for its narcissistic appetite. Having the courage to stand is what I learned about addressing opposition.

While fear's purpose is to make us uncomfortable, it isn't always negative. We can also report that fear speaks to us in ways that keep us safe. For some, fear may say, "Don't skydive." The hair that stands on the back of our necks warning us to leave a place or stay put is also fear. Therefore, we should view fear as information; that's all. Fear is a source, a tipster that lets us know that something is off that demands the courage to correct it. We should also embrace fear as commonplace. For instance, mentioning "Don't be afraid" or "Do not fear" 365 times in the Bible was not arbitrary. Nor is it a coincidence that we have a verse for every day of the year. Fearful events occur every day, and as simple as they sound, these scriptures reassure us. It is on this foundation that we can build strength against frightening events. It is time to change our mindset regarding fear.

Finally, my epiphany in college extended beyond courage and fear. Sure, I pushed back against a part of an antagonistic system that made itself visible. Valiant effort! Still, getting my grade changed was like upgrading an alligator's diet from goldfish to mice if I were the alligator. In other words, I gladly accepted a slightly improved academic reward and a bigger fish tank called graduate school, only to learn that I continued to feast on table scraps. The places where limits and fish tanks (aka boxes) exist can take time to identify. Spoiler alert! America is full of larger boxes. We can find them in every aspect of our lives. Everywhere rules and pushy people live. Our families, patterns of thought, decisions, and even systems like judicial, employment, housing, medical, and government are all ripe for sabotage. Will you dare show up in all these spaces as "you?"

Nobody offered advice on getting Dr. Collin's face out of my head or the echo of his insult provoking me with that lousy C. But how could they? A mixture of anger and embarrassment prevented me from sharing my story—for a while, anyway. But let's be completely real. I wanted to beat his ass like he stole something because he did. Dr. Collin stole my academic innocence by revealing bigotry's ugly truth. Depravity is everywhere.

Engaging my professors was my trademark until then. After that, I pulled away from all my teachers for my sanity. But I never became a class discontent, although every class has a few. The lesson here is that we either believe in our power or not. And the time to test your resolve is facing challenges. Allowing it to change your ways too much would mean foolery won. It's never about what we face, only how we face it.

Therefore, by exercising your right and ability to self-define, you can chip away at barriers central to reaching your goals: doubt, worthiness, fear of failure, self-sabotage, et cetera. For example, 1970's martial artist-turned-actor Bruce Lee points out that we stand in our way because of how we see ourselves. Lee said, "Man is constantly growing. And when he is bound by a set pattern of ideas or way of doing things, that's when he stops growing."[1]

In essence, personal growth and advancement are mental and physical battles, according to Mr. Lee. The real test, however, is whether we're willing to accept such challenges. When I was a child, every kid wanted to be like Bruce Lee: competitive, fiercely independent, and trained to whoop ass if provoked. Or so I thought. Neighborhood boys and classmates playfully challenged each other in their yards or school bathrooms. Popup fights happened at a moment's notice. I wanted that life until I got my head-kicked a few times while sparring. I confirmed my change of heart after I wrapped myself while practicing with homemade nun-chucks. I thought, "No wonder everyone isn't doing it and there's only one Bruce Lee." Few people have the desire or appetite to invite pain or embrace the idea of struggle for self-improvement or bragging rights. It is easier and less embarrassing to blend in safely or never strive for anything.

Falling and Getting Up

I remember the first time I went roller skating: a school outing for my fifth-grade class. My mom dropped off my friend Keith and me at Skateland. We never had roller skated before, and it showed. We could barely stand up on our skates. I cautiously made my way around the rink until my balance was less of an issue. The two or three times I fell were embarrassing. After that, I thought, "Spare me the bruised knees and sore elbows from busting my butt. I'm done." I changed into my shoes and watched the skaters as the first slow music set began. Kids coupled up and slow-skated, holding hands, one skating backward and the other forward.

In contrast, Keith was a maniac. He skated faster than his ability, which caused others to fall as frequently as he did. Keith was my best friend and neighbor, and everybody knew it. Skating for the first time made him a target for jokes and belly-aching laughter, one fall after another. He had established a reputation as reckless, a person you'd better watch or be next to go down. Still, somehow, Keith convinced a woman, an experienced skater, to skate couples with him during the first slow music set and the four or five that followed. She rolled backward and Keith forward until he adapted to the synchronicity of skating with a partner. Then, they switched. Keith even caused her to fall a few times, and you could tell by her outfit that the rink was her no-fall zone.

---

[1] Bruce Lee. (2015). *Bruce Lee Jeet Kune Do: Bruce Lee's Commentaries on the Martial Way.* Tuttle Publishing.

Keith's partner skated in pearl white skates, personalized with pink wheels, pink laces, a small, flashing headlight on each toe, and her name, Tracy, written in cursive down each skate's rear spine. Tracy also wore a fitted all-white jumper and two barrettes tied at the top of her two long braided pigtails that fell on the sides of her face. The reflective sheen of her outfit sparkled under the spinning balls of psychedelic lighting, which the DJ activated for slower tempos. Indeed, any person who would put that much thought into an ensemble could not have foreseen falls.

During the ride home, my mom asked about our adventure. I chimed in immediately with jokes about Keith falling, and rightfully so. We all laughed. At one point, I volunteered that I had only crashed two or three times. With both eyebrows raised, my mom seemed visibly surprised either by my low number of falls or that I counted them. Then, Keith responded.

"I don't know how many times I fell. I just knew that I wanted to learn, and that meant bustin' my tail. So, instead of learning how not to fall, I learned how to skate. Now I can do it fast, slow, bouncing and dancing, or as a couple. A girl even taught me how to skate as a couple and tips for skating backward and stopping. Now, all I have to do is practice."

"What was in it for Tracy?" I asked.

"She's the baby of the family, and always wanted to teach skating to someone the way her sisters and bad older brothers taught her. Since dudes feared her family, nobody dared ask her to skate. They only watched."

I verbally acknowledged that everything he said made sense while silently vowing that I would be braver and leave Skateland with more bruises next time.

Many of you live your lives like I approached skating that day. You go through cautious routines and wish for more progress than your risk will allow. You keep moving without goals—activity without purpose—somewhat comfortable with an average, predictable pace. As a result, you have lived the equivalent of balancing on your skates. You will move in careful, recurring circles, calculating every forward motion. You have chosen comfort and are almost grateful in communicating that you are not experiencing falls.

There may be legitimate reasons for cautious behavior in adults, such as a tragic past moment or a lifetime of disappointment in certain areas. However, it is also valid that you can change the effect of misfortune if you're still alive after its cause. In other words, if that thing didn't kill you, it has prepared you for what's next. My first understanding of this concept smacked me in the face as a young adult in the church. A well-educated man who earned two doctorate degrees, Bishop Kenneth

Ulmer, held a crisp $20 bill high above his head. He teased the congregation by asking those who wanted the money to raise a hand. Hands shot up all over the assembly. A few people jumped to their feet and raised both hands. Then dramatically, Bishop Ulmer crushed the new bill in his hands, rolled it into a ball, and threw it on the floor. Some in attendance laughed as he repeatedly stomped on the money. Finally, Bishop Ulmer bent over, grabbed the balled-up bill, and asked, "Who wants this twenty-dollar bill now?" Seeing only an increase in enthusiasm for the cash, he tossed the money into the hands of an eager member. Then, he spoke slowly and convincingly into his microphone:

"Some of you have been beaten, crushed and stepped on, and just like that $20 bill, you have never lost your value."

The crowd approved. I watched as the congregation applauded. Some stood, and others shouted. I heard several "hallelujahs." A good number yelled, "That's good pastor," and there were one or two "amens." Bishop Ulmer nailed it if he intended to demonstrate why we must stop letting people hold us hostage for past mistakes. I will take it a step further and say we must stop holding ourselves victim to events in our past. No amount of therapy or grief will permit us to reconstruct our memories to reimagine our visions. That would be flat-out lying; there's no sense in lying to yourself. Instead, our aspirations must be more significant than our memory of bad or good events.

CHAPTER TWO
EVENTS DO NOT DEFINE US

The tutor admonished the young boy through clenched teeth, "You can do better than that, or we'll just sit here." Then, she moved away from the boy's blank face and reiterated the instructions, jabbing her index finger into the table to amplify her words.

"Construct one sentence at a time by using the alphabet. The subject of each sentence must start with A, then B, until you reach the end. Now start over and speak louder."

I shook my head and didn't think much more about them until a deep, ominous voice interrupted,

"You skipped Q."

"Oh, my bad. Make a sentence for Q now," she said.

Then, the tutor reclined and closed her eyes while the child collected his thoughts. Each time he began to say the following letter and corresponding sentence, his tutor exhaled deeply, broadcasting, "It's about damn time," if a hard breath could speak.

Bam! I slammed my pen and got her attention. Then, I gestured by tilting my head, shrugging my shoulders, and raising my palms. Even though I knew it meant "I don't know," universally, I wanted to communicate that even well-meaning educators could reinforce children's deficiencies and diminish their effort. No chance of that happening. When they reached Z, the woman motioned for the child's father to join.

"Time for real talk," she said.

I sat up, ready for what would come next.

"This doesn't make sense. He should be reading by now. His teachers must be passing him from one grade to the next because he clearly cannot do the work. Right now, he is not learning. He needs to be professionally tested for a disability. I told your wife last week that he needs to be tested. The testing people and the teachers are professionals. You and your wife are not. They can deal with this, and you can't."

Time stood still. He'd submitted to stifled contemplation for seconds longer than he should have. "Say something!" I silently urged because it was becoming apparent that I must intervene. I will ask permission to escort his child to the bookstore's children's section, which was in plain view of our tables. Moreover, my action might cue them to stop even if the dad answers, "No." Finally, the man covered his mouth with one fist to clear his throat, "Ahem, ahem."

I would not dare interrupt his moment to defend his child. He was undoubtedly about to let the woman and everyone within earshot know he had his son's back. He'd express that although he and his wife may not be "education professionals," they could lovingly nurture and share with their son: "If your teachers can teach, you can learn." The boy also needed to see his dad champion the moment so he could walk out with his head up and his young chest out. Instead, the man said,

"Yeah, it goes in one ear and out the other."

"You can pay me electronically," she said.

Then, it was my turn to stew quietly as the man left with his son. The tutor followed them out. After spending 23 years in higher education, I could not believe I would let that scene play out. I thought of how I could have changed that moment for the child. I should have come to his defense. Then, my brother's famous words popped into my head: "It ain't too late." I bolted to the parking lot like I was late for a flight. The man and child had gone. However, the tutor was texting in her running car with music blaring. I introduced myself, briefly shared my educator's background, and gave her my phone number to pass on to the child's father. She said, "I will text him your number right now." I knew that negativity could cost the child his academic future. Unfortunately, the boy's dad never called.

I fumed over the father and tutor's characterization of the child's aptitude. Whatever truth it held might haunt the child because he overheard them. Negative words take their toll and can manifest in a loss of ambition or a child no longer believing in themselves. They are dream killers. Loss of purpose and dignity breeds resentment and diminishes hopes and dreams. The same is true for labels. While I understand the importance of testing to establish a baseline, we cannot trust a child's test results after you've told him he could not learn. Instead, the adults in the room should have focused on the young man's strengths and explored ways to make his learning engaging, even fun.

Soon, this child will be a young adult. Then, he will have opportunities to change course. Silencing past noise will play a significant role in changing his mindset. For example, rejecting the notion that information goes in one ear and out the other must come first. Unlearning such negative social labeling that bends his will leads to accepting the force of attraction that restores and gives. Gives what? Everything worth having.

Engineering Your Will

Many years ago, I met a group of young men during the last summer orientation before school started. I introduced myself when I approached the group and said, "Who wants to go next? Please tell me your name, your hometown, and your major." Then, I pointed to one student and said, "The first to look away draws the short straw; it's your turn."

"My name is Cameron, and I am from Charlotte, North Carolina; my major is engineering."

"Whoa, engineering! That's awesome."

I shook his hand and followed up with a fist bump. When I finished my theatrics, he pointed to the next guy, who jumped right in. As it were, the first four students declared engineering as their major. I was performing my fourth Oscar-worthy scene of overexcitement. Then, I noticed the last remaining guy in the group nervously wringing his hands and shifting his weight from one foot to the other. I turned toward him.

"Alright, let's have it," I said.

"Uh, Ahmad and engineering."

I must have hit the ceiling, giving the most nervous of them all my grand finale. Then, I told them a story about a similar group, all men and engineers, who graduated a few years earlier.

"Look guys, you have a rare opportunity, a ready-made study group. If you take all your classes together, you will set the curve and earn straight A's. It's been done before. Try it!"

They looked at each other, and a chorus of "Let's do it," "I'm in," and "Yes" followed. They shook hands. Soon, they took the same classes with the same teachers at the exact times. Amazingly, they achieved similar success, earning straight A's during their first two years. Then something happened. Ahmad knocked on my office door after the first semester of his junior year.

"Uh, excuse me. If you have some time, I would like to talk with you," he said.

"Yeah man, come on in and have a seat."

I was excited because it wasn't often that a straight-A student came to visit. In my role, I was more of a fixer. Part of my job was running peer mentor and academic advancement programs. I mainly dealt with students with compatibility issues or those who needed educational support. Eager to hear what he had to say, I dropped my pen and leaned forward. "How can I help you?" I asked.

Then, with his elbows on his knees and his hands positioned in a V-shape, cupping his chin to hold up his head, he began speaking:

"I want to tell you an embarrassing story, and I don't want you to stop me until I finish. I might lose my nerve. When we met during orientation, I met the other guys before you approached us, like seconds before. I had no idea what I would major in until I saw how excited you got when they said 'engineering.' So, since I was last, I parroted 'engineering.' I didn't even know what engineering was. I only attended the last orientation because it took me all summer to complete my high school requirements. Everybody thought I should have been a better student because my mother is a teacher. Unfortunately, I found it more attractive to be the class clown. I don't know how I graduated. I suspect that my mother knew some people, and they pushed me through. I know she pulled strings to get me into this university. Besides my mother, nobody ever believed in me academically. I thought she was only faking it because I am her son. I got kicked out of school for fighting and other bad behavior, just being disruptive. I didn't want school. Now suddenly, I am a straight-A student in engineering, and I feel like an imposter. I don't know. I don't feel like I deserve the praise that everybody gives me. I am embarrassed by it because I don't recognize this as me."

I hadn't heard this much rambling in years. Ahmad also recognized that he was repeating himself because he stopped talking unexpectedly and looked up. When he saw me, I was already nodding to communicate that I understood his point and knew it was my turn to speak.

"You have excelled in one of the most challenging majors at this university. So, your academic performance in high school was not due to a lack of ability. You disconnected in high school and will have to figure out why. Nobody will ever ask again how you performed in high school. Ahmad, I respect your humility; however, enrollment means you belong. You've earned A's and the respect of your teachers and classmates. You're not an impostor. The Engineering Department doesn't frivolously give away money; you've earned academic scholarships because of your efforts. Your mom did not pull strings for those. You've made the Dean's List and mentored others to excel. Come on, man. Today, you are a young scholar people look up to. Ahmad, why did you think I needed to know all this?"

"With all due respect," he said. "I don't even like engineering. I wanted to know if changing my major would be okay with you."

I laughed loud and hard. Then, finally, we stood, and I shook Ahmad's hand while saying, "Yeah man, yes," and we both laughed. After that, we sat back down and discussed possibilities for his new major.

I have had countless counseling meetings with students and adults trapped in time and past conflicts involving family, friends, church officials, teachers, coaches, and colleagues. It's hard for me to dance around the advice of getting over it without saying, "Get over it." So I tend to tell individuals and groups this: In general, people worry too much about things that aren't important, and importance is relative to control. In other words, the less control you have over an issue, the less critical you must rank the concern. Some matters are life-shaping and looming, such as love, loss, abandonment, neglect, betrayal, or other deep wounds. I am not negating the feelings caused by those events when I say rank the issue. Nor does the strategy I propose involve repressing feelings. Nobody in their right mind would suggest that the sensitivity disappears without addressing it. And ignoring trauma is not a cure. So instead, I am saying that you must willfully and deliberately examine everything within you linked to sending you back to that place of despair. No blueprint diagrams your route from returning to the pain, getting stuck in that pain, and traveling through healing. What lies between your pain and recovery involves your deliberate dealing with your stuff. There's likely a profound freedom associated with envisioning the future you want while living in the present. For example, academic success didn't move Ahmad beyond what hurt him in high school. As academically decorated as he was in college, he didn't begin to deal with his concern effectively until our meeting about changing his major. Then, he initiated a step toward healing and reimagining his future.

Likewise, the boy in the bookstore must one day believe in his abilities more than past labels. This change will motivate him to build on small wins and recapture the will he long surrendered to others. Redefining pessimism and scarce optimism mischaracterized by teachers, parents, and tutors comes next. In plain English, something transformative will happen when the young boy awakens and discovers his true self. Then, like Ahmad's process of repeatedly making the Dean's List, the young boy will want to build upon "aha" moments when "I think I can" turns into "I know I can."

As I have said before, the cause of a mindset shift is whatever compels someone to take charge of being themselves—the discovery of will. However, reaching a new stage of development doesn't keep you there. Doubt festers. As observed with Ahmad, continued emergence takes drive, support, and nurturing.

Furthermore, discovering your truth is often startling and overwhelming, making experiencing self-doubt during this period likely. Feeling like an imposter or undeserving of success is also commonplace. However, anger is the most prevalent response to learning the truth. Empowering his truth may lead him to forgive those who let him down, academically and personally. If not, the proverbial chip on the shoulder will motivate him just fine.

What follows is a soul-stirring readiness to shine while rejecting the limits others placed on his abilities. He cannot hold on to both. Finally, in a usual manner, he may write a new script and establish his unique vision—one that draws bona fide conclusions from the new ways that he sees himself. Thus, his action enacts healing, representing enhanced strength, confidence, and joy. Other resulting behaviors may follow, such as:

- Refusing to allow low expectations to ever again become prescriptions for making daily decisions
- Vowing not to allow past performance to dictate how he will live
- Moving past the need to address events that may trigger pain hidden in the background in the name of reconciliation

The point I will make here is that accepting and knowing himself dispels the notion of inferiority and the need for nonsensical conversations about closure. Such a confrontation may further frustration, like someone requesting a final meeting with an ex-partner hoping for an explanation for why they cheated. There's no satisfying answer. Besides, such meetings rarely happen or help those betrayed. What happens to closure, then? He would be better off writing a screenplay of the scene he wishes to have with all those who underestimated him. An alternate ending that he designs would script closure flawlessly. So might burning it or trashing it as a final step. Moving past closure is for him, nobody else.

It would help us deal with hurt and pain as we deal with other essential parts of life, giving ourselves closure. This way, we conclude that decisions to turn pages are on our shoulders. Thus, let's presume an issue is out of your hands. Place it out of your mind (or tucked in the back of it).

Since few do well at self-evaluation, I suggest beginning with answering the questions of purpose and letting them guide you: Who am I, what is my essence, what contributions will I make, what am I capable of achieving, what is important to me, what do I need to improve, and what is my power? We will discuss more strategies to regain control in later chapters.

CHAPTER THREE
WE ARE WHAT WE ARE

Baby naming can take on a life of its own, from family names and traditions to taking suggestions from me as godfather. Naturally, I wanted to help, considering how long the little guy had been in the world. Therefore, I burst through the hospital room door to make good on this opportunity.

"It's been three days. Name the boy!"

Cynthia shrugged. "You sound like the nurses." Then, she crossed her arms in apparent frustration. "Let's pick one now that you're here."

"You're on." I moved closer to him for clues.

"I understand you're looking for a strong name with meaning?" I said, holding up my godson for ideas as if observing him at eye level would help.

I knew he couldn't process the moment. Yet, I'll never forget his reaction. First, he seemed to look me over, laugh, and squirm; then, he did it once more to assert that he was checking me out too.

He was at the age of innocence, not pretense. He wasn't trying to impress as we matched his squirms and looks to definitions from the baby's names websites. Then, mightier, more enduring looks passed; they were his looks, not mine. And finally, when the corners of his mouth curved into a smile, his name picked him: Ahkeil (ah-keel).

The occasion of naming Ahkeil made me concede a common expression: "We are what we are." Somehow those words ranked right up there with gibberish until Ahkeil came. Of course, who doesn't know we are what we are? Duh.

Now, I understand that the expression refers to our spirit. It is our core being, which may have existed at or before birth and operates in spaces independent of lofty titles, considerable accomplishments, or displays of bravado. In other words,

"We are what we are" is us when our superficial layers vanish.

For example, my dear friend from Oakland, California, has two beautiful daughters. Let's nickname them Daphne and Loni. Daphne is the eldest; she's also my godchild. She has a sweet spirit, is even-tempered with a spicy kick if provoked, and has a solid drive to do the right thing. Daphne will calmly and compassionately go with the flow of a group, content with whatever the moment brings.

However, Loni exudes high energy all the time. She is playful and demands attention, even if she must break a house rule or two to get it. Loni is only calm when she's asleep, and if there is no excitement, she will create some. Then, everyone, even Loni, will laugh hysterically or stare bewildered; there's no in-between.

These are two examples of kids being who they are. Neither child was born with successes or failures. And adding layers won't change what lies beneath. Daphne will retain a sweet spirit, and Loni's will be highly charged; it's who they are. Some people can acknowledge a sweet baby as a loving child. Others may identify a young person as having an old soul. People like me can choose a name that would be a perfect fit, like Ahkeil, which means "intelligent, thoughtful, and wise." These are the kinds of descriptions at the center of who we are. Other things, ranging from earned titles to dumb decisions, are only events.

Suppose Daphne and Loni grow up and start a law practice. Daphne may focus on branding, marketing, and research, specializing in behind-the-scenes work. In contrast, Loni may thrive in litigation and basking in the attention of lights, cameras, and headlines. Still, their professional successes and failures are only events with lawyer titles. When the deeds and titles are gone, one person will remain sweet and calm, and her younger sister will be highly charged and energetic. In other words, their endeavors would not change what lies at their core. Of course, I am projecting. We all do.

Raise your hand if you have looked at a child's behavior and predicted what they might be like as adults.

"Look at how all the kids follow her. She's going to be a leader."

"Aw, look at how that baby gives his toys to other kids. Make sure people don't take advantage; that one is a giver."

Right or wrong, we do this primarily because of what we may see at their core. For example, my childhood friend, Keith, who taught me that falling on my skates was okay, showed that resilience might be at his core. He is a go-getter, someone who conquers obstacles because, to him, advancement has everything to do with going for it. Thus, there was no surprise when I met up with Keith during college.

He described a nontraditional path toward becoming a surgeon, including stops-and-starts and financial creativity. That was long ago. Still, something told me that Keith would inevitably cross the finish line. Winning is in him.

The reverse is also true. When we see how some adults act, we may say things like, "I bet you were a tattletale growing up, a brat, or worse—a spoiled brat," among other things. Being know-it-alls, interrupting people talking, lying to get out of trouble, and throwing tantrums round out my shortlist. There are always clues, no matter how much people change. And faking it till we make it rarely works. We are who we are.

On this matter of our essence, our core, I only acknowledge that we are not failures solely because of inadequate parenting, bad grades, or divorce—no more than we are successes because we earn valedictorian status, attain advanced degrees, or marry and start a family. Success and failure are only about something we've done or not done, not who we are.

Nevertheless, we tend to accept that we are ex-something when we shed a title. We may recall our time in those roles when reminiscing with friends, small talk with acquaintances, embellishing for sure. Still, we can acknowledge the experience as a closed chapter and that we have moved on. For example, Shaquille "Shaq" O'Neal was a professional basketball player. He often speaks of the glory days with the Lakers and his epic championship runs with the late Kobe Bryant. Currently, Shaq is an active investor and owns restaurants and fitness clubs. He is also one of the star analysts of the Emmy Award-winning post-game show *Inside the NBA*. Therefore, Shaq would not say to someone, "I am a basketball player and a business owner." Instead, he would lead with his current titles: father, Hall of Famer, investor, sports analyst, and entrepreneur.

On the other hand, we treat former titles differently from past behaviors or actions considered shameful. For example, when we do something "wrong," that moment is unfairly deemed our life companion. We allow society to label us; if they don't, we assign a label to ourselves. Instead, we should purge the event from our self-imposed storage file, like when the department of motor vehicles drops tickets and accidents after we stop violating or crashing long enough. In the words of one of my former pastors, "We are all ex-something." The implication is that if we are an ex, we are no longer what we used to be or do. Our hands are washed clean. I will share a grim, once-painful example:

A woman I presumed to be Kim rushed through the courtyard lined with tables and chairs and took her seat. She grabbed a black felt marker from her bag, reaching away from my table. With it, Kim drew a thick, equal sign through the name "Kim" on the table-tent nameplate. "Oops, she's not Kim," I thought. That's what I get for peaking. Then, while writing in her name and without looking up, she said, "I am new. I am so new that whoever printed this name—." She caught herself. She thought better of complaining, especially on her first day. Negativity circles like a burning fuse through college campuses, guaranteed to find a multitude of interested listeners before returning to sender and detonating.

However, her initial response seemed justified to me; it was the first thing we had in common. I knew how frustrating it might feel when anyone screws up your name. It is one of the things that I do not let slide. "We must always respect how someone chooses to identify themselves," my favorite uncle once taught me. Therefore, I kept quiet and tried to apply stoic face management.

She said, "Uh, my name is Evelyn."

I nodded, smiled, and said, "Hello."

Evelyn took more time to settle her energy. Nothing intensely frazzles a person on the first day at work like a morning traffic jam. Added frustrations include getting lost and seeing the wrong name in your place upon arrival. After a few moments, we exchanged pleasantries and checked our watches. Then, with simultaneous exhales, we acknowledged it was time to start and set off in opposite directions.

Along with faculty and other administrators, Evelyn and I maneuvered through the crowd representing our respective colleges to parents of prospective students. Unfortunately, this college fair was unstructured—crowded mingling—and I found it impossible to reconnect with Evelyn. Nevertheless, we exchanged smiles throughout the morning when one of us caught the other stealing an extended glance. We were equally curious and smitten in the few hours since our awkward introduction. Then, amid the madness, I heard someone call my name. In came my colleague, arriving quite late. She had learned the hard way that a 30-minute drive could take three and a half hours in LA traffic. Unfortunately, while Evelyn spoke with a family, I passed my duties to my colleague minutes before my next meeting. As a result, I did not have a chance to tell Evelyn "goodbye" or exchange contact information. I only knew her campus was blocks away and not close to my routine business.

However, the fact was that every new administrator's initial duty was to visit sister colleges in the area and make introductions. I learned my office was on Evelyn's list a few days later. She had met the rest of my team by the time I arrived. We masked our excitement with a firm handshake and a standard greeting while the staff watched because liking the newbie is also news that would travel. They did not see the lightning bolts exchanged through our grip or notice that I would be the last administrator she met on tour that day. Throughout our re-introductions, we maintained straight faces.

"Don't you run an internship program for students on your campus?" I asked.

"Yes, here's my card. I would be happy to involve your students. By the way, do you have a list of programs your department sponsors?"

"I have a brochure upstairs. Do you have a few minutes?"

And just like that, we went to my office to fake business as our priority. Evelyn and I created collaborative opportunities to benefit students. Our dual agendas meant spending time together was an equal benefit, and the electrical energy was palpable between us. I was a workaholic. She also had a lot of time on her hands and threw herself into work to fill that time. We embraced our apparent attraction and began activities unrelated to work.

First, there were off-campus lunches. Lunches turned into dinners. Then, after-work excursions such as riding my motorcycle up the coast on weekends became a thing. Evelyn and I talked about everything and nothing well into most nights. Still, I worked hard to keep us in the friend zone. I wanted to be known as someone other than the administrator with his personal life in a fishbowl. I got this, I thought. I even created professional boundaries. It was the only way to remain rational during avalanches of emotion.

My first line of defense was to discourage hugs. I recall reaching for preemptive handshakes for weeks. That's weird, I know. Indeed, I had to try. However, it was tough to greet one another and part ways by shaking hands outside work. Predictably, soon, handshakes became increasingly unnatural. Secondly, we had to stay on task and on time because I intentionally sandwiched our meetings between other commitments. Or we'd risk turning our workdays into long dates. I think we both knew that would be inefficient. We spent too much time veering off-topic. Therefore, we eventually agreed to schedule our meetings as the last of the day or connect after hours, whatever best fit our schedules. Finally, I was steadfast in keeping an open-door policy when we met. Ha. We ruined that strategy after the first conversation we deemed confidential. She would step inside my office while simultaneously closing the door behind her during subsequent visits. Just like that, it became clear that I was in over my head. My boundaries had fallen like dominoes, each of us toppling the first piece at opposite ends.

Neither of us anticipated the growing emotions triggered by spending time together daily. We should have counteracted its intensity with responsible conversations. Instead, we allowed feelings to guide our dialogue, disregarding opportunities to go deeper than small talk. In hindsight, I intentionally avoided common relationship questions by steering conversations away from deep, personal matters. I didn't want answers because I found contentment in my assumptions. We were on the same page, Christian and ready to date each other. I concluded further that Evelyn could not be involved with anyone else if I had all her time.

Nevertheless, uncertainty yanked at my soul and advanced the notion that something was off about Evelyn. It was a gentle pull that I chalked up to our emotional secrecy at work. We were careful not to give people the wrong impression, which felt like we were sneaking around. Yet, I knew that feeling of uneasiness was not about work. It was Evelyn. The moment I felt that tug in my spirit would have been a great time to ask open questions about feelings, intentions, and past relationships without overstepping the friend zone. Yeah, yeah. Instead, I carefully filtered her every word. As my bouts of apprehension accrued, I asked fewer questions and volunteered nothing. A free-flowing exchange might have risked our bliss, and I was unwilling to sacrifice that she may have been too good to be true. Reasoning that "nothing" (intimate) had happened made it easier to opt for ignorance. We were friends.

Meanwhile, our desire was a moving, attractive force that fed on the energy that masked our feelings. What lay beneath was clarity. Her allure proved too much for my attempts at composure. The id part of my mind convinced me that Evelyn also desired me. At that point, nothing stood between us. We finally progressed from platonic to intimate.

We all think we can control heart matters. The following scripture clarifies the reason we cannot. The Bible says in 2 Timothy 2:22, "Flee also youthful lusts: but follow righteousness, faith, charity, peace, with them that call on the Lord with a pure heart" (KJV).

When I first read the word "flee," I saw someone running away from a situation. The text implies that whatever is present calls for urgency. Get far away and fast! In other words, we cannot win the battle of our senses; the urge for our desires is too strong. So run before they take hold. You cannot flirt with those things that trigger you.

Notice that the text does not say to run aimlessly. Instead, the words provide direction: Run toward righteousness, in the direction of faith, with the aim of charity and peace, in the presence of other people who call on God and mean it.

As prescribed, I called on Christian friends to pray for me. Something felt wrong telling them everything because some also worked on campus. I was too ashamed of myself for losing control. Therefore, I never told them what I had done, which rendered them accountability scarecrows, protecting nothing. Then, I involved myself heavily with my church. I always attended Sunday service. I participated in a ministry, which was coaching the youth basketball team. I even attended Wednesday night services at my church or another with a fantastic midweek program. These activities kept me busier and provided less free time. Honestly though, they proved nothing except that we can have direction without focus. Sure, my life was going somewhere; that's the direction. Still, I needed more focus.

In other words, none of my running around changed the fact. Moving beyond friendship broke an arbitrary rule I set for myself: Never date anybody who also works in higher education. That meant ignoring our flying sparks and lowered guards. I disregarded self-control. Then, with caution nearly in the wind, justifications came. "Lots of couples meet through work," and "I knew I would likely find my future partner through work since I was a workaholic." So maybe breaking that rule wasn't the worst idea, not when the other broken rule was catastrophic: Never entertain a married woman.

Like most single men, I searched her hand for a wedding ring before our first words. It is one way to determine if a woman is available or off-limits without being forward. I searched my memory and confirmed. Evelyn did not wear a single piece of jewelry, which is not something I would have overlooked. I studied her every time I saw her. Then, while collaborating on a project, I noticed her wedding band months after our introductions and after we were intimate. Thus, I might have felt less guilt if I had shut down all future interactions right then. But instead of fleeing, I lingered.

"Hey, wait-a-minute, is that like a family heirloom or something?"

"What?"

"That ring," I said as I pointed toward her finger.

"No, it is my wedding ring."

I stood up from the table and walked toward the window. The silence made what I had to say harder and harder. Somehow facing the window made my words more accessible.

"I didn't know that you—."

Not letting me finish my thought, she said, "We slipped . . . We can still work together."

"I wasn't aware that the dictionary included 'slipped' as a euphemism for adultery. And my thoughts and our conversations have also crossed lines. I would like to think we could still collaborate on projects. Working together means we will only have conversations we would have if your husband were present. Do you agree?" I turned to face her. "I don't want to be known as a homewrecker."

"I agree," she said.

It never occurred to me that Evelyn might be married. She wasn't wearing her ring when we met, nor did she wear it again after our confrontation. Still, I would stare at Evelyn's bare left hand, which bore no tan line or blemish. And my mind perpetually looped back to the moment I saw the platinum band and the impact of its meaning. My mind's eye searches for such things. And the act of looking for it shamed me for my wrong. I kept wondering whether I intentionally avoided asking about a potential significant other. Are you dating anyone? It is an obvious question. By avoiding the "man in your life" question, I must have known the answer was "yes." She would have told me if she wanted me to learn about another man. I also suspected that any dating she might be doing would dissolve since we spent so much time together.

Eventually, Evelyn divulged more of her story. She married her high school sweetheart. Neither had ever dated another person. He was a "dot.com" executive who focused all his time on making money. I didn't know that he would encourage Evelyn to spend time with me so she wouldn't be bored and alone. Although we never met, he insisted I take Evelyn on short trips and drive his new Mercedes convertible, which we never did. Again, I did not know he existed. On consecutive Saturday mornings, "You should ride motorcycles today," he suggested. He was happy that she was pleased. He would do anything to keep her from complaining about him having to work. Evelyn had a different point of view. Whenever her husband encouraged her to be with me, she figured he loved her less. And the more she shared, the more manipulative I saw her.

I hated what I did and feared that was who I had become. Caught between two hard places offered a no-win scenario: I can lose love, or I can love Evelyn and lose myself. Unfortunately, I took too long to decide, which amounted to a choice. When working together, we caught lingering stares like before, only now, much less innocently. Our expressions communicated that we meant everything we were thinking. Then, a hello hug progressed into hugs coming and going. Our embraces grew longer and tighter. There was only one direction this would go.

And we both knew it, wanted it, and would not stop it, given the opportunity. So finally, after a couple of weeks of mounting guilt and gut-wrenching moral conviction, I told Evelyn that I could no longer see or talk to her.

"We have to stop interacting altogether. Only devious lust can be this wrong and feel right.

We fell for a deceitful con where everybody loses. You are everything I've ever wanted. That's the con. The deception is that I think you are perfect for me. But God would not have me slither to get what is perfect and destined. That is one reason I know this match is not the work of God. The other reason is that now when I look at you, I see the devil himself. My shame opened my eyes."

Undeterred, she spoke: "I don't want to stop seeing you." Sniffles followed.

Her tears broke through my conviction. I reached out to hug her, console her, and, if I told the truth, the hug also comforted me. Then, when I touched the proverbial hot stove only to learn that it was still hot, we nervously kissed like the world was watching, judging. It was like I was doing something wrong in front of all the people I cared for: my parents, my grandparents, my siblings, my closest friends, the students I counseled, and my pastor; all their eyes were on me—disappointed.

"I will leave him for you," she said. I could tell she had given considerable thought to divorce because her sharp tone added certainty to her pronouncement. Not at all like someone who would say whatever to hang on to what was slipping away. She meant that without fear or flinch, just raw assurance. Her words sobered me like a broken spell, and I snapped back to reality with my own certainty. I pushed back to arm's length and then another full stride from her personal space.

"There is no future for us, Evelyn. God would never bless a relationship that started like this. Belief in this reality is how we know everything about us is wrong. We cannot go back and do it right."

More tears.

I had also considered Evelyn's potential divorce before her tearful reveal. Although haunted by my conscience, I tried vainly to legitimize my affair. Marry her, I thought, hold hands, and walk into the sunset. It is an apparent thought for cheaters. However, marrying someone you've cheated with is rarely the right choice. Therefore, I narrowed my considerations to two options. The first was to stay together and endure the long-term pain we would carry by further ignoring our beliefs. The second option was to part ways, bringing short-term heartache—still pain, nonetheless. My mind worked non-stop, thoroughly muddied by potential outcomes such as seeking forgiveness and perhaps living blissfully or cursing our children not yet born. No matter how I looked at it, option one was forever dirty and cold-blooded to the innocent man involved. Option two meant an imminent loss. My revelation eventually came.

Hearing Evelyn's tearful plea for potential divorce was the epiphany that provided renewed understanding. There is no strength in accepting a bad situation as fate, whether self-created or not. Therefore, I saw permanent involvement with Evelyn like earning compound interest on my worst debt. Simply put, we would earn guilt and shame for our original misdeeds, accumulating future regret and misfortune as karma in perpetuity. No thanks. I'll pass.

There was another week of long goodbyes and mixed messages. I blocked Evelyn's number and then unblocked it daily for consecutive days. I did not want her to call and hoped she would from one moment to the next. Meanwhile, I knew that my beliefs must take precedence, which prevented me from ever reaching out to her. Unfortunately, we were two depressed Christians struggling with what we saw in our respective mirrors and hating it. In addition, an innocent man was robbed of his wife's fidelity and potentially his trust in her. "What would happen if he ever learned of our betrayal?" I thought. Still, I was too deep to get out on my own. What can we do when our beliefs are at odds with what is physically in front of us? There comes a time when you're too powerless to run.

Still, anybody who has ever been in dark places knows that there are some things through which only God can draw you out. Evelyn and I knew that she was my drug. I was addicted and struggling with my spiritual sobriety one day at a time. Then, one night, Evelyn's call snuck through my intermittent call block. And I answered rather than resist, which I had done six consecutive days. "Dammit," I thought. I was close to a milestone, one week of moral repair, blown by answering the call.

"Hello," I said.

Then, I heard sniffling on the other end. No words.

"Where is your husband?"

"He's in the shower."

"No, no, no. Hang up. I told you not to call me anymore. I meant that."

Then, she delivered a sobering line best suited for a Hollywood drama: "But when I'm with my husband, I feel like I'm cheating on you."

Silence.

A flushing sensation soaked my face and rippled through my core and to my fingertips. Then, a warm current of guilt-filled sweat gushed through my pores. I wondered if Evelyn intended to flatter me or communicate how deeply I mattered to her. I shrugged. Her words brought the murky depth of my transgressions sharply into focus. I screwed up big time.

"Do you hear yourself? This is out of order. I'll say it again. There is no future for a relationship that started like this. Please do not call me anymore."

Click. I hung up. The following day, I got a call from Evelyn's closest co-worker. She called to relay a message from Evelyn.

"Evelyn was crying when her husband finished his shower last night. After he asked why the tears, she confessed that you guys once made a mistake. Then, he forced her resignation. Evelyn resigned this morning by phone. She also changed her phone number and said they were moving. Her husband's message to you is, 'Don't call yourself a Christian.'"

Nobody could call what I did anything less than a catastrophe—a gut punch sure to cause a counterpunch—as violence would be an apt response for the only victim. So, I would not blame him if he tried. Instead, he told me not to call myself a Christian. His call-out reminds me of when a child hurts a parent's feelings. And rather than punish the child, they say, "I'm disappointed." That guilt always hurts worse.

It took some time, but eventually, I rejected the parting shot from Evelyn's husband. I knew I had to own how I sullied his marriage and disregarded my values. However, just as I could not let Dr. Collin's behavior define me academically, I could not allow Evelyn's husband to define me personally. In other words, whether right or wrong, I choose how I identify myself, as my favorite uncle told me. Thus, of course, it's not as simple as I stated. If it were, nobody would take responsibility for their actions. Instead, they would make accountability a matter of convenience. However, knowing that all my actions are between God and me is simple. I once heard someone in church say, "You don't know how awful you can be because you haven't thoroughly analyzed yourself. You also don't know how good you can be because you listen to other people."

Thus, I returned to my questions of purpose: Who am I, what is my essence, what contributions will I make, what am I capable of achieving, what is important to me, what do I need to improve, and what is my power? Ultimately, it was by embracing the Christian identity that I began healing, even though I initially felt like a monster. I needed to feel human again, to pull myself out of the muck and from feeling the sting of lingering grief. To do this, I leaned into a scripture. As I have said, nature and scripture present guidance and critique applicable to human events. Therefore, I use both to dissect the most confounding elements in my life accordingly. Ephesians 2:3-10 (NIV) reads:

> *(3) All of us also lived among them at one time, gratifying the cravings of our flesh and following its desires and thoughts. Like the rest, we were by nature deserving of wrath. (4) But because of His great love for us, God, who is rich in mercy, (5) made us alive with Christ even when we were dead in transgressions—it is by grace you have been saved. (6) And God raised us up with Christ and seated us with him in the heavenly realms in Christ Jesus, (7) in order that in the coming ages he might show the incomparable riches of his grace, expressed in his kindness to us in Christ Jesus. (8) For it is by grace you have been saved, through faith—and this is not from yourselves, it is the gift of God— (9) not by works, so that no one can boast. (10) For we are God's handiwork, created in Christ Jesus to do good works, which God prepared in advance for us to do.*

In other words, by knowing who I am in Christ, I could move beyond the mistakes that I have made. Sure, we get bogged down occasionally, and it is easy to get into a rut. Still, getting unstuck starts with introspection and answering your first question of purpose: Who am I?

Someone reading this book may have dealt with frustration in maladaptive ways, such as shouting, swearing, slamming doors, or screaming into pillows. Others have shadowboxed and wished their circumstance was on the other end. And more than a few indulged in stress eating, drinking, or illegal substances. But with few exceptions, there is a time when we must admit that we have learned all we can. And then declare it is time to move on. No longer letting the thing that had you stuck impact how you move or think.

One of my mantras is, "You're only as good as your next decision." The words speak to the future by using the present continuous tense. For example, the act of making decisions always continues in the mantra. In other words, the saying describes an action that repeats. Notice that it does not say to ignore past actions. Instead, it places a value on operating in the present, moving forward or backward, by making the next single decision, each being the most critical.

I did not write this story seeking penance or redemption. God forgave me long ago. Instead, every thought, account, and detail included in this book is to help someone free themselves from what may be holding them back. 1 Corinthians

10:13 (ESV) states: "No temptation has overtaken you that is not common to man. God is faithful, and He will not let you be tempted beyond your ability, but with the temptation, He will also provide the way of escape, that you may be able to endure it."

CHAPTER FOUR
PEOPLE-PLEASING IS SELF-SACRIFICE, NOT LEADERSHIP

I met Alan, who worked at another university in town, at a professional conference when I worked as Assistant Dean of Students. I was in my late 20s. He was older. Still, we were early in our careers and optimistic about our futures. Many of our conversations centered around his job. He had all the traditional academic credentials for his position and enough positive work experience to warrant his rank and then some. However, when I asked about pay increases and promotions, he offered flimsy excuses and towed the company line. He could have explained why he would not consider the job market more explicitly, even though it was common knowledge that college administrators achieved higher rank and salary by leaving. To keep things somewhat light between us, I didn't push him. Instead, I accepted that he was a man committed to mediocrity. First, though, I needed help figuring out why.

Then, two work situations exposed his fear. One student issue may have led to bad press; the other involved a staff conflict that might have required him to intervene and mediate. By any measure, these were mid-level cases, relatively easy; however, ones Alan must address swiftly and judiciously. Since it was common for colleagues to share strategies, I went along with him picking my brain. Heck, everybody gets stuck sometimes. And I served as a university hearing officer and a certified conflict mediator on campus, who contributed more as a mentor to Alan than a friend. Unfortunately, there was a problem with his tone and proposed remedies. I couldn't put my finger on it. Again, tiptoeing around conflict did not match Alan's powerful physical presence.

Alan was well-spoken and built strong like he wore a muscle suit. But his meek, docility would make you wonder if he'd even be helpful if the building were burning down. Such a people-pleaser, he may run if someone says save yourself, and stop if another person cries for help. Ultimately, all three of them would burn. No surprise that he felt my way of handling drama was too strong.

Slowly, Alan withdrew his energy as I pitched potential strategies. "If that doesn't work, you may try this," I continued until I sensed apprehension. Then, doubtful and wimpish, Alan meekly offered a bland counter to my suggestions. Admittedly, it was eyebrow-raising to see him water down my proposals by making them less direct. He was reluctant to take a side and expressed middle-of-the-road approaches, which was his apparent effort to be a people-pleaser and blend in. Unfortunately, Alan's conformist strategy implied his inability and unwillingness to lead—two unintended consequences.

Then, he confided in me. He had spent 10 years in federal prison, and he could not do the things that I could do because he was less "marketable" as a felon if fired. His last performance review was mediocre. He considered himself lucky to have his job and would be neutral in all interactions to keep it. I encouraged him to share his thoughts and opinions at work and let his principles guide him. Since he was more apt to be fired for not being himself, he may as well go down operating as he believed.

"I have to handle things differently than I would if not for my past," he said.

I quickly responded: "My question is, why operate in the job like you don't yet have it? They hired you to be you, to bring your unique perspective and ideas. If you can't do that, your supervisors may discount your input. They may render your presence ineffective and find someone who can add to the campus dialogue and not just agree with it."

His credibility as a leader improved when he stopped allowing his negative past to guide his decisions and trying to please everybody. Presumably, we all agree that people-pleasing is a fear that leads to certain doom.

Fear of Failure

My first awareness of the fear of failure came in the fourth grade when a teammate refused to shoot free throws that would potentially tie or win our game. With seconds left on the clock, his butt stayed fastened to the bench, following the opponent's time out as the players from both teams lined up on the lane lines. Still, he wouldn't budge, couldn't budge. The free-throw line remained empty, and the opposing coach's strategy of icing the shooter worked. We lost.

I attended a fantastic play rehearsal in junior high school a few years later. The young actors recited their lines on cue, indicating that things would go smoothly when the curtains opened. Unfortunately, one of the actors refused to come on stage on opening night. So much for preparation to calm stage fright.

A guy refused to try out for the football team in the seventh grade. He claimed that he could not handle the humiliation of getting cut. Interestingly, nobody ever got cut from the football team. Had he gone to tryouts, position coaches would have salivated and fought over dibs on him. Instead, he was not playing even though he was the second biggest guy in his grade and the fastest in the school. We learned he was the fastest once he ran track three years later and didn't lose a race during the season. He surprised himself with his talent. There was a lot of talk around town about whether he would remain undefeated. Alas, we can only speculate because he punked out by not participating in the regional track & field meet. "This way, I stay undefeated," he said. Ironically, his consistent sprint times would have qualified for advancement to the state contest had he run.

Each person was more than capable, and they knew it. The question is, what comes between what we know and what we ultimately do? Rather than rush to the answer, let's hang out where the tension lies for a while.

By and large, Americans confuse who they are with the things they've done. Then, changes to their so-called achievement or status often present identity challenges. For example, changing things like marital status, social class, body image, celebrity status, or rank can shake people to their core. In other words, who we say we are and how we answer the other questions of purpose should not depend on the precarious ways others may see us. Simply put, labels can support and undermine an individual's self-esteem, hamper their ability to progress, and cause unspeakable pain.

However, the truth is that whether you forget your lines, make the team, lose a race, or get a divorce doesn't define you. Instead, how hard you try reveals whether you have given them power. Some of us are familiar with the plot in old karate movies (or The Matrix) where the best student doesn't believe he is a master. After acing all tests, he pleads with his teacher to give him more tests. Think briefly about what might happen if the student decided not to try. Besides the movie ending prematurely, the student would never realize their progress and power. Maybe they never answer the questions of purpose for themselves, which they do by the movie's end. "I am the master," they proclaim. When you know who you are, you know better how to meet your needs. That is the definition of self-knowledge and the basis for all positive human interaction.

I taught history in a Saturday Program for Academic and Cultural Education (SPACE), attracting middle-school-aged Black children focused on science and math. Not surprisingly, the reasons students shouted for having little excitement for my class were long and varied. They declared that history was boring and irrelevant to their futures. One student said, "I don't want to waste time learning about dead people." I told them that we would cover thousands of years and that history would be their favorite class by the midpoint of the term. Then, what began as honest speculation, quickly elevated to boos, laughter, and dismissive waving gestures.

I laughed along with them and seamlessly moved into the beginning of the lesson. I called a student's name and asked, "Are you a genius?" There was a moment of stunned silence. Then, I went to the next student on my list, who answered, "no." After five students answered "no" in succession, I changed the question. "Why aren't you a genius?" I asked five or six different students. They returned silence! So, I changed the question one last time and asked the remaining students to shout out the characteristics of a genius. With two students posted in front of a whiteboard, serving as scribes, I directed which words or phrases they would write. Students were all shouting at once:

- Someone who gets straight A's
- Someone who is smart
- Does all their homework
- Does their work without being told
- Confident
- Has ability

In the strongest, authoritative voice I could muster, I yelled, "STOP!" Principal Joe Clark of the movie *Lean on Me* would have been proud. Then, in a scene fit for an Academy Award, I communicated disappointment as I asked my scribes to sit down. The room was quiet. I looked earnestly into each student's eyes and tapped the desk of those who tried to look down or away. Then, I went through their list in a still yet firm voice, pointing to a different child each time.

- Can you get straight A's?
- Are you smart?
- Can you do all your homework?

- Can you do your work without being told?
- Can you develop confidence?
- Do you have ability?

Collectively, they answered "yes" to each question. The energy in the room picked up with each answer. So, are you a genius? "Yes," they responded. My smile showed my approval. Then, I handed each of them a poem that spoke of the reader as a genius in the first person. We began and ended each class reciting the poem in unison. Eventually, the class memorized the genius poem. It was the first of many lessons where students placed themselves at the subject's center. They were fueled by seeing themselves (and later their ancestors) as participants in scholarship and religion, inventors and entrepreneurs, musicians and artists, and rulers, all of which spoke power into them.

This history class may have changed self-esteem for some. Then, the increased value in self greatly improved relationships with their families, friends, teachers, and others. Focusing on their past sparked a hunger for more exploration for other students. Together, we drew a line from antiquity to the present day. We ignited a burn to learn. Eventually, I had to force students out of my classroom, or they would stay too long after and miss lunch. Their paradigm shift toward history class was evidence that they saw connecting the contributions of their ancestors as affirming their existence. I was satisfied knowing that history became their favorite or most important class. Either was a win. I taught that knowledge of self was critical to their survival and instrumental in answering questions of purpose. It helps to learn these things as children because they absorb new material faster and often with less skepticism. Often, teaching adults is like trying to use new software on an antiquated computer. Without significant upgrades, the adult brain may reject new knowledge, simply unable to compute it. Drawing the best out of children is where dreams are born.

Section Two

SECTION ONE • TRANSCENDING BOUNDARIES

ACHIEVING THROUGH DREAMING

Surrender to Your Dreams

When you're reluctant to shoot for your dreams,
You're holding on to somebody or something, it seems:

Bad memories,
Situations,
Past hurts,
Hesitation,
A collection of lies masquerading as your fate.

But when you become the architect of your perception.
You'll trade the ball and chain for emancipation,

Such as constraints for release,
Swapping anger for peace.
Expelling ego for humility,
Being stuck for utility.

In other words, you cannot hold on to your nightmares
If you dare to surrender to your dreams.

Hughes Suffren

CHAPTER FIVE
TAKE YOUR THOUGHTS AND DREAMS CAPTIVE

He was approximately 8 feet tall and pulled one booted club foot with the help of one hand behind his thigh. His boot had a metal tap on its heel that scraped on the concrete when he dragged it. "Skrrrrreeeee, pause, pause, pause, skrrrreeee." The sound was getting louder and louder. So, without looking, I knew he was gaining on me as I frantically tugged and pulled to free my pant leg, stuck in my bike's chain. Once awakened, I was too scared to go back to sleep. The giant man might be there, at my bike, waiting for me, and if I close my eyes, I'll see him.

"It's true," said the calming voice in the dark. "If we put our minds to it, we always dream about the last thing we were thinking before falling asleep."

That's what my older sister told me after she quieted my screams by gently patting my back.

"Are you sure?"

"Yes, I do it all the time."

She recognized I needed more encouragement as I sat slumped in a cold sweat. "Try it. Just think of something fun," she said. It was sound advice to a child haunted by a recurring nightmare. Besides, I had tried everything else. Plus, she was my big sister. Being two whole years older made her a genius. Therefore, I embraced her guarantee and directly made my nightly verbal request to the dream makers: girls, girls, girls, girls. A fourth-grade boy wouldn't have much else on his brain.

When it worked, I credited my sister: "That was the best advice ever!" After that, I blamed myself for not focusing enough or letting my mind wander when it failed. Then, as I grew older, my technique evolved into a method far more reliable. Foolproof.

I stumbled upon my advanced method during an October trip to a haunted house with my sister and two cousins, who are brothers. The building had the outdoor furnishings one would expect from a haunted house. Cobwebs, skeletons, orange balloons, and black balloons lined the entrance. We walked through a dark, narrow passageway to enter and toward a supposed dead end. The surround sound chants of a séance echoed, and the room was damp and drafty. Cold. Then booming footsteps grew louder and faster, like something or someone was running toward us. In the same split second, we realized there was nowhere to go, and a flash of light illuminated the face of Dr. Frankenstein's monster. It appeared in front of our faces, closest to me. As the screams left our mouths, a trap door that blended with the walls opened. My cousins and sister made a break for it and could not return to check for me once through. Instead of running, I punched "the monster." It was a nervous reflex to someone quickly invading my personal space rather than a sign of fear or aggression. Standing there, frozen, I was more afraid that I hit him than I was of him.

He pulled off the rubber monster mask with one hand and revealed that he was a balding, old white guy. For a moment, he looked uncertain, perhaps stuck somewhere between reporting me to the authorities or hitting me back. When he opened his mouth, he babbled while shooing me with his free hand. "You're supposed to run," he said. While I watched, he shook his head, put on his mask, and reset his trap and spooky soundtrack. Of course, he had not intended to expose spookhouse trade secrets. Now the jig was up. He waved me away again. This time, I slipped through the door that looked like a wall, which opened long enough to get through and then closed behind me. I caught up to my family and explained why I was far behind. I wasn't sure if they believed me when I told them I had punched the monster. Their mouths fell open. With gasps as the only audible sound between us, a second or two passed. Finally, one of my cousins broke the awkward silence by excitedly saying, "Man, you're crazy." We celebrated with high fives and laughter and continued cautiously walking through a winding path toward the next manufactured horror. I found myself faking being scared by running when they ran, only to stay together.

During the car ride home, my mom asked if the haunted house was scary. My two cousins and my sister shouted the most frightening parts for them, and one of them added that I had punched a monster. "That's awful," mom said with a curious gaze. She found the news more credible when I told her an old white guy was under the mask. Her expression turned accepting, nodding. Knowing I was too small for my punches to hurt anyone, she laughed, permitting us to laugh too. Maintaining the smirk of trying to contain laughter, mom looked at me,

"Why didn't you—?"

"Run," I interrupted. "Not from an old dude wearing a mask," I said.

That was the day horror movies were no longer scary, and neither were my nightmares. During the scariest shows, I would say out loud, "That ain't real," which ultimately triggered a calming sensory response, like the feeling that follows a deep breath. Even for a child, horror movies disobeyed common sense and rules of physics, and their storylines were generally worlds away from my reality. Every sane person I knew would run away from the danger of a field of zombies or a chainsaw starting by itself and not toward them. Such scenes were always too far-fetched for me. My nightmares were far scarier but no more real, I thought. So, I applied a similar strategy to my dreams that I did for scary movies. When my dreams turned stressful, I'd wake myself up by saying out loud, "This is only a dream." My eyes always opened, and I felt safe and satisfied.

The ability to order consciousness was evidence that my technique was evolving. I was no longer cautious or concerned about experiencing nightmares. Instead, I enjoyed the extraordinary strength of coming to my rescue. It was like my bad dreams were bullies, and the ability to wake up was my superpower. Having newly acquired enhanced natural ability is one thing; however, controlling its use makes it an advantage. For example, the Incredible Hulk reached Avenger status when he could freely turn himself into the Hulk. His friends could not count on his power if he had to wait until something made him mad enough to become unstoppable and still out of control.

One hundred percent of the time, my power worked at my will until I became an adult. It isn't that my strategy stopped working. Instead, I further refined my skills as I grew older. One night, I must have been too tired to wake up. Then, it happened; I accidentally stayed asleep while awakening inside my dream. Seamless. This one providential event, this seminal moment, was all I needed to recognize that I held improved power. First, I began capturing stressful moments with cat-like quickness. Then, I changed the course of my dreams from anguish to something favorable. In other words, just like Frankenstein's monster reset his trap, I could redo segments of my dreams. With practice, I developed the skill that led me to return to any point in my dreams and create new scenarios, much like when movies flashback and create alternate endings. This ability was a game-changer because it meant uninterrupted sleep, thus no longer trending toward becoming depressed, or worse—an insomniac.

Nobody ever believed me when I spoke about the phenomenon of altering dreams. Young people, older adults, teachers, family, and friends all skeptically challenged me like I said I saw an alien or Big Foot. I regretted telling anybody and thought about how negatively people react to those with differences. Being young, Black, beanpole skinny, and the brightest student in my class triggered unwanted attention. So, I stopped talking about dreams and my ability to control the bad ones. I accepted the fact that God gives everyone gifts. Why and how people use their talents is between them and God. Nobody is obligated to believe in our dreams or abilities; both are personal. God revealed this gift so I may have perspective, sanity, balance, and insight. Revelation is still coming. I would be remiss without explicitly saying that human beings can control their thoughts, actions, and realities, even when asleep. I say this because it is not reasonable for me to have the ability to alter dreams alone. Other people must share similar abilities in circles other than mine.

With a bit of internet research, confirmation came. I learned, for example, that "lucid dreams" is a term that academically supports what I discovered experientially. Historians traced lucid dreaming to ancient times. Africans in Egypt analyzed the meaning behind dreams and studied dream symbols, searching for messages and prophecies from the gods. The Greeks and Romans copied. Still, the extent of early versions was glimpses of reality and the ability to wake up. Finally, in 1975, researchers proved (in a laboratory) perfect recall and moving freely within dreams. Advances in the field gained momentum in the 1980s. By then, I had already perfected control over redirecting my dreams.

Now, there are techniques for lucid dreaming, complete with pros and cons. Researchers are looking to make the method a practical tool for self-improvement. And commodify it, no doubt. We'll see whether scientists eventually will market altering dreams as a blue pill/red pill prescription. Take blue to awaken during moments of elevated stress and red for an adventure. Nonetheless, I have moved on because I completely control my bad dreams; I change them if my dreams aren't positive. I also change negative thoughts, and you can do it too.

Nature and biblical scriptures often answer questions that may go unanswered if left up to us. In nature, for the most part, animals operate on instinct—reactions that automatically occur well below their conscious level. The same is true of fauna. Flowers bloom in their season, trees bear fruit, and both live and die. Unfortunately, that explanation tells us nothing about people's ability to develop their minds—that we operate beyond instinct and that our actions can be voluntary.

Perhaps scripture might address the prospect of controlling our subconscious. The Bible says in Proverbs 23:7 (KJV), "For as he thinketh in his heart, so is he." It seems that if God holds us accountable for our thoughts, then we must be able to control them. I'm no theologian. Nor do I have a monopoly on the truth. Therefore, if I have misinterpreted the context of Proverbs, I will offer another scripture.

Several other scriptures speak about changing our thoughts. For example, Corinthians 10:5 (ESV) encourages us to "take every thought captive to obey Christ." The biblical emphasis on the linear relationship between thoughts and action is revolutionary in its application. In other words, whatever we think, we will do if given the opportunity. For years, I understood these scriptures as threats not to sin. But now, I see them as diagrams for success.

For example, people allow the essence of their true selves and their life direction to be twisted and confused by outsiders. There's just too much noise in our day-to-day lives. However, revelation often makes our paths clear in our minds. If it needs to be clarified, we can create clarity in our subconscious, claim it as our truth, and what follows is a higher self-concept. In other words, a path to emerging is to take control of our minds. New understanding will produce elevated aspirations and positive human experiences.

CHAPTER SIX
DREAMS OFFER PATHWAYS TO ACHIEVEMENT

Dreams are only one area in our minds that may influence our actions. Another is our imagination, including daydreams and visions. For instance, I could handle most challenging situations if I saw a path to overcoming them. Vision-land elevated my creativity, processing, and experience. These thoughts also reduced stress and fear. Moreover, the experience allowed that hard thing to be something I had conquered before, even if only in my head. Thus, dreams and daydreams are indispensable tools that offer pathways toward achievement.

My belief in dreams and daydreams began the summer between fourth and fifth grade. When arriving at the basketball court on our empty neighborhood playground, I would practice my ballhandling and dribbling drills as if my coaches were watching. First, I spoke their dialogue aloud, mimicked their tone, and answered with my voice. Then, before leaving the court, I would dramatize an imaginary scene after hours of ball-handling drills and shooting jump shots. One of my favorites was the closing moments of a basketball game, which I voiced out loud in the third person: "He gets the rebound and dribbles up the right side of the court. The crowd is counting down—five, four, three. He crosses over to his left to avoid the double-team and gets off his shot. Three, two, one, aaaaaaaaaaaaaaaah, the horn sounds."

If the shot went in, I'd go into my celebration, which ranged from virtual high fives to a victory lap or a version of the famous pose of Muhammad Ali standing over Sonny Liston. I changed my celebration if I deemed it lame or uncool. If the jump shot missed, I continued narrating an alternate ending: "He misses, but he's fouled on the play. He needs to hit both free-throws for his team to win."

If I made them both, I would go into my rehearsed celebration. If I missed one, it was overtime, and I started the countdown again. You see, I always win in my dreams and daydreams, and experiencing success through visualization led to actual achievement.

For example, at the end of that summer, I won top awards for ballhandling and dribbling at a basketball camp sponsored by a local university. And in the camp's final scrimmage, I scored the game-winning shot without nerves or hesitation because I had already rehearsed the scene hundreds of times in my mind and on the playground. My fifth-grade season also bore more success, which I also attributed to changing my thoughts. Statistically, I recorded the most consistent and productive numbers of any player in our league. I earned the "Most Improved" and "Rebounder" trophies. The head coaches gave the latter award to the player who snatched the most rebounds for the season. Whatever validity those trophies symbolized fell short of the prize I knew I'd worked for and earned, Most Valuable Player (MVP). After our banquet, the MVP award winner could not look me in the eye when he said, "Man, you deserved MVP." I shrugged and offered the weakest, most insincere congratulations. "I know" is how I should have responded. Indeed, I saw myself throwing that "most improved" trophy in the trash. That wasn't visualization; it was a fact. I trashed it. Every year after that, I earned MVP honors to go along with a state championship in my senior year of high school.

Another example of the power of thoughts came when my sister's track coach, Mr. Kline, told her she needed to change her walk and run. Her toes pointed outward like a penguin when she walked. Mr. Kline suggested that she practice walking deliberately and straight "like an Indian Chief." Before political correctness was mainstream, he said it and then demonstrated the walk. His toes pointed forward as if he were walking on the outer edges of a straight painted line 2-3 inches wide. He recommended that she do it when she thought about it, which would soon become a habit. She practiced her new walk, and when she wasn't practicing walking or running that way, she visualized winning by running that way. Mr. Kline was correct. She formed a habit and developed a more efficient gate by the seventh grade, one year later. Without a doubt, my sister's efforts of focused thoughts and visualization were factors in her success. She went on to win four gold medals at the state championships for track and field during each year of high school, never losing a race.

More than the success that followed was understanding the relationship between controlling my dreams and producing good thoughts. This formula led to peak performance. Accolades such as winning awards and basketball games were byproducts of the inner work that partly defines who I am. Thus, the strategies I thought I found, found me, which means there were no external hand-me-downs. I could not order a side of dream control. God only brought out of me organically what He placed inside me, which laid dormant.

What power or ability do you overlook because self-reflection is too hard? Do you bypass natural innovations for external breakthroughs? Unfortunately, answering these questions in a maladaptive way led me to a severe case of John Henryism, a cultural drive to do everything alone at significant personal risk. I later learned that mine was one of many cultures to embrace this strategy. Nevertheless, that was how I rolled during my early college years.

Back then, I thought nothing of coordinated activities for self-improvement because most of what was available had come from my imagination. The rest came from my family. Thus, getting outside help was taboo. Why are they trying to study me, and why would I allow it? I thought. Then, gym classes and work added to my disapproval. I considered icebreakers and team builders prying or worthless attempts at forced fun. I deemed organized guided meditation methods bland attempts of pseudo-self-awareness. In other words, activities void of authenticity and substance were not for me. After all, visualizing the end-of-game countdowns and last-second shot celebrations was, in fact, natural and innate.

For instance, one day, my college football coaches met with our team in an auditorium. They announced that we would gather there every Monday afternoon during the off-season. Then, the head coach mentioned some sketchy crap about preparing our minds for success. Next to him stood a guest speaker. Just let me tell you how he turned loose the skeptics by introducing him.

Bedlam ensued as he stepped to the microphone. It was as if the entire room was having a party, and he was there, uninvited to his celebration. Surprise! Suffice (it) to say, there were skeptics and agitators, and I was both.

We all knew that our head coach did everything for one purpose: to win. He glossed over personal matters such as injuries and academic progress toward degrees. Instead, he focused on whether we were healthy enough to play and academically eligible—proof that his care for our players, personally and academically, was conditional and secondary. We had a fractured program. Our athletic director had lost confidence in our coaching staff. Our coaches did not get along with each other; coaches did not get along with players, and players did not get along with players. Yet, the head coach tried everything to unite us, albeit for selfish reasons. That's why nobody took him seriously when he announced that our guest speaker was a hypnotist. We thought even less of the hypnotist.

After the hypnotist babbled about his background and offered a few words of context, he asked for volunteers. I thought this guy must be a fraud, and there was no way I would participate. However, one of the five players he chose from raised hands was my roommate. He went through the familiar ritual of hypnosis: "Follow the medallion with your eyes. When I snap my fingers, you will stand at attention and do as I tell you. When I snap my fingers twice, you will awaken, and you won't remember what happened."

Then, he "put them under" as a group. Next, he asked the volunteers to perform certain acts individually, such as running around the room, jumping up and down, barking like a dog, and other silly acts of obedience. Complete nonsense! We all laughed, and nobody believed the volunteers were under his spell. During the recap, the volunteers took turns denying being under his control. All but one said they were having fun with it and just faking. The one outlier was one of our backup quarterbacks. He wanted our team to win so badly that he would not admit that the spell did not work until days later.

Our coach was grasping at straws. Watching him was like watching the end of a movie. It is the scene where the people closest to the villain cannot take any more of his lies or slimy acts. Simultaneously, the villain sees his world shrinking and offers nonsensical alternative endings, trying to prove to everyone in the room that he's not the problem, all while they look at him with disgust. One by one, they leave the room, passing by authorities coming in to remove him. That could eventually be our coach's scene. He was cancerous. Thus, in the minds of our team, the "powers that be" would soon remove him. Coaches cannot lose their locker rooms and keep their jobs. Even so, the lame duck offered guided meditation as his next bright idea.

Mondays became meditation days for our college football team, and I sat as far in the back and as close to the exit doors as possible. It was garbage psychobabble, I said to anybody who would listen. Our facilitator turned on the elevator music and spoke softly. I joked with teammates that a séance would be next. Our coaches were anxious to win games, and I saw these sessions as desperation. What we needed were better players. Lights coming on signaled the end of our mandatory session. I would bolt at the first flicker of the fluorescent lights, making sure the team manager marked an X next to my name on the attendance list as I'd run out. The sessions lasted the winter of my sophomore year. During spring practices, I saw a difference in some of our players.

"Tough catch, man. You've been making a lot of those lately," I said to one of my teammates.

"I owe it all to meditation days," he said.

"What. How?"

"I've seen these plays many times by visualizing making them. Didn't Meditation Mondays work for you?"

At that moment, all I could think was that I had blocked my progress. My skepticism and pessimism toward organized reflection allowed my competitors to close any talent gap I may have had. I might have tried meditation the following year if another losing season hadn't influenced our coach's decision not to offer it.

We were perennial losers—every team's wishful opponent for homecoming. Therefore, again, coaches stood to lose more than games. So then, agitated and desperate, our coaching staff took the fatal step of violating the rules for recruiting. Their coaching futures and integrity, already on life support, had flatlined.

Thus, shortly after the NCAA penalized our team, the university president fired the staff. Then, it was evident to me then that I played myself. I realized late that guided meditation was another form of playing out scenes on my neighborhood playground, whether organized or not. Visualization is essential. I used it to help me become a two-sport college athlete. Unfortunately, I believed in the power of dreams, daydreams, and visualization but mistakenly thought they lost their value when organized.

Moreover, commodifying the technique for selfish gains stripped away the unique, personal quality of reflection and follow-through for me. So, I condemned the strategy before giving the guided, commercial version a chance. Missing out served as a cold reminder that insight comes in many forms; these skills are powerful, and we must realize when we are in a moment to gain or sharpen them.

Nevertheless, I have successfully checked off nightmares and daydreams from my list of tools to redefine, transform, and apply for my good. It came directly to me, not from books, classes, psychological theories, or ideologies. It is not weak to seek help when you know you need assistance; it is resourceful. There will never be a prize for muscling through and underachieving. For example, I used to tell all students: "If you cannot get through chapter three in a textbook without a teacher's help, secure a tutor before the class begins. You can drop the tutor when you have a solid grasp of the material."

I suggest learning what you need in any way you can. My effort here is to share an important truth. We have extraordinary power to mold whatever enters our minds into future achievement. Therefore, listening to your dreams and using them to inform conscious realities may be instructive. And who knows? Now and again, a deep-thinking strategy may work for you.

CHAPTER SEVEN
DREAM OF THE WORLD YOU WANT TO LIVE IN

There is, of course, one annoying thing I have yet to uncover—how to finish a dream accidentally interrupted, especially if it needed changing before I awakened. Yes, I admit it. I join the masses who are annoyed by disrupted good dreams. Let us be truthful. We have all stayed in bed, hoping to finish a dream that was so good. Lightly closing your eyes was your attempt to remember or perhaps fall back to sleep. You may have taken deep breaths or inhaled through your nose and exhaled through your mouth, trying to prevent distractions. This type of dream appears infrequently and falling back to sleep offers no guarantee of its return. Still, you try. You focus hard because losing the moment means the fantasy will be gone forever if history repeats itself.

The good ones rarely recur. Ultimately, your efforts fail. So, you're sitting there trying to piece your dream back together. You may recall parts of the dream vividly. Other elements may make no sense and border on being weird. When this happens, as I know it does, don't become frustrated and begin to doubt your ability to redirect a dream before you wake. The real issue is that some dreams are so factually relevant and historically accurate that you want to see them through. Others are haunting because they feel so real that what follows in real life isn't the dream's direction. It leaves the dreamer stunned and searching for answers as if part of their soul is stuck until they find them. Both were true for an older teenager named Sultan and his dreams of self-sufficiency, entrepreneurship, and one day having a family of his own.

Sultan and his parents and siblings worked and lived on a large farm owned by someone else. Sultan had nine siblings, some of whom rubbed in that he was the least favorite of his parents' children. He understood that his favorability rank was precise and not alleged because his mother clarified it. She gave her other children the best she and her husband could offer in clothes, privileges, and accolades when she spoke of them publicly. Sultan wore the rags of a farmhand—raggedy overalls and busted shoes—and his mother barely mentioned him. Most children might develop esteem and confidence issues, sink into social isolation, or acquire another emotionally or mentally significant condition. Retaliation is also common. But not for Sultan. He didn't engage in the ribbing or feel the need to ask his parents why. Without bitterness, he understood that he was a child of God first and did not bother with how anybody thought of him, not even his parents. He accepted his position and did not let it affect how he treated his siblings. He loved his family unconditionally.

I listened as Sultan retold events authentically, even sharing that he was not considered intelligent by academic standards. He had a fifth-grade education but more "good sense" than most scholars. From swimming in the local creek as regular exercise, Sultan maintained incredible lean musculature. Undoubtedly, his fitness came from also working the farm with his family. There were many days when Sultan had to skip school to work, which accounted for significant gaps in his schooling. Still, Sultan and his family saw an incredible opportunity in their arrangement. His parents would share the crops according to their agreement with the landowners. Then, at the end of each year, Sultan's family would earn profits after paying the balance of their expenses to the landowner, such as food, lodging, and supplies.

At the end of their initial year, the landowners delivered the startling news to Sultan's family that they broke even. Breaking even meant that nothing was left for profit, that there was barely enough to live on. Consistent with the "pull yourself up by your bootstraps" philosophy, Sultan and his family focused on working harder. For them, depending on each other was motivating. Sultan dreamt that the next year would be their year. Indeed, the weather cooperated. He dreamed and daydreamed that his family could afford land of their own one day. Sultan spoke expectantly of sprawling acres with vegetation and farm animals. He claimed the future blessing as if God said the words directly into Sultan's ears. Throughout this particularly fruitful year, Sultan spoke assuredly about profits and how his family could use the money to do things differently to get ahead. He would ramble a list of things, like how minimum wage earners speak about the function of their tax returns. When we get the money, we will do this and that with it.

The prospect of plentiful harvests that year also meant incredible sacrifices. For example, there was only time for work, which halted all activities Sultan's parents had not deemed urgent. Thus, sacrificing school was the cost of eventual self-sufficiency. It was a dreadful compromise but an obvious choice in the South. So much rain and extraordinary growth almost tripled their previous yield. Everyone was thrilled because the business arrangement at its core meant both parties would make a lot of money.

Sultan's father met with the landowner at the end of the year. While he was away, the rest of the family spoke words filled with anticipation—eager for verifiable progress toward their goal. They were sharing plans for saving, buying, and celebrating. Then, Sultan's father returned. The look on his face and his body language were unreadable.

The energy in the room dulled, and Sultan's siblings shushed each other. Nobody moved, and seemingly time itself stood still. Palpable was that eerie, uncomfortable quiet like when the anticipatory moment of truth meets the dreaded cliffhanger. Finally, the patriarch mustered three words that would change the lives of his family forever: "We broke even." Everyone in the room knew that this was theft and a violation. However, no one spoke the words. Instead, they went back to work, realizing that they were trapped.

Exploitation is a heavy, painful burden when you have perceived yourself as powerless. Many sharecroppers learned that truth and justice were moving targets, and the landowners ensured it. However, the bad news did not dash Sultan's dreams. Instead, he got clarity from such blatant deceit. It is such a moment when a person experiences so much pain and heartbreak that it motivates them to say aloud, "That ain't gonna happen to me no more." Well, that's what Sultan said. He started thinking creatively and strategically. Still, despite leaving the farm for a few weeks each year, Sultan worked hard daily. Sultan's countenance had changed. He no longer joked, played games, or discussed plans to leave or their futures. They worked harder and harder, and each year, the landowners told Sultan's father that his family broke even. The prospect of going under kept them working hard to keep a roof over their heads; they maintained the cycle of dependence.

A few years later, Sultan called his family into a room at the end of the contract year. Calling a family meeting was unusual because Sultan was not the eldest or the head of the household. Nevertheless, he briefly shared the nature of his whereabouts when he left during specific periods throughout the years.

"Each year, I took some of what the landowners would steal from us, sold it, and saved the money. I have half built a home for us on land that I purchased. Pack your things. We leave tonight."

Sultan Moore was my grandfather. The least favorite child who would deliver freedom to his family is biblically recognizable. Fairytales, Christian movies, and children's stories also feature the last finishing first plotline. However, granddaddy did not think about such things. Instead, he fought clever oppression disguised as a fair business agreement because it was the right thing to do. Without granddaddy's bravery, his family could never enjoy inalienable rights. It was more likely that they would have wallowed in generational poverty. Still, once delivered, granddaddy did not boast. Nor did he seek retribution of any kind. He never said, "I told you so." It was more critical for him to remain authentically himself and further address deceit leveled at his family. In other words, granddaddy channeled his initial rage into change. Self-sufficiency was his goal. Respect and accolades were byproducts of resistance, which sprang from his vision of a better future and accepting that he was "built differently."

One key to granddaddy's motivation was his early observation that the host rigged the game. Imagine playing poker, and you noticed that the dealer dealt an ace from the bottom of the deck every time a sizable pot was on the table. And the house wins. You would stop playing the game. However, in the sharecropping game, refusing to play could cost families their lives. Still, anybody in their right mind would seek a way out. Granddaddy was an unschooled field hand and a genius in practical matters. Things had to make sense to him, and people had to treat people right.

In those days, granddaddy kept his thoughts, feelings, and plans. He also deployed diplomatic skills to avert suspicion. I can only imagine what he would think of everybody putting their business online, down to meals they eat, only for attention. Granddaddy would disapprove of public feuds and common conceit. Protecting his vision and improving his business acumen remained keys to success. To maximize his family's return, granddaddy calculated and adjusted the gross return of the product. He factored in losses to lower overall gains but not enough to cause unwanted suspicion. He also controlled waste. In layperson's terms, granddaddy skimmed product off the top. The only difference is that he was only taking a fraction of the income landowners owed his family in yield and seed.

Don't you get all Texas justice on me or holier than thou. There wasn't a Better Business Bureau or worker's union for sharecroppers. Take a moment and imagine going to work every day for a year. Then, to get any money for your efforts, you must devise a plan to steal a small portion of your paycheck. Paleeeeeeze! Besides, revelation through prayer clarified and activated granddaddy's dreams and enabled him to move toward them without guilt or fear. He also reconciled his biblical understanding of being God's child by resisting the Southern viewpoint of Black inferiority. To accept Christ meant to denounce second-class citizenship. He used to say, "I put my pants on the same way as the next man."

Our family discovered that granddaddy had purchased approximately five acres of land and partially built a house before arriving. As a result, the accumulated annual profits from sharecropping went far. With the help of neighbors, they quickly finished building the house that granddaddy started. The entire neighborhood pitched in. Teaming up to construct homes was a neighborly act for Black people in the segregated South, and so was sharing resources. They used scrounged-up supplies, such as scrap boards of different shapes, sizes, and weights. Nails, screws, and wire also came in handy.

Even newly constructed houses looked dilapidated because farmers were not skilled builders. We can also credit the slummy look and shoddy construction to substandard building materials, which lacked uniformity. Their home may not have been any more appealing than an abandoned shack. It had uneven corners, no paint, and a galvanized tin roof with some pieces already rusted. However, the land was theirs, which mattered most to the Moore family. They were free from the economic dependence of sharecropping. My grandfather and his siblings no longer had to choose work over school. There was no more working from sunup to sundown or swindling, lying landowners. Our family converted "It looks like you broke even" into a punchline for progress, and family members repeat it when they retell our story.

Manifest Your Dreams

The family lived together until the children grew up and left home one by one. Granddaddy was second to go. He went from the family farm to working as a pullman on a train. Then, my grandfather married my grandmother. Soon after his nuptials, he quit the train business, which was similar to corporate sharecropping in how workers were mistreated and not correctly paid. As soon as granddaddy quit his job, the US Army drafted him to serve in World War II. I was never sure if granddaddy's military injury was actual or imagined, but when granddaddy returned home within a year, he purchased ten acres of land not too far from the original family plot.

He built a house for himself and another down the road for his mother. This land was ripe for expansion, especially for a dreamer with high business acumen. He began to farm the land and raise animals. Eventually, he built a convenience store complete with two gas pumps. Then, he paid a company $600 to dig a well, $1 per foot. That was a lot of money in the 1940s. It was the only well of its kind within miles. From the well, he ran pipes to his house for running water. He also ran waterpipes to his mother's house. Granddaddy's store anchored the town, and the United States Post Office noticed. An agency representative convinced my grandfather to build an extension to his store with a separate entrance to conduct government business. When he did, they awarded the town a United States Postal Service branch and named my grandmother the first Black postmistress.

The Moore family was a fixture and a benefit to the community. In addition to the store, gas station, and post office, granddaddy secured benches near the street in front of the store so people could sit and wait for the bus. He installed a spigot near the well and never charged anyone a penny who wanted to draw water. The Moore family also had the only telephone, and it was in the store. Neighbors miles away would give their relatives the Moore family phone number. My grandparents would send my uncles all over town to alert folks when their loved ones might call back. No charge. Finally, the Moore family had a television and movie projector. Neighbors would poke their heads into the windows to watch boxing matches. Some nights, my grandfather projected movies onto the wall outside the store. People throughout the town brought chairs and blankets and sat and watched.

To thrive is what granddaddy always expected of himself. During the dark days, the heaviness of hope did not stifle his joy as some people once thought. Instead, he channeled his lighthearted side into unyielding grit. He knew that he could also live his dream if anybody in this world lived theirs. He only needed to rewrite the scene.

Granddaddy emphasized his abilities, not shortcomings, and he achieved much as an adult. Still, I often wondered what kind of young man my grandfather must have been. To convince his sharecropping parents and nine siblings to risk their lives to follow him, at age 21, uneducated, and the least favorite. Yet, his parents must have recognized his strength and leadership. I learned that granddaddy was not a bully. He stood up for himself and his family. He meant what he said, and you only had one chance to cross him. Granddaddy's trust in God was so strong, along with his obedience, that his reward was also generations of productive citizens whom God would protect. We are still living in granddaddy's favor.

Fortunately, I learned a great deal about my family. This priceless knowledge spans generations. Some accounts predate my grandfather. How much do you know about yours? Someone's memory might give you a deeper appreciation of who you are if you go beyond loosely understood family trees. For example, how your ancestors dealt with history's hardships is essential. Did they overcome, squeak by, or fail? Because it is likely that relatives in your lifetime, or you, will deal with similar challenges because history is cyclical. You can't argue with that. It isn't a matter of liking what you learn. Instead, you may glean resilience toward achieving your goals. For instance, I have learned from family members who overcame recessions, pandemics, misanthropic political figures, and societal unrest as entrepreneurs. Therefore, events from 2016-2022 were do-overs for them and familiar to me. In other words, their stories helped me avoid missteps as I pivoted professionally, including positive, powerful energy while implementing new visions.

CHAPTER EIGHT
LIVING THE DREAM

Granddaddy communicated our family history and the power of God's provision through his storytelling. And we listened. We identified the relationship of each narrative to dreaming, faith, and achieving. It is one family formula. In addition, Granddaddy's oral history would inspire generations to have a deep understanding and commitment to justice, integrity, and faith as values. We understood that values aren't slogans for refrigerator magnets. Instead, they are guiding principles for making decisions. Granddaddy also emphasized a much larger point about who we are in this world, who we are as God's children, and the unlimited possibilities of what we could become if we believed. Storytelling was his way of laying our foundation so that we may answer our questions of purpose from positions of strength rather than lack.

I claimed a special bond between us from my earliest memory of my grandfather. Even though I wasn't any more special to him than the other 28 grandchildren, he still had a way of making each of us feel as funny as he was. It was the way he included us in his jokes. We felt as brave as he was when he retold stories of dealing with racism in the Deep South. He paused just enough to communicate that we would have done the same thing and then continue. We also felt powerful because he spoke strength into us, making us proud of our family name. In some way, each grandchild felt like they were, in fact, the most special to him. However, this notion of "special" was absurd. After all, he had seven children, whom he often reminded, "Ain't none of y'all no different than the rest; I love you all the same." Maybe granddaddy was overcompensating because he knew the feeling of not being favored. He could have meant that for his children, but he still preferred me. I held on to the latter for a long time.

I made this claim of being the most special because I was the spitting image of my grandfather. For example, a portrait of granddaddy hung in his dining room. As I grew older, my younger cousins thought it was me.

At a family reunion in 2018, 10 years after my grandfather passed away, a 94-year-old woman, who I'd never met, peered at me through a crowd. I noticed that I was the object of her stare when she tapped a younger woman on the arm and motioned toward me. The younger woman looked at me, took her cues from the older woman, and started walking toward me. Acting as a guide by resting one of the older woman's arms on her arm, she guided her walk. I asked my mother, in a whisper, if she knew the two women. But I could tell by my mother's reflective stare that they were unfamiliar. As the two women inched closer, the older woman waved her free hand toward me. As her free hand finally touched me, she looked into my eyes and said, "Sultan Moore still lives." Again, she looked at my mother, and this time, grasping my wrist, she repeated, "Sultan Moore still lives." Then, she spoke of moments with my grandfather that seemed familiar to my mother. For a few moments, the woman reminisced about my grandfather. Then, she shared memories of my mom that would transform her look from bewilderment to reflection. My mom replied, "Oh yes, I remember that like it was yesterday." As it turned out, my mother knew the woman when she was much younger, when my mother was a preschooler. Pride filled me at that moment, and I laughed loud and hard as I listened to stories about my mother. We all laughed loudly. Loud laughter may well be a family trait.

My grandfather had a hardy laugh. His bellow reverberated throughout the house when he told jokes or reached the punchline of one of his familiar stories. His tales included growing up in Alabama, marrying and raising children there, and running his business. Each story is a life lesson and an excerpt from our family history. Somehow granddaddy found humor within those painful tales, which I learned first-hand is more accessible in reflection. We laughed every time we heard them, even though he always told them with the same tone and emphasis. He did not add or subtract any details or emotion, no matter who listened. He retold them verbatim. I bonded with granddaddy and experienced his fearlessness by learning about our family's history. I gasped during dangerous parts, sucking in a chest full of air and not releasing it. And I also cheered by firmly saying, "Yeah," when granddaddy showed them unsavory characters a thing or two. I prevailed with granddaddy in his stories as if I were there. Sharing stories of the deep Southern racism and how he challenged and overcame it planted a resilient spirit in me that grew visit after visit.

We knew all about granddaddy as the first entrepreneur in our family. He built, owned, and operated a combination full-service gas station and convenience store. It was a focal point on the main road that runs through Beloit, Alabama, only approximately eight miles from Selma, Alabama. Like all gas stations back then, granddaddy's station was full-service.

Nobody pumped their own gas anywhere. Instead, as a vehicle pulled up to gas pumps, the tires would run over a thin rubber hose perpendicular to the pump approximately 8 feet long. The pressure of the front and rear tires on the hose triggered the bell twice for the front tires and twice for the rear tires: "ding ding, ding ding." Then, an attendant would hustle toward the driver, "What'll it be?" Next, the driver would call out the amount of money in dollars and cents to indicate the amount of gas and anything they may want from the store.

Typically, the attendant checked the oil, tire pressure, radiator fluid, wiper fluid, and brake fluid. Next, he sprayed the windows with water from a small spray bottle they would hook to their pants by the nozzle. Then wipe the glass dry with a brick red cloth rag they kept hanging from a back pant pocket. Once the attendant completed the service, the driver paid cash at the pump.

I remember how granddaddy told one of my favorite stories about a man who refused to pay him:

"A well-dressed, white man pulled up in a fine automobile. I walked out of the store and toward the car, and the man yelled, 'Fill it up, boy.' I didn't think too much of being called 'boy' in those days. We didn't worry about such things. Shoot, I called them 'boy' right back when they did it and watched their faces turn up. 'Sure thing, boy,' I said. It meant something to have a Black man refer to a white man as a boy. People were scared, but I'm a man just like they are a man. I didn't argue the point. They knew it."

However, all men who knew my grandfather called him Mr. Moore. That meant something too. Granddaddy continued:

"Now, all gas stations were full-service in those days. You could not pump your gas, you see. So, I unscrewed the gas cap and placed it on the car. I yelled, 'Regular or ethyl?' The stranger said, 'Ethyl.' So I put the nozzle that poured ethyl gasoline into the tank and started pumping gas. I squeezed the nozzle until the tank was full because if you weren't squeezing, you weren't pumping any gas. Gas pumps didn't have automatic shutoffs at that time. Then, I checked the oil and cleaned the windows and windshield; that was part of the full service."

"When I finished, I yelled that it'd be $2.10. You see, gas was only about 21 cents per gallon in those days, and $2 was a lot of money. Then, the man said, 'I'll pay you next time,' as he walked back toward his car after getting out to stretch his legs. I said, 'Just a minute,' and got my pistol from the store. 'You're going to gimmie my money right now.' My voice was strong, and I looked the man in the eyes. His eyes looked at my gun barrel aimed at him. He knew I wasn't playin'. I meant business. 'Put my money on top of the car.' His hands shook as he pulled the money out of his pocket and laid it on the hood. He was scared, man. He was so afraid that he couldn't get in his car fast enough. Then, when he thought he was safe in his car, he looked at me and said, 'I'm gonna get the Klan on you, and I ain't never coming back here, no mo.' I said, 'I didn't tell you to come the first time. Now get away from here.'

At that point, grandaddy would laugh. We'd all wait for that familiar punchline, "I didn't tell you to come the first time," and laugh too. I'd imagine the stranger driving away, humiliated and hearing my grandfather's laughter until he was at least a mile away. I'd hoped that granddaddy's bellowing haunted the stranger's dreams forever. After that incident, my grandparents were worried that the Klan would come. So, the family prepared for it as best they could. Granddaddy had his guns ready, and so did his shotgun-wielding mother, who lived down the road. Grandmama warned the children not to wander too far and to be inside before dark. Then, they figured the stranger was probably too embarrassed to reveal to his associates that a Black man treated him disrespectfully. There was no retaliation, and the stranger never returned.

Any family member within earshot of my grandfather telling one of his stories would stop and listen as if they were hearing it for the first time. At once, everyone would hysterically laugh when grandaddy laughed. We all seemed to have a little of his laugh. It often starts with a long "oh" or "ah." Then, the laughter erupts into an eardrum-shattering roar, which may cause tight abdominal muscles, shortness of breath, and a complete loss of composure. A case of the giggles sometimes follows.

The only person who found little humor in granddaddy retelling the past was my grandmother. Grandmama would sometimes leave the room. Other times, she would dismiss granddaddy as crazy and reckless. Sometimes, grandmama mentioned how people respected granddaddy because he always treated people fairly. Still, she rarely laughed at the stories; she was mostly serious. To grandmama, those stories represented the dangerous and precarious times of the 1940s and 1950s for Black people in rural Alabama. She didn't like to discuss times when white people normalized lynching, false imprisonments, and Klan activities. Granddaddy's bold behavior could have left my grandmama a widow with seven children, which is a fact that granddaddy would leave out until we asked. My grandmother sometimes quipped that granddaddy wasted his time voting. Still, he never missed an election. Still, she laughed because Alabama had separate ballot boxes, one white and the other colored. "They just throw your votes in the trash" was her punchline. Even though we laughed, voting was courageous activism. Therefore, I took sides, always opting for granddaddy's fearlessness over caution, justice in place of the status quo, and standing out rather than blending in. I loved granddaddy, and I knew I would be like him.

Because the children in my family correctly learned our history, we understood there was always struggle and injustice. There was always resistance; we were the product of grandaddy's dreams. I relished the time I spent with granddaddy so much that I wanted to be courageous like him—assertive, moral, and not to be messed with for any reason. We never had cliché conversations or talked indirectly. The straight truth was liberating and strengthened my developing principles and normal tendencies. So, as I grew older, I considered how grandaddy would handle situations and patterned my actions accordingly. I felt his energy when I held my ground during neighborhood conflicts or school confrontations.

However, my upbringing could not be more different from his. I grew up in the city, and school was a priority. I also considered consequences like school detention or suspension. There was also my parents' wrath if I earned low scores for poor conduct, whether I was technically correct or not.

One of Granddaddy's most recognized characteristics was that he was his own man. His lessons taught me that I should be myself and that who I am plus God is more than enough. So, rather than try to be like Granddaddy, I strove to be the most authentic me. The trials and triumphs of my family's legacy, narrated by Granddaddy, conveyed the culture and cohesion that continues to guide me. However, I took one thing directly from Granddaddy: I will be courageous in everything, especially in my dreams.

CHAPTER NINE
CARL TAYLOR'S DREAM

Coach Carl Taylor stopped his car in front of my house. It was rare that I was the last player he'd drop home after practice and rarer still that I would have one-to-one time to ask personal questions.

"Nobody likes you, coach. You're a fringe group of one, a loner. You have nothing in common with other school administrators. Why did you choose this high school to coach?"

He was about to laugh, before noticing my seriousness. "Don't worry, I'm not going anywhere," he said, answering the question I would have asked next. Then, he switched off the ignition.

"And I don't give a damn who likes me or not. I am here to fulfill my dream of coaching a team to a state championship win. That would mean the world to me. You'd better believe that I've already rehearsed how I would throw it in their faces."

"Whose faces?" I asked.

"Everybody who said I couldn't: old friends, parents, and everybody smilin' in my face and doing things to hold me back."

"Then what?"

"I would get the hell outta' here!" he yelled and laughed.

My mom pulled back the curtain to see where the loud voice was coming from. So, I went inside. Coach Taylor had a particular way of yelling at his players. His powerful voice was heavy like a freight train, just as loud and uniquely baritone. When he shouted, Coach Taylor's words delivered earthquake-like tremors, which scared players to either do the right thing or do the wrong thing as hard as possible. Plus, in close range, he stirred souls, disturbed spirits, unsteadied nervous systems, and weakened knees. If there ever was a voice made explicitly for the outdoors, God created that voice for Coach Taylor.

However, despite his signature voice, Coach Taylor's smooth, urban swagger made some of his players want to prove to him that they could sweat through his pressure and succeed. Proximity may also have privileges. His image of cool might rub off on his team. Without direct evidence that cool can transfer cool, some players still hung in there for it.

Taylor's coaching style was intense and demanding, causing thin-skinned mama's boys who desired the basketball court to join the band or cheerleading. It became clear that those activities would bring them the closest to Coach Taylor's basketball court while wearing a school-issued uniform.

Therefore, playing for Coach Taylor was not for the feeble or potential bragging rights. Anybody who tried out for the team half wanting to quit never lasted. You had to desire basketball in an irrational way like the screw-loose thinkers who become Navy Seals, separating themselves from those who merely try out for the title. There needed to be more than initial inertia to sustain tryouts or preseason conditioning. Any thoughts to convince yourself to stay another day already sank you.

Nevertheless, the pervasive attitude in our high school was timid and reticent about anything that mattered. Even so, playing for Coach Taylor legitimized a person's toughness in a way that awed non-ballers when team members walked the halls. Everybody saw that we were savagely brave and never scared, even though that wasn't entirely true.

Still, players who wanted to play badly enough learned that there was mad love behind Coach Taylor's bark. When Coach laughed with you, he did it intensely. Nothing about coach Taylor conveyed a calm. He only knew extreme or the 100 at the far right of the spectrum. He fiercely stood up for players and students off the court, too.

I watched Coach Taylor say, "I will beat ur' ass," as he squeezed the neck of a parent like a vice. Eyes bugged in terror; the man offered paralysis in place of resistance. Then, Coach cocked back a tight fist, sure to break more than the man's black rimmed glasses.

"Please, no, okay, don't!" the man said as his hands sprang to life in a surrender pose.

"I'm puttin' you on notice," Coach said. "Next time I'll beat you to an inch of your life."

It was the first time I saw a grown man plead mercy to another man's threat. Because where I came from, there weren't threats and pleading, just beatdowns. Nevertheless, it worked out for the man, all except the part about losing his dignity, self-respect, and manhood altogether.

However, Coach Taylor did not punch the man after he publicly punked him. We later learned that school officials knew the man Coach Taylor snatched up was a parent who bullied and abused his child. Yet, Coach Taylor stood in the gap for that student by showing the courage to do something. That's Carl Taylor, always doing good work and keeping his benevolence under wraps. He seemed to thrive on adults being uncomfortable around him. Cowardice was their problem.

They don't make em' like Coach Taylor anymore. Too often, we go back in time and spit up crap about what we would have done in big moments and how we would show up now. Huh! But there's far more evidence to allege at least three things: (1) that nobody would stand up for the abused child these days; (2) there would be a stupid video of the incident circulating on social media; and (3) some idiot would be in the comments talking about what they would have done instead of record. PALEEZE!

Nevertheless, even though our paths would inevitably collide, I met Coach Taylor sooner than I had imagined. He was the varsity basketball coach, and all ninth-grade players played on the first-year team. Therefore, I didn't predict Coach Taylor would see me in action that year until I was blindsided by a series of events.

My ninth-grade coach called in sick and missed his first game in twenty-six years. Then, Coach Taylor filled in as his backup. Nobody informed our team of the change until just before game time. It was the third game of our season, and our opponent was a rival school. Players were getting tight, nervous, and scared when Coach Taylor entered the locker room. Not me. I scrapped with older kids and grown men on city playgrounds to harden my game. So, I saw Taylor's presence as an exciting opportunity. I scored 30 points, snatched 18 rebounds, and collected blocked shots and steals to round out my stat sheet. We won by a single point. After the game, Coach Taylor asked me to dress for the junior varsity game the following night. I beamed as I told my mother that I might get to play, and we both made predictions about how much playing time I may get in quarters.

To my surprise, Coach Taylor played me as a starter. I played all four quarters and finished with 27 points and 15 rebounds. Next, coach Taylor asked me to join the varsity team's pre-game talk. Excited and focused, I listened as if he were talking directly to me. I nodded as Coach went over the game plan. I also responded with the team's collective "yes" when he asked whether we understood our roles. I knew he noticed that I was focused and involved because he requested that I sit on the varsity bench afterward. This moment was surreal, and I was enjoying it minute by minute. There was no time to feel proud of myself, and I saw no satisfaction in sitting on the bench, even if it belonged to the varsity. I wanted to play.

There was no pressure, no nerves I couldn't check. I went through the layup lines feeling loose and almost giddy, communicating to all who watched that I belonged. Still, in my mind, I had little chance of playing. Juniors and seniors filled our varsity roster. Nobody getting playing time feared losing any of it to a first-year student who had already played a complete game. Plus, we were on the road, and there's some truth to younger players playing better at home. Even so, I figured I would only see action if we started blowing out the other team on the scoreboard.

Mark was the only natural scorer among Coach Taylor's eight-man rotation of players. So, it was unlikely that we would blow out the other team. Mark was an all-conference player and would have been an all-American if it weren't for his temper. Watching Mark turn angrily on teammates for a bad pass was painful. He berated referees for calls made and ones they didn't. He also retreated into his head and mentally gave up when things weren't going his way. If I knew this about Mark, so did the opposing coach, who loaded his team with talent and employed a defensive scheme that frustrated and neutralized Mark. I remember that at one point, the score was 20-1, and we were losing. Our team grew irritated with each careless turnover, reckless shot attempt, forgotten assignment, and lack of hustle play by our starters. Embarrassing! Each mishap also lessened my chance to play.

I had never seen Coach Taylor so angry. He paced the sidelines, yelling at our players as they ran by. Maybe he thought they could only hear him if he were closer. The truth is that the whole gym heard him and perhaps the bus drivers in the parking lot. When his blood reached its boiling point, Coach Taylor looked at the end of the bench and yelled my last name. I didn't recognize that he was talking to me. I mean, dang. I knew my name, but why was he saying it? I slumped down and covered my mouth with a towel to hide my expression—bewilderment. I'm not going to embarrass myself by getting up. I need to make sure that he said my name. Better yet, I thought he would have to come to get me.

Coach yelled, "Timeout." The five players on the floor ran toward the bench area. Players and managers on the bench jumped to our feet to form a huddle. Nobody sat. Before speaking a word of strategy, Coach Taylor snatched open my warmup jacket, yanked it down until it fell to the floor, and yelled, "Check in!" Then, he pushed me toward the scorer's table. Because I was frozen, I did not remember that Coach Taylor spoke to the scorer for me to check my sorry butt into the game. So, I had to rely on how Coach Taylor retold the story to fill those empty spaces.

The first play I made was a rebound that I snatched with one hand in an intimidating swooping motion, slapping the ball with my other hand to secure it. That play sent a message to the opposing team that I meant business, and I sensed their fear. After that play, I blanked out and went to work. I do not remember being in the moment. Only that everybody seemed to move slower than I did. I chalked it up to nerves, though this was weird, like an out-of-body experience. Everything that I dreamed I would do in such moments I did. I set out to score, snatch rebounds, block shots, and get steals, all within the confines of Coach's pregame speech. Unfortunately, I could not figure out why I could not remember.

When the horn sounded, indicating halftime, I had scored 15 points and grabbed 11 rebounds in less than one-quarter of play. Unfortunately, I could not play the second half since the league rule limited a player to play a maximum of five quarters in one day. Our assistant coach told me the provision as we went to the locker room to brace for Coach Taylor's halftime wrath.

With Coach Taylor, a verbal beatdown could happen in practice, in a game, or outside of a class if he caught you walking in late. While yelling, sometimes his gum would fly out of his mouth, and he would grab it in mid-air, return it to his mouth, and without pausing in speech or looking away, he continued making his point. Coach Taylor sensed if any player disagreed with him. There was also no hiding from Coach if a player felt sensitive or embarrassed about how he yelled at them. He called out anybody not on the same page, his page, by questioning the behavior and always giving them choices. During halftime, Mark faced complicated decisions.

Mark stood away from the team. Panting quickly with clenched fists, Mark's eyes beamed at Coach Taylor like he was contemplating a costly option. The rest of the group sat and listened as Coach yelled a summary of his pregame compared to what the starters did in a point-counterpoint style: "I said pick up in a full court press. Instead, y'all ran down court. I said force the point guard to his left. You gave him three right-hand layups."

At about that time, Coach looked into each player's eyes to ensure we paid close attention. He panned from left to right and finally noticed Mark. He looked at the group again and then back to Mark as he saw Mark standing to his right and approximately 10 feet away. Coach Taylor's questioning look turned into a scowl on the second look of his double-take when he saw Mark's fists in a fight-ready position. Coach mumbled, "Awe shit, here we go," under his breath, walked into Mark's personal space, and stood nose-to-nose. "Oh, you don't like me yelling at you. It looks like you want to do something about it. Go ahead and hit me if you want to.

Go ahead, hit me. Then, after I whoop your ass like the man you think you are, I'm gonna' finish telling you to do what the hell I want you to do. Now if you don't want to listen, you can take off my uniform and take your ass home."

After taking a moment to contemplate his choices, Mark took off his uniform. He emphatically threw down his jersey after a full wind-up, like when professional players spike the football after scoring touchdowns. The air left the room, along with Mark's pride and decorum. Our team's collective gasp was audible as Mark walked away. Coach Taylor ordered him back by saying, "Give me my shorts too."

I never understood quitting. To give up or quit is unnecessary, like death by suicide. Those who choose that end may think they have made a more significant point, but everything moves on without them. And so did our team. After Mark's dramatic exit, wearing only his underwear, Coach Taylor turned to me and extended his hand. I reached out, and as we shook, he said, "Welcome to varsity."

The choices Coach Taylor gave Mark were his to give, but Mark had them independent of Coach Taylor. We always have them. Let's pretend Mark wanted to stay on the team. How could he grow if he didn't overcome the obstacle standing in the way of what he wanted? For example, Mark's parents could have sought help from a therapist or counselor and reframed his mindset to focus on positive outcomes rather than letting emotions control his behavior. He could also have worked on self-awareness, developed techniques to recognize triggers for his temper, and learned to respond healthier.

Additionally, Mark could have surrounded himself with positive influences and sought support from friends, family, and other coaches. Instead, ego and pride triggered Mark's temper. He could not overcome those without dissonance and humility. And Coach Taylor gave both in spades. It may sound sappy to mention how Coach Taylor could have focused on positive reinforcement, emphasized player development over winning, and improved communication with Mark. He could also have taken a more patient approach, knowing Mark needed help. Unfortunately, sometimes the hard way is the most helpful.

The first time a Christian told me not to pray for patience because God gives patience by making people wait, I looked at the person like they had two heads. I've heard this from people of all faiths and religious traditions. With his logic, people won't ask for strength because you might get difficulty. Few would ask for courage because they don't want to face danger. Asking for wisdom may mean problems to solve.

You cannot believe God reveals everything in His time and be a spiritual wimp about your growth because the costs scare you. In other words, if you believe God's grace is sufficient, why be a sucker about becoming who you can be? Here's my advice. Speak with God about growing you, and don't concern yourself with His delivery system or somebody else's opinion. Otherwise, you'll surely ask for God's help with regret after opportunities pass like Mark, who never played organized ball again.

… SECTION TWO • ACHIEVING THROUGH DREAMING

Section Three

BEING IN
THE ZONE

I Got This

"You don't know what you don't know,"
Was an epiphany that had me shook.

Thus, a headline is not the story,
And a cover is not a book.

Fools fake it till they make it.
Fraud is making it hook or crook.

Being captivating is different from
"Ha, I made you look."

If you can read, you can teach.
Playing small is the only risk.

What mainly determines achieving results
Is knowing you got this!

Hughes Suffren

CHAPTER TEN
SLOW MOTION, PART 1

School officials met fierce protest because Coach Taylor promoted me to varsity. Some of the parents of my new teammates expressed their anger to our school's athletic director and our principal. Rightfully cautious, they did not lodge complaints directly to the Coach. Coach Taylor had a way of being right in the worst way by putting whomever was wrong on blast. He also earned a reputation for ferocity that scared people. For example, it was common knowledge that Coach Taylor shot a man in the ass who attempted to steal his car. The bullet was a message not to mess with him and a warning of what would happen if you did because a perpetrator running away is no longer a threat. Ergo, parents didn't like Coach Taylor's style, nor did they want his wrath.

Angling to round up support, some parents hinted their concerns about how Coach Taylor handled the halftime of my first game. Feigning kindness, other parents lobbied the Coach to reinstate Mark. He was the best player on our team, they presented. A few parents tried to block my advancement by telling the athletic director that Coach Taylor moved me up out of spite and not merit. In addition, cowardly attempts to intimidate coach Taylor included threats of pain and death. Of course, all aggressions were anonymous and written, never spoken. There were also murmurs from specific teammates who opposed my presence. Coach Taylor addressed them publicly in a team meeting:

"I didn't cut Mark. Mark quit and I don't have time for quitters. Now, I don't give a damn what you think or what your parents think. I don't care what your friends think. This is my team. I will run it the way I see fit. If you don't like what I am doing, you can get the hell out because I don't need you!"

That was a seminal moment. Before then, people treated my older sister and me like two token Black kids because we moved into the district from Kansas City, Missouri, and were subsequently bussed to their nearly all-white high school. We were unknown and the odd people out. Teachers ignored us. Most white kids mocked or feared the stereotypes they blanketly assigned to inner-city children, such as uneducated and violent. But they all played nice and put on their plastic smiles during track and basketball season. Even Coach Taylor was surprised school officials hired someone bold, outspoken, and Black like him.

My sister was the first in my family to attend that high school, and I was the first to enroll in the town's junior high school. It can be lonely being the first. Most white students and all teachers and administrators ignored us. Fortunately, Black classmates and support staff welcomed us. Besides Coach Taylor, my sister was the only person who gave me a fraction of cover from politics, bureaucracy, and hidden agendas at school. Since she blazed a trail in track, her talent and last name served notice to haters that I was coming. Once there, I could not help but think how different my high school experience might have been if not for serendipity, supposing it's okay to refer to my ninth-grade coach getting sick as beneficial.

Nobody video-recorded my first game. It was an away game for our team, and only a few diehard fans traveled. Who am I kidding? Any varsity coach playing a ninth-grade hooper coaches a team that sucks too bad to have fans. Thus, our only recognizable support included the parents of a few players, some of our team's girlfriends, and our junior varsity team, who sat in the stands after showers. Still, expectation gaps contributed to significant communication breakdowns as people shared many accounts of what happened that day. I remember one story's version describing a sellout crowd in our favor. Unfortunately, discrepancies like that ran the gamut. In place of historical accuracy, people altered much of my performance to fit the dramatic retelling of the larger story about Mark. There was a familiar plotline: I was the savior, the hero figure in their narrative, causing massive disruptions. Notoriously, I would have to endure scorn and ridicule because white parents wanted their sons, who were juniors and seniors, to play in my place.

I think that makes me the protagonist, which would make Mark the antagonist. Understandably, there is something utterly distasteful about a hot-tempered villain who makes you—and everybody else—his target. Therefore, Mark played the role of the hot-headed brat who wasted his talent. Finally, Coach Taylor portrayed an enforcer like Joe Clark from the old movie *Lean on Me*. The movie's main character was a bold, well-meaning principal of an underachieving high school. Joe Clark spared nobody's feelings and was the ultimate disciplinarian. The film is a true story about Joe Clark, Principal of Eastside High School in Chicago. History credits Clark for leading the academic turnaround of children who needed someone to believe in them. Expelling nearly 300 underperforming students who were rotten to their core had a widespread impact on the school and community. Most bullish accounts of Clark fit Coach Taylor's narrative and what happened with Mark because that train wreck was imminent.

However, the way people described my first varsity performance disregarded facts in place of fiction. Because the location of my high school was a small rural town, any gossip was like dropping a lit match into dry brush. The stories about my game and Coach versus Mark spread like wildfire: hot, dangerously shifting, and out of control. I did not dare tell people that, at best, I had a spotty memory of my performance. Let alone being in a daze; as outsiders, they might consider beginner's luck. Besides, that admission would be like pouring a cup of water on the blaze. Therefore, when people asked, I would tell them, "I was just playing basketball," I did not mention my stat totals.

I nodded and smiled when I overheard how people retold recycled versions of my performance that day. They were two-faced people, as we'd call anyone back then, who smiled in the faces of those they spoke severely about behind their backs. Thus, I only fully acknowledged the accounts of those present at the game: the local newspaper, my new teammates, and Coach Taylor, who said, "You proved that you were ready for the moment." In other words, my performance had nothing to do with luck and everything to do with preparation.

Meanwhile, my summary matched what Coach Taylor said. I remembered being in the zone. The scene was in slow motion, and while I was moving slower than usual, I was moving faster than the other players. Getting to whatever loose ball I wanted, snatching every rebound I eyeballed and declared mine, and knocking down shots I deemed routine from practicing them. But I never had the linear game-time experience of being in the moment. Instead, the game was a strange series of slow-motion highlights I had mostly forgotten when the buzzer sounded.

The rest of that year was rough, and so was the following year. Even though veiled threats to hurt Coach Taylor professionally fell short, and the death threats toward him had subsided, the pressure to win remained. All could see that we were better each year. We improved from a single-digit win team to winning half our games in my second year. However, it was after the last game of my second year when Coach Taylor shared his dream in my driveway.

I'll never forget how he yelled, "I would get the hell outta here," referring to winning a state championship. After his belly-aching laugh that disturbed the neighborhood and my mom, he said, "When you are a senior, you know we're going to win my state title. Then, everybody will have to shut up. You will get a basketball scholarship anywhere you want to go. Coaching opportunities also will open for me. So, when you leave, I will also leave. I'm riding your coattail."

It was motivating to think of myself as pivotal in Coach's dream. However, identifying me as a sidekick in his dream was no pressure because he was my sidekick in my dreams of winning it all. Moreover, external forces never pressured me because Coach Taylor took all the heat. His stoic public demeanor and resting scowl face belied his private benevolence and nurturing. In retrospect, Coach Taylor saw something good in most students and quickly identified those who needed his protection or assistance. So, I was not alone. In addition to providing athletes rides home from practice or games, Coach gave us lunch money and plenty of personal advice. One year, he bought football and basketball shoes for a few players who needed them. There were many beneficiaries of Coach Taylor's good side. However, the closest to him were a student-athlete named Grady and me.

Grady, a quick-witted, outgoing linebacker who starred on our varsity football team, lived at the end of my block. He pushed me out of the way to make a tackle during our first game together. Afterward, he explained that the football scene changed before he viciously snot-bubbled a ball carrier. Suddenly, everyone else appeared to move at half-speed and back to normal when the crowd reacted to the hit. My "this happens to you too" look in response was our bonding moment, even though I cannot remember sharing my slow-motion event with him.

College coaches and news organizations recognized Grady as a standout football player. Universities from all over the country offered Grady football scholarships as early as his first year of high school. He was a year older than me and played varsity basketball by his third year. Unfortunately for the opposing team, Grady was a bruiser who constantly exhausted his allotment of fouls. After each infraction, Grady would look to Coach Taylor bewildered, hands raised, communicating that he did not touch the guy. There could be a trail of blood, or a mangled opponent, sprawled on the floor in the aftermath of contact, and Grady's expression of surprise would be the same. He didn't need to do much to be our enforcer because his football reputation followed him to the hardwood.

Obnoxious and often untimely, Grady's humor tip-toed on the line of insubordination. Sometimes Coach Taylor would laugh before he ordered Grady to run stairs or suicide line drills for his comedic antics. Naturally, coach Taylor also extended a fight option if Grady pouted. He would say, "We can always settle this another way, if you think you're man enough." Nonetheless, there was never a question that Grady was ready for that challenge. An athlete devoted to the weight room, Grady was the only student big enough, strong enough, and crazy enough to think a physical altercation with Coach Taylor might be worth it. Therefore, during practices, he became an unyielding contrarian with a score to settle. Needling coach Taylor was Grady's mission. Thus, a trainwreck was imminent. All that remained in my mind was whether the future altercation would be a slow-motion episode for Grady or an old-fashioned beatdown.

CHAPTER ELEVEN
SLOW MOTION, PART 2

Coach Taylor shouted, "Okay, everyone spread out on the baseline!" That meant the end of practice and time to run suicides, an apt name for the drill. You remember those sprints that take your breath and make you feel that death might be better.

"Oh my God! Oh my God! Oh my God!" Grady yelled. "This is making me skinny!" Next, Grady threw up his hands demonstratively, turned away from the team, and yelled again, "This is making me skinny!" Perhaps he thought having his back to players and coaches emphasized that he wasn't speaking directly to anyone.

Everyone stopped and stared. Of course, he and everybody else knew this outburst was different. Grady was escalating, on purpose, it seemed. Then, Grady bobbed and weaved to the baseline shadowboxing. Finally, Coach Taylor took the bait.

"You wanna throw some hands? Coach Taylor asked.

"Let's go!" Grady snapped like he was expecting the invitation.

The two led the way to the locker room, where their first fight would go down. There was excitement in the air as the team followed to watch. Most of the group sided with Grady. A few of us declared Coach Taylor would win. My healthy fear of Coach Taylor and respect for elders compelled my loyalty to Coach. We whispered bets as we hurried down to get a spot in front of the designated locker area where varsity basketball players dressed. We called it the cage.

The cage was a rectangular enclosure with black, metal chain-link fencing for walls. Its dimensions approximated a free throw lane area—15 feet long and 12 feet wide. The walls stretched high and connected to the ceiling and its door. This design provided only one way in and out of the cage. I know it doesn't sound like much, and it wasn't. Of course, players stepping around and over each other wasn't ideal. Still, to have a locker in that tight space was an honor, and earning the right to be there was distinct.

Coach Taylor would walk into the cage and punk a would-be challenger by locking the door with a padlock behind him. Before that day, one hundred percent of the opponents lost their nerve when the padlock clicked shut. However, this time was different. It came down to Grady's respect as a man, and he was willing to fight for it, especially if it meant shutting up Coach Taylor. Grady was the biggest, most muscular guy in our school. He also had the competitive temperament to be in the cage. There was no turning back.

Once in the cage, Coach Taylor closed the padlock that cinched the heavy chain looped through the fencing and the door. Then, Coach Taylor presented the key to the lock with one hand, which he wore on a chain around his neck. With his other hand, he pulled the neckline of his shirt and dropped the key inside.

"If you get the key from around my neck and get out, you win. Now, if you think you're a man, go ahead. Hit me."

Coach Taylor baited Grady into throwing the first punch until one landed flush on Coach Taylor's jaw with a loud thud. Then, Coach Taylor threw video game-like body shots, too fast and vicious to count. It was like those fake wrestling punches, where the guy getting punched is lifted off the ground when each blow lands, only faster. We shouted like crazy without cheering on either of them. Finally, Grady turned his back in retreat and found himself in what I thought was a headlock. After years of watching mixed martial arts, I can distinguish the hold as a rear naked choke. From behind, Coach slipped his arm under Grady's neck. Coach Taylor was moments away from putting Grady to sleep by clasping his hands for power and leverage. I know now that the maneuver restricts blood flow and oxygen to the brain and would have quickly caused Grady to pass out. Instead, Grady frantically tapped Coach Taylor's arm, a universal sign of surrender. We oohed and aahed. Nobody cared that the fight fell short of our expectations. Coach Taylor quickly won by forcing Grady to tap out. When Coach slightly loosened his grip, there was something in his eye I hadn't seen before: enjoyment! He smiled as he commanded Grady to repeat a few "I will never" statements after him:

"Say, 'I will never disrespect my coach.'"

"I will never disrespect my coach," Grady responded.

"Say, 'I will never disrupt practice again.'" Coach looked at us while commanding Grady to respond.

"I will never, disrupt practice again," Grady relented.

We got the message Coach Taylor's stare communicated—that any of us could be next. Coach humbled Grady the hard way, indeed. He demonstrated the mantra my dad forced on my siblings and me: "If you can't hear, you must feel."

Moments like that became our stories, laughs, and the foundation of bonds we created with each other and Coach. I took a few turns in the cage with Coach Taylor. He jammed me up a couple of times. Once for getting in trouble for talking in class and another for misbehaving at home. I couldn't get away with anything. Coach Taylor held me to a higher standard. It didn't take much for him to employ swift discipline, which my parents authorized. One day, I walked into my house and nearly panicked when I saw Coach Taylor in the living room talking to my parents. I covered my mouth when I heard him ask them for permission to discipline me. My father responded in a heavy Caribbean accent, "Sure, whoop him good." That was Coach's green light; he knew that structure was what I needed. He laid down his laws and relentlessly enforced the wishes of my parents, teachers, and our school's code of conduct. I got no breaks. Our team also came together because I didn't get leniency or special treatment for being the best player. In some ways, they felt terrible for me. To them, Coach sought to keep me humble by unfairly punishing me.

Nevertheless, Coach Taylor could not care less about appearances. That was for outsiders. Instead, Coach Taylor focused on creating a family environment. His system worked. Holding me accountable bred personal accountability for each player. Grady had graduated, and nobody wanted to take his place or mine in the cage. Coach Taylor was undefeated. Soon, more than 15 basketball players from different backgrounds moved in unison. Each hooper knew their role and began to self-regulate their behavior. A shift in the atmosphere made Coach Taylor smile: a growing allegiance to each other—all for one and one for all.

We started hanging out with each other off the court. We also checked each other for behavior detrimental to our team, no matter where it happened. For example, we would question and help a teammate who was underperforming in class. We admonished others for habitual tardiness or for submitting late or incomplete assignments. Indeed, any teammate's class, home, or social problems were team problems. This "steel sharpens steel" mentality diminished the need for cage time with Coach Taylor. We had become our brother's keeper. In other words, our team bought into doing things the right way, Coach Taylor's way. It was our collective change that eliminated punitive responses from our coaching staff. Suddenly coaches treated us like men, producing a motivational climate that led to many successes. In my senior year, we won our preseason and Christmas tournaments and beat our conference rivals. We began to believe that for us and all who follow us, and perhaps future generations because of us, winning will be what they know or remember.

It is incredible how I can explain minute details of events that led to the state tournament. Still, I can't remember the basketball game of my life—my high school state championship. I do, however, recall fragments from the beginning of the game. I didn't feel pressure from college coaches in the stands. Coach Taylor's desire for better coaching jobs didn't enter my mind. I was ready for the moment. I looked at my opponents. One of the players was 6'9" tall and played on my traveling basketball team in the summers. They had other tall starters. One stood 6'6" and another 6'5", respectively. As our team went through warmup drills, a new motivation to play well came over me. My father and grandfather sat in the stands. Nobody told me beforehand that they would attend. My father's life was the epitome of hard work. My grandfather's life was the epitome of seizing big moments. On my most significant stage to date, I would get to show them what the hype about me was about. They would soon see why the papers wrote stories and college coaches kept calling. Therefore, this game was the moment Coach Taylor and I had dreamed about so many times.

However, trying to remember the game was like piecing together a weird, disjointed dream. For example, I remember winning the jump ball and shooting a 15-foot bank shot over the 6'9" center. He closed the distance between us and raised one arm. I slowly changed the shot's trajectory and shot over his fingertips. In the next offensive play, I took him off the dribble and reversed the layup to the other side of the basket when he leaped to block it. Later, I made another bank shot off the left side, and that's all I remember from the first half. I only remember missing the front end of two bonus free throws in the second half.

Another weird example is that I don't remember Coach Taylor telling me to do anything. I thought he just let me hoop. There were times when I performed in a dreamy, slow-motion state, like my first jump shot and reverse layup. Beyond that, the game started and ended. Most everything in between was a blur.

While I played the game, there were no familiar sounds of cheers, boos, or hecklers. Instead, I heard static like the monotonous haze of a television without a cable signal. This sound was steady and continuous. It was not rhythmic or loud, but it was dominant. However, when I watched the video weeks later, I experienced the game for the first time, minus the few plays I recalled. I scored 36 points, 18 in each half. I made 16 out of 18 shots from the field and four free throws. Yet, it was an out-of-body experience that I wish I could say I enjoyed. I didn't feel robbed of the event, though. I made those plays, and everything went my way, like in my dreams.

Moreover, I knew that I hadn't run on adrenaline. That's a different feeling altogether. Instead, this was a moment when God took over. I'm not sure what He was trying to tell me. What I took away was that if I give up myself (ego) and let God perform through me, I am unstoppable. There it is. However, Coach Taylor said, "You proved that you were ready for the moment." In other words, my performance had nothing to do with luck and everything to do with preparation. Nevertheless, this episode supports other players who recall similar experiences.

I tried to explain my slow-motion interlude to a reporter, "Well, that was great," he quickly cut me off and moved to a question for another player. Note to self. If the answer to a question is unexplainable, "say less." Still, I knew what NBA Basketball star Kobe Bryant meant many years later after scoring 81 points in a basketball game. "The game slowed down," Kobe said in a postgame interview. Other athletes have experienced such moments as I did. For example, Steph Curry and Damien Lillard, among the best scorers in the National Basketball Association, have echoed Kobe's account that the game slows down when they've gone "into the zone." But, like Kobe, they know to give only a few details. No matter how they explain humbly, people only want to hear that they dominated. Still, entering the zone will work for anyone:

1. It starts in your mind, believing that you can excel.
2. Changing daily practices to support excellence must come next, leading to elevated thoughts and significant improvement in your endeavor.
3. Your work and faith meeting opportunities manifests outcomes

When I put it like that, you also understand that emerging in this way doesn't happen overnight.

The Flow State

"Being in the zone," is also known as the flow state. This is a mental state where a person is fully immersed in an activity and feels a sense of energized focus, complete involvement, and enjoyment. During the flow state, individuals absorb themselves in what they are doing; they lose track of time and may even forget about their physical needs. Psychologist Mihaly Csikszentmihalyi was the first to describe the flow state. He noted that people who experience this state often feel a sense of control, confidence, and creativity. They are wholly focused on the task and may even feel that their actions are automatic or instinctual.

Therefore, the blur or time slowing down described by legendary athletes' performances is consistent with the account of a future legend—American Olympic sprinter Sydney McLaughlin. In an interview with Sports Spectrum, McLaughlin talked about how her faith helps her stay grounded and focused on what matters: "I think it just comes down to knowing who you are, and knowing who you're competing for. At the end of the day, it's not about me. It's about what God's placed me here to do."[2] Regarding the flow state, McLaughlin adds, "When you're in that zone, it's almost like you're not really thinking. You're just reacting. It's a very spiritual experience, honestly. You feel like you're in tune with something greater than yourself."[3]

After repeatedly breaking her world record, Sydney McLaughlin was the world record holder in the 400-meter hurdles as of 2023. Finally, although dreamers cannot always tell what happened, dominating the moment was years in the making. Thus, without action (e.g., work, commitment, resilience, and faith), dreams are no more than fantasy. But if you put in the work, you can break through ceilings.

Consider, for example, a pattern in which slow motion has occurred thus far. We found it in people striving for something with all their might. Athletes were great examples. They examined their paths and pursued goals like they were retrieving something stolen from themselves. Their spiritual enlightenment also reflects a combination of additional attributes. Among them are:

1. Wanting to accomplish something so ridiculous that few people other than your mother will believe it is possible
2. Becoming a student of what it takes to achieve that thing
3. Going for it with courage and resilience, proclaiming victory in advance
4. Internalizing an unwavering faith that teeters on insanity

In other words, an irrational elevated state of consciousness is arrived at through a rational process of determination. Therefore, the way itself is clear about the role of those who operate on their elevated frequency.

However, another explanation for spiritual intervention might be a calling on your life that is bigger than you imagine. The idea that nothing can stop you from elevating or being spared, regardless of your actions. In the next chapter, let's look at slow motion in this context.

---

[2] McLaughlin, S. (2021, August 2). Sydney McLaughlin: The Tokyo Olympics, Faith, and Finding the 'Flow State.' In J. Romano (Interviewer), Sports Spectrum. Retrieved from https://sportsspectrum.com/podcast/2021/08/02/sydney-mclaughlin-the-tokyo-olympics-faith-and-finding-the-flow-state/.
[3] (McLaughlin 2021).

CHAPTER TWELVE
MOTORCYCLE DAYS

While my experience with slow motion remained spiritual, it was not limited to athletic performances, even though I had an outrageous number of sports encounters. Put briefly, God's favor was always the outcome for me, such as the following example, which had nothing to do with reaching far-fetched goals and working hard. Faith was the way.

I was riding my motorcycle on the Los Angeles 110 freeway traveling toward Pasadena. If you know this stretch of highway, you are familiar with its narrow, winding lanes and how the furthest left lane suddenly separates and becomes an onramp for Interstate 5. I was driving in the lane to the immediate right of the one that would soon become an onramp and behind a mid-sized SUV, a Toyota 4Runner. It was a perfect California day. The temperature was in the high 70s with a light breeze and, of course, no humidity. Traffic was moderate, so moving with the pace of traffic meant exceeding the speed limit by five to ten miles per hour. If anybody were on the fence about buying a motorcycle, days like that would inspire their bike purchases.

Motorcyclists typically egg on one another to perform risky maneuvers, which was one reason I never joined a motorcycle club. I chalked them up as groupthink. However, I rode with my friend Mario from time to time, and he lived in Pasadena. Riding was purely recreational for us. I never commuted to work by motorcycle, nor did Mario cycle to medical school or residency. He kept his bike secret for obvious reasons. I was a college dean, and Mario was studying and training to become an orthopedic surgeon. For the most part, we were responsible riders with one compelling vice. Mario's indulgence was popping wheelies. When he came to my house, he would ride his wheelie for blocks. The intermittent roar and gear changes let me know he was close long before arriving. He would drop down his front wheel when he reached my driveway and laugh.

I had an occasional need for speed. I opened the throttle on Sundays at 6 AM on empty California freeways, if at all. A substantial speeding ticket eliminated my speed habit. A state trooper cited me for traveling 98 miles per hour (mph) in a 55mph zone. Even that was after slowing to exit. My top speed was 183mph. The officer almost arrested me for reckless driving. Instead, I paid a hefty fine and went to traffic school.

Traffic school scared me straight. First, I learned that the odds were against my survival if I continued to speed. Then, an officer shared the story of a speeder who lost control and side-swiped a chain-linked fence. The fence grated the rider's body like cheese. He died with no chance at an open casket. Next, I learned that the most common cause of motorcycle accidents is the failure of other motorists to detect motorcycles on the road. Therefore, if I move too fast, I might surprise an unsuspecting driver.

As a result, I spent multiple weekends studying evasive maneuvers taught to advanced riders and police officers. However, I needed more than that and anecdotes. It was necessary to change the physical aspects of riding. In other words, I must practice good habits and fine-tune my mental awareness to survive distracted LA drivers.

So, I put cones down in large parking lots, mimicking setups from training courses I saw online. Since the layouts emphasized cornering, braking, swerving, and managing traction, I realized the only way to perform the maneuvers was to ride within posted speed limits. Therefore, I slowed down and got to where I could do almost anything on a motorcycle. I even studied how to fall.

Likewise, Mario had an encounter that diminished his urge to ride recklessly. During a rotation in the emergency room, Mario picked up the leg of a motorcyclist who crashed and tossed it into a large container the size and shape of those used by homeowners for city waste pickup. That amputation was enough. Mario lost the desire to pop wheelies. For a moment, we claimed to have been luckier than most. We'd had a good run and spoke of those reckless days as ancient history, with no intention of bringing them back.

I remember riding on Los Angeles' 110 freeway years later. I trailed a Toyota 4Runner at a safe distance. I maintained my lane without splitting between other cars and followed all rules for safe motorcycle driving. I always trailed vehicles on the outer third of the road to remain visible in the driver's side mirrors. I kept consistent speeds and constantly looked for escape routes in case of driver errors. There were always errors.

I noticed the left turn signal flashing, and the SUV gradually maneuvered into the far-left lane. I began to pass. When I reached the SUV's rear door, I noticed the SUV starting an abrupt lane change back. After that, the scene went into slow motion. The driver seemed unaware that her initial lane change would take her onto a different freeway. Then, without looking, she returned to the lane she had left. I knew she didn't look because I could see her through her side mirror, which meant she could also have seen me.

While in slow motion, I checked the lane to my right, and cars were moving faster than cars in my lane. I checked behind me, and the risk of getting hit from behind was too significant to slow down. The only option left was to brace as the 4Runner's side mirror was in the position to hit my shoulder. Once I braced for impact, time changed to regular speed. The distance between me and the mirror closed fast, and bam! I crashed hard into the mirror. Because of the narrow lanes of the 110 freeway, I did not have any wiggle room. If I veered in any direction or slowed down, I'd be in the middle of a pileup.

There was no panic in me, though. The slow-motion scene was familiar, reminiscent of moments when I overcame obstacles. So, I believed that no matter what, I'd come out on top, as always in my dreams. The distance between the right side mirror and my left shoulder and chest area quickly closed. Thump! The impact of the collision lifted me out of my seat a little. The bike quivered and moved roughly a half inch right and quickly returned left, approximately the same half inch. I have swerved more from driving over a pothole. I slowed and kept pace, again next to the rear door. This time I saw her looking at me in her rearview mirror. Her mouth was wide open, panicked. She knew then that she had hit me. I slowed a bit more, wanting to get behind her, but the cars behind her followed closely.

When her brake lights illuminated next to me, the scene returned to slow motion. I guessed that her reflexes made her slam on her brakes. More people would employ that instinct in an accident. Her side mirror wasn't adjustable like the mirrors drivers can turn in when they park. Still, I broke through the mirror on my second impact regardless of the auto maker's intent to make it impenetrable. While in slow motion through both crashes, I felt a gentle pull from above. I felt tethered, as if God had attached a line to me and my bike and towed us. Now in front of her and past the onramp, I led her to a grassy area just off the shoulder on the left. She jumped out of her vehicle in hysterical chatter, and I was extremely calm, just like when I woke up from my dreams.

    I cannot explain the onset of slow motion or why I experience those moments. I only know that whatever happens in my subconscious—such as dreams, daydreams, and slow-motion—has a chance when I allow God to work through me. What happens after that is always remarkable.

Section Four

PERSPECTIVE, PROGRESS, AND STRATEGIES

Fascinating, Isn't It?

Consider society is more "connected."
Yet, more citizens are unprotected.
More people, more phones, what's next?

I miss voices and seeing faces.
Freedom to learn about all races,
Making connections based on nuances, not texts.

Harmful foods and medications,
Attributing beauty to operations,
Society's quick fixes and their whine.

The doubtful seek fantasy and quick fixes, but
Emerging flows from mental remixes.
Satisfaction arrives in God's time.

Like "progress," perspective is fascinating.

Hughes Suffren

CHAPTER THIRTEEN
THE STORY OF MARY ANN, PART 1

A woman paused at the top of the stairs to catch her breath and bearings. It was just after the Club's grand opening, and this moment was the woman's first time on the second floor. She scanned the room until her eyes locked on mine. Then, she marched directly toward me. She must have acted on a perfect description of me. However, her confidence was a different kind of act. I stood behind the personal training desk and faked typing a text message on my tablet. At the same time, I held the woman in my peripheral vision and awaited her arrival. She wore mismatched clothes that were intentionally baggy, oversized, and not the current style. The woman also carried a tattered piece of paper, loosely gripped between her thumb and forefinger, like something dirty to be tossed into the trash. Her walk was sure and confident. However, how she transported the page, which she had folded into a small, uneven square, raised questions she intended her strut to answer. Faking it did not work. Instead, she communicated awkward indecision like the space of time between standing at a pool's edge, wanting to jump, and refusing to leap. Perhaps she had not fully committed to sharing its contents. My best guess was that each stride built the woman's courage and speaking with me was akin to jumping into the pool's deepest end.

    I could see through the folds as the light hit the creased squares. My gaze revealed faint outlines of tiny print, and the writing filled the page from one corner to the others. It was clear that whatever the woman wrote was agonizingly detailed.

    She did not know my background as a former collegiate athlete, a counselor, or a college dean. The woman only knew my reputation as a fitness professional and that I was certified to help her. Likewise, I had not met the woman before. Nobody told me that she was on her way to see me. Nevertheless, from one look at her, I knew that I would rely on tools learned from those varied life experiences if we were to begin a successful wellness journey. I must also borrow lessons from great motivators and examples of success stories to keep her engaged.

"Hi, my name is Mary Ann and from your nametag, I know you're the person I came to see."

"Good morning, Mary Ann. It is a pleasure to meet you. Is that for me?" I said as I glanced

at the hand that grudgingly held the form.

Without another word, Mary Ann handed me the tattered page. Her reach was slow, falling short of full extension. Picture an alligator's arms' reach as she handed over the form, which contained her handwritten health summary, current physical limitations, and fitness goals. I opened and flattened the page, and my cursory glance confirmed my initial thoughts. Mary Ann was a mess, and she had a long road ahead.

I had met many people who believed they wanted to change and significantly transform physically. But our opening energy exchange did not feel any different from those who failed. Suddenly, I was somewhere between a struggle with face management and what to say next. I did not lose my words; there was no chance of that. I had plenty to say. However, my pause bought me time to filter what I should and should not mention. Mary Ann's written summary produced many competing thoughts. I wanted to know if she was a quitter like so many others who succumbed to the arduous journey and gave up, or maybe I wanted to know why. Why did she show up, and why would this start be different from her others? There had to be other starts. Indeed, nobody would grow to her size without a few failed attempts at diets or exercise. So, I began a series of questions:

"What made you come in here today? Did a doc—"

"I don't want to die," she said, cutting me off before I could finish.

I paused. My face must have been blank, undaunted. My expressionless reaction to hearing Mary Ann's desperate plea may communicate cynicism. And I was, indeed, cynical. That's because I recalled a story my mother shared about a man. He was a family member, married into it on my father's side. There's no drama like family drama. Anyway, after repeated lung cancer treatments and refusing to quit smoking, his doctor said,

"You are going to die. If you smoke one more cigarette after today, I will not treat you again."

"Thank you, doctor," the patient replied. "I don't want to die, and I am scared to die," he further assured the doctor.

Toward the end of their visit, the man remained adamant about strictly following the doctor's prescribed treatment plan. Then, the man lit a cigarette from his appointment to his car. He continued to smoke until he died a few months later. So, one might say I was unmoved by Mary Ann's admission. It was true.

A hush fell between us, which I would not disturb. The moment craved thought and anticipation, not impatience, hurry, or force. Besides, I wanted Mary Ann to take charge of her vulnerability by initiating the dive into her story. So, I took my sweet time, again doodling on my tablet, until the only reasonable action was for Mary Ann to break the heavy silence. The strategy worked. Mary Ann read my expression and began to share her story. Without thought, shame, or pretense, Mary Ann started much in the flow of an Alcoholics Anonymous meeting. But her words were not rehearsed: "My name is Mary Ann, and I'm here to lose weight. Just tell me what to do, and I will do it," she said.

Mary Ann noticed me nodding and waving my hand toward me—like saying come here—a clear indication that I needed more. Then, she continued to speak, adding much-needed context for her appearance and written text: "I am 5'5" and 370 pounds, and I have a lot of issues. Let's start with my back; my spine is curved. So, suppose I drop something on the floor. In that case, I have to think about how I will pick it up to limit physical pain and strategically maneuver around to reach it. My knees constantly hurt, and I wear orthotics and special shoes for flat feet. I told my podiatrist that sometimes I feel like I have a broken heel. Then, he gave me a boot to wear at night to relieve the pain he diagnosed as plantar fasciitis. I also have high blood pressure, high cholesterol, and stage two hypertension, which means I'm on a two-drug regimen to bring down my blood pressure. My doctor says that I am at risk of an early heart attack or stroke because of my family history."

She paused and forced a clinched-lip smile with an expression that did not match. "Wait a minute, Mary Ann. I want to make sure I get all of this," I said. I was feverishly typing notes and follow-up questions into my tablet. A few moments passed. "When were you in your best shape, and what did you do to get there?" I asked.

"I have always been big. Whether playing soccer, softball, or swimming, I was the girl who could move well for my size. At 5'4" and approximately 180 pounds, I lettered in all three of those sports in high school."

"Hold it. I thought you were 5'5"?" I asked.

"I grew an inch in college," she said.

"Ahh, got it. Please continue."

"Now, I'm 33 years old, and I've had more starts and stops with diets and exercise than I can remember. My mom, who earned a PhD in Special Education and whose specialty was testing, diagnosed me with ADHD in first grade. She decided to test me because I was disruptive in class. Teachers would report that I would wander the classroom and talk nonstop. All that and I still earned straight A's. Diagnosing girls with hyperactivity was rare in 1985. Knowing full well that there were rules against treating your family, mom sought an independent specialist who later confirmed her diagnosis. I felt powerless over controlling my weight. It was bad enough that I would have to fight genetics of being big from my mother's side of the family. But I also began gaining weight from medication. First, I took Ritalin, which proved ineffective for anything other killing my appetite. My parents were always telling me to eat. So, my doctors switched me to Prozac at 16-years-old for depression, and Dexedrine for ADHD. Prozac worked medically. Physically, however, I gained 75 pounds. Weight gain is a side-effect of the drug. I joined weight watchers at 13, along with my mom."

"Stop! How did it feel to be on Weight Watchers at such a young age?" I asked.

"It didn't bother me at all because it felt more like a game. That's it; it was a food matching game. When I got tired of playing the game, I stopped Weight Watchers and began battering myself for not doing more to prevent getting fat. Brutally and mercilessly, kids bullied me from middle school through high school. I never had any friends or self-confidence. It was just me and my homework."

It was rare to exceed an hour on a new client intake session. Mary Ann was different. Therefore, our meeting was the only time I spent two hours. Then again, I hadn't experienced a potential client being so open, vulnerable, and just laying it all out there. No secrets. Therefore, I felt I should listen to and document her whole story, understand Mary Ann's habits and her way of thinking. Of course, there was more to the conversation than what she shared. Maybe it was her convictions that converted me. Still, somewhere between my initial curiosity and the end of our talk, I believed 100% in Mary Ann. She wanted to change badly, and my presumptions about appearances, such as her baggy mismatched outfit, focused stride, or tattered paper, were unimportant.

I suppose I should have felt guilty for prejudging, which brings up indoctrinated ignorance toward people with differences. I frankly submit that fitting into the status quo is ludicrously essential in the United States and that encoding affects everyone. Therefore, it is naive to assume that positive values are our first thoughts when considering obese people. We automatically place heavy people on a continuum behind wherever we see ourselves. This practice affects their employment, social activities, travel, and political aspirations. In other words, there is a hierarchy in the American mind. Our skewed mindset creates distance between Americans we deem "normal" and those who do not fit the propagandized American physical profile. I am not saying that I am the portrait of the status quo. I would not dare. Rather than debate whether there is such a thing as normal, let's concede that the American masses regard people who are obese as different. "Different from what?" you may ask. The fantasy of the norm is your answer. Obese people are fringe elements that Americans treat harshly, ridicule as lazy, and characterize as undisciplined. Most Americans readily assign them labels and behaviors to satisfy our collective conscience. Complacency over striving, reckless eating over well-balanced diets, and their usefulness undervalued and overlooked. They are telling all who will listen that overweight people want to be unhealthy and choose to be overweight.

At the same time, we sneer upon considerations such as injuries, medications, or other medical causes. Summarizing that if they weren't overweight, they would not have medical issues. Never mind that how they got big is none of our business. Sometimes judgment turns to pity when we see overweight people in a gym or working out. Still, we judge when we see them eating something other than a salad. We are all guilty. Yet, standing before me was someone who was fed up with caring about what people thought. She clung to the objectives of small, progressive changes with the end goal of saving her life. Finally, I asked Mary Ann a series of leading consent-styled questions:

"So, you will do whatever I ask?"

"Yes."

"Do you realize that I will give you homework that may include exercise, diet, stress reduction, and sleep tracking?"

"Yes"

"You're committed to showing up early to warm up and not miss sessions (because consistency is key)?"

"I'm ready!"

"Then, I would be happy to be your trainer."

We exchanged our availability and settled on set days and times to train. Neither of us knew exactly what lay ahead. The information Mary Ann handed me was the cornerstone from which I would build out the framework of our plan. Her written history immediately eliminated groups of movements and machines. For example, her deconditioned system required us to slowly elevate her heart rate and train it for faster and faster recovery before increasing it more. Therefore, up-down movements were out. We also had to stretch and strengthen her back, which eliminated rotation exercises. She was too heavy to perform squats or to lie on the floor safely. You get the picture.

Both the written information from the questionnaire and her explanation helped me better create our initial three-month plan. Her progress dictated the next three months and so on. Although Mary Ann's notes did not provide a perfect blueprint, they made clear the physical and mental limits I should avoid and the tactics I should include.

For example, when we first started training, Mary Ann's health issues dictated my exercise programming. We did not engage in any fancy exercises, clever moves, or strenuous activity because if her heart rate were to reach 160, she would get so dizzy that she could not regain her bearings during the same hour. Sadly, a brisk walk of 15-20 feet would cause the room to spin. So, we took baby steps. literally and figuratively. My goal was to keep Mary Ann moving slowly. We acknowledged weight loss in 5-pound and 10-pound increments, and she never regained any weight that she lost. That sounds simple, but it is rare not to fluctuate. She often reminded me that her weight would only go in one direction—both encouraging herself and making sure that I wouldn't forget. I saw a determined woman when I looked at Mary Ann. I knew that working with her would be low-risk and high return for her and a fulfilling experience for me. And perhaps the most important consequence of our collaboration would be that she defied medical probabilities and continued living better.

Although our sessions were monotonous, Mary Ann never complained about what I asked of her. If her energy dropped, I would bark borrowed words from my high school basketball coach, "Do it and like it," and she complied by picking up her pace. In contrast, the "Do it and like it" line caused my other clients to respond differently. They would yell a variation of, "I'll do it, but I don't have to like it." The subtle difference speaks loudly. Their slight pushback represents a need to feel powerful. Exercising any semblance of control was essential to them. In other words, they could not or were unwilling to check their egos at the front door. Now, perhaps you understand another reason why Mary Ann and I got along so well. She was the ultimate "yes" client, while others annoyingly responded, "Yes, but…"

Mary Ann's training was slow and incremental, like a patient rehabilitating an injury. Still, Mary Ann trained with the mentality of an elite athlete—hardworking and dedicated—and she immediately responded to coaching and feedback. It was my job to keep her fire lit. So, I trained her as a throwback, hardcore coach. Sometimes I zinged her with other clever one-liners. For example, when she had a random pain while going hard, I would say, "Tape an aspirin to it and keep it movin'." We would laugh. However, I remixed some encouraging Coach Taylor-like yelling in quiet moments, minus his occasional colorful vocabulary. It may sound silly to yell at someone whose top speed was a snail's pace. Still, I found ways to mix up our workouts and maintain her healthy fear of disappointing me.

I liked that Mary Ann responded to tough love through current sports references, something we share from watching *SportsCenter* on ESPN every day. Mary Ann is a sports nut. She remains current with rosters, trades, injury reports, and standings. We banter through text messages mimicking *SportsCenter* insiders and give our little monologues before or after our sessions. I also found her accumulation of Georgia sports history interesting. Mary Ann could grab an unsung historical fact, connect it to something current, and do it organically.

Born and raised in Atlanta, Mary Ann proudly qualifies for the title of Georgia Peach. She is also an alumna of the University of Georgia and Georgia State University as well as a loyal fan of her hometown's professional sports teams. Mary Ann can talk about sports nonstop, and she loves it; however, when it was time to train, she trained as if nothing else mattered.

Mary Ann treated our bond as her last option. Of course, Mary Ann had moments of doubt, as anyone in her position would. She had tried and failed with strategies from infomercial personalities, magazine columns, and self-help books. None of those endeavors helped any more than the faddish diets that followed. They all encouraged excitement, which amounted to a few measurable pounds lost initially. However, each attempt waned and eventually ended with new, stronger cravings. Each failed diet left Mary Ann weighing more than when she started, compounding her frustration each time. She also failed at measuring food, whether using online trackers or Weight Watchers. Loved ones mournfully salvaged Mary Ann's emotions after each weight loss strategy nose-dived. Coddling is one reason parents may make lousy support groups. Parents are protectors, and it is deeply embedded into most to make life easier for their children. This assertion is especially true when one or more parents personally share their child's hardship, emotions, and perhaps, the guilt that may come with it.

I will never forget the first training session after Mary Ann's accumulated weight loss reached 45 pounds. She seemed less cheerful than usual that morning, less talkative, almost depressed, which was odd for someone who reached such a milestone. I took an extra step back as Mary Ann worked. I didn't initiate unnecessary conversation, only directions, cues, corrections, and commands. She needed space, and I gave it to her. "When it is time to talk, we will speak," I thought. Deep breaths and eye contact were clues that she was working up the nerve to speak. Finally, we reached the midpoint of our session. Then, Mary Ann shared what her mom said to her that morning: "I can't tell that you've lost any weight. I don't know why you waste so much money on personal training." Unfazed by her remarks, I pressed Mary Ann to keep working as she paused to talk.

"Less talk, more work!" I barked. Smoothly and efficiently, I transitioned her from one exercise to the next as tears began to well in her eyes. I am a trained counselor, undaunted by tears. So, instead of handing her a tissue or towel, I gave her a dumbbell to curl.

In a pissed-off tone, she said, "It's too heavy," as she strained to budge the dumbbell.

Not one for a pity party, I firmly and sharply said, "Curl the dumbbell."

"I can't," she said.

"You're not going to quit. Use both hands if you have to," I said.

A growing number of people walking slowed their pace to watch, and Mary Ann knew that attention was growing. It must have been upsetting for Mary Ann to hear her mother rebuke her efforts and those words have the opposite effect on me. Her vision now blurry from tears and her voice quivering from emotion, she said, "I can't."

Even though she was mad at me, the last thing she ever wanted was to disappoint me. So, she followed my orders to try and still could not budge the dumbbell. I could tell she gave it her all because each try produced less. She was burning out. Then, in dramatic fashion and devoid of empathy, I let out a frustrated gasp. When I felt more of her disappointment than anger, I snatched the dumbbell from Mary Ann's hands and turned it on its side so that she could read the number "45."

Now with a compassionate tone, I said, "This is the 45 pounds you lost, Mary Ann. That's 45 pounds no longer on your back, and 45 pounds no longer on your knees, and 45 pounds no longer on your feet. Everybody in your life may not be in your corner now, but there will be a day when they jump on your bandwagon."

Knowing that more words may ruin our moment of perspective and progress, I pointed toward her workout towel. Her face was wet from sweat, and she needed to address her loose sniffles, snot, and tears. Finally, after a minute or two of pulling herself together, Mary Ann was ready for her next milestone: the next five-pound increment of weight loss. Still silent, I motioned to a lighter set of dumbbells.

CHAPTER FOURTEEN
LIFE IS A JOURNEY

Who doesn't throw up in their mouth a little every time someone says that life is a journey? It is an annoying catchphrase, although valid at its core. The problem is that it is not helpful; it tells us to wait and is somewhat preachy. Upon hearing it, my instinct is to oppose the distance between their words meant for surrender and those I speak as my reality. While forcing a rancid swallow of warm spit, I think, "Miss me altogether with that raggedy cliché, and give me something I can use." I do not doubt that 10 people out of 10 would sum up that pitch as the beginning of the dreaded "Take your time because you have all the time in the world and your whole life ahead of you" speech. In deference to elders, we listen as if anyone knows what is best for someone except for themselves.

Moreover, the way you may want to approach an endeavor or the speed at which you want to achieve it may have happened differently for them. So, it is common for such people to say "slow down" to those perceived as wanting too much, too soon because it's often personal. Therefore, the typical discussion turns to examples of the speaker self-reflecting. Then, they point to random senior citizens who made a great life for themselves after 20 or 30 years of incremental progress. Unfortunately, my eyes are out of focus, and I'd rather be elsewhere by this time.

My reaction may be a harsh way of viewing advice. But advice should inspire, encourage, or creatively address constraints, not oppose them as final. This chapter will prove that anybody may find themselves on either side of the conversation, even with the best intentions. They may embody the go-getter and the dream killer, with both sides believing they are right. Not only that, but I will also provide an approach go-getters can use to navigate their journeys.

Several years ago, I set a lofty goal to referee men's college basketball at the highest level. Even though I had never blown a whistle, I sought to ascend and join the officiating staff somewhere quickly. From referee blogs and internet searches, I learned that I could develop intangibles at my pace. I figured I could nail those things, look the part, and present myself as the next logical choice as a college hire. The prospect of earning great money served as great motivation. Besides, refereeing basketball was my way to remain involved in the game that gave me so much. I was all in.

Meanwhile everybody I asked about calling college games told me California was different. Initially, every referee had to work for a high school association. This step scared away a lot of people who wanted big money fast. Not me. I joined the prestigious California Basketball Officials Association LA Unit. I wanted legitimacy as I parlayed the best high school training into college contracts and long-term success. Everyone I asked agreed that I was in the right place.

We met in the gymnasium of a local middle school. Each week, after listening to a guest speaker or two, the Unit president dismissed us, and we hurried to our assigned classrooms. Any delay would be akin to being late to a game. Some instructors would lock their doors and count anyone who tarried as absent.

The Unit's most accomplished officials led our mandatory certification classes. They all were incredible men and women, and they wanted to know us personally. So, our instructors asked open-ended questions. After answering the initial question, students could say "pass" to avoid follow-up questions or "play ball" to accept a deeper dive. That was one of our ground rules. We did not have many. Specifically, we had no scripted ground rules and very few follow-up questions. Our exchanges eventually led to the veterans sharing their war stories and encouraging us to share ours.

There was a proud, shared history of the Unit. It was the first Southern California Unit, and it comprised the most competitive teams in the state. Make it in LA, and you can make it anywhere because you will be battle-tested. Students felt the veterans' camaraderie, loyalty, and sense of family. They demonstrated an overwhelming reverence for basketball and reciprocity to the LA Unit. They walked and talked boldly, and we wanted to be a part of that. Each facilitator testified to the long, arduous road toward refereeing the high school playoffs and disclosed that earning those assignments would take us years. College officials taught the veteran sections. Since ours was a beginner to mid-level class, only one facilitator could talk about college basketball from experience. He worked at the small college level.

"Get college ball out of your heads," one instructor said. He was laughing and serious as he admonished our class. All because one student asked about something that happened in a televised college game. "Some of you are in a dreamland. Thinking you can ascend to that level anytime soon is the height of folly." He continued firing shots and (unknowingly) spoke of my goal as fantasy. He vehemently upheld his paradigm as our reality in his next breath: "If you were bigtime, you wouldn't be in this class," he said.

The other facilitators cosigned with nods and chimed in with, "You got that right," "Yeah," and "Amen." In the minds of our instructors, only high school ball lay in our futures.

I knew that I did not have the patience for what they described, but I sat quietly and listened. Finally, they asked us to share our goals, one by one, publicly.

I felt somewhat disrespectful when I boldly said, "I am on a specific path to referee Division I basketball within three years." Note that Division I is the highest level of college athletics. As soon as I made the statement, I remembered that the facilitator who called on me had recently made it to the junior college and Division II levels after six and eight years, respectively.

He nodded and took a deep breath. Then, he folded his arms against his chest and said, "I've already been where you're trying to go. Most referees want to move up fast. Now, let me tell you how it really works in Southern California. You will spend four to five years working high school ball, three to four years working junior college, another three to five years working Division II, and if you're still a rising star, you may make it to Division I, mid-majors."

I don't think he noticed I was looking past him and into a fog because I pretended to listen out of respect. I gave a few insincere nods, and uh-huhs meant only to hurry him along. Then, he finished.

"Any questions?" he asked as if he had made his point and dropped the mic.

"Pass," I said.

And he walked off his stage to sit at the teacher's desk.

Meanwhile, nothing changed in me when he completed his lecture. In my mind, he was another person of authority telling me that average was good enough. Rather than respond, I made working on my skills my protest. I didn't share with anybody that I was at a gym at 6 o'clock every morning practicing mechanics such as blowing the whistle and calling fouls and violations in the mirror room. I spent countless hours rehearsing how I would point to where to put the ball back into play and reporting fouls and timeouts to an imaginary table crew. I was determined to "look the part" from my first game forward. Thus, I went beyond practicing mechanical duties. I hit the weights hard to bolster my athletic look and paid a tailor to alter my uniform.

During pregame warm-up, a coach once remarked, "Hey ref, you look like you can still take the ball and finish above the rim." I smiled, knowing that I had his confidence and deference on close calls due to my look. The summer that followed my first season, I earned the "Best Referee" award at a high school camp sponsored by two Division I officials. The award included an all-expenses-paid scholarship to a college camp of my choice. A year and a half after my first game, I accepted positions on the staff of two Division I conferences. I also got an offer to join the NBA training program, which included refereeing its development league. With that, I broke the Southern California mold.

Just like that, I was a hot commodity as a guest speaker and clinician at referee camps nationwide. My message centered around one central idea: Nobody can deny what is yours if you act like you want it. When I said "act," I meant that you must be proactive and do things that will accelerate your ability to accomplish your goals. That may require doing what other people are unwilling to do. For some referees, that may mean instituting a 5:00 AM wake-up call to go to the gym. For others, it may mean continuously studying the rule book. Many young referees may practice a confident, athletic run; study one-liners when responding to coaches; or get a mentor. I started with a decision to define and orchestrate my narrative. Then, I chose to improve upon all the areas that involved refereeing at the level I strived to reach. In other words, figure out what is for you, do the necessary work, avoid the naysayers, and you will emerge through faith.

That veteran referee who spoke patience to me did not realize how fast times were changing. If so, he would have known that more Americans seek to disrupt the traditional career path, no matter the industry, and fewer people appreciate the classic "patience" speech. That's not just me being hypersensitive to empty rhetoric. Or maybe it is. Either way, let's not pretend that "life is a journey" espouses profound revelations for you, even though you may agree with its meaning.

Reminders to work harder and wait longer perpetuate the status quo by suggesting systems dominate individual will. I don't see it this way. I accept each person's path as theirs to choose, and there is power, protection, and provision when the path you choose is also the path God wants for you. Belief produces positive results. We often underestimate the importance of our decision-making power and God's hand in our endeavors, whether becoming lean and fit or writing a book. When we sync our desire and faith to God's will for us, the floodgates of blessings open, and nobody can deny that which is ours. It is also one way we can explain unmerited favor. I am sure you have confessed similar experiences, such as, "I can't believe I got that job," or "I overslept but still made my flight because it was delayed." We shouldn't be so quick to misidentify favor as luck.

Learning From Mistakes

Again, when something is for you to have, nobody can deny you; sometimes, you can't even mess it up if you try. For example, a collegiate athlete dreamed of playing in the NBA. Let us call him Julien. Standing 6'7" tall, with broad shoulders and a sprinters gate, he had the prototypical body of an NBA small forward. Averaging 16 points per game as a sophomore, Julien had a guard's shooting touch and ballhandling skills. He was also strong enough to bully players with his solid post-up game. For those reasons, everyone, including pro scouts, knew the league was his for the taking. However, nobody anticipated the armed robbery and kidnapping charges he earned following a trip to the NCAA tournament.

Julien was young and impressionable. He did not weigh his options or pause and take a breath when a football player mentioned a robbery. Instead, Julien bypassed his home training and agreed to tag along, which allowed the law to write the next chapter of his story. He committed the crime with a gun-wielding, bona fide hardened criminal. During the arrest, Julien was shot by police and charged with two felonies. Lucky for Julien, his basketball coach believed in him. The coach used all his influence to get him acquitted by testifying on his behalf. Then, he called in a favor and got Julien a scholarship to play at a university on the West Coast. There was no returning to his original school, and his coach knew that Julien needed a fresh start. Then, shortly after arriving on the new campus, police began investigating Julien for "false use of a financial instrument and sexual misconduct." He never played a game. The new coach kicked Julien off the team and sent him home before being charged or attending a class.

I heard rumors that Julien's mom had to take a second mortgage on her house to cover his mounting legal fees. This guy's life was another sad tale of talent and opportunities wasted. There is more. One Saturday night, I was in a Chicago nightclub and saw Julien surrounded by a group of women. Like old friends, we greeted each other with a tightly gripped handshake and embraced with the other hand. Then, after he returned to his seat, I could tell he read my look of sadness and disappointment.

"Man, what are you doing to your mom?" I asked. I intended that to be the first of a series of questions.

Instead, with the voice control of a slurring drunk, Julien cut me off: "Yo yo yo, don't even trip, bruh; I got this. It's been over a year since I've played. I still have two years of eligibility. Imma go to a junior college next year and average about 40 on them fools. Then, a major college is gonna' give me a scholarship to play one year, and I'll drop 30 a game. Then, imma get drafted to the league."

I felt sorry for him. Denial does not look good on anybody, especially not on an inebriated falling star wasting away his shine. Since I wasn't good at face management then, I looked at Julien with dismay. It was a curious stare like he was an addict who told me he was quitting his habit (again), for real, this time. So palpable was my wilting energy and posture. He had to have known that I disagreed as clearly as anticipating a "but" coming when contrarians speak.

Then, I noticed his eyes glaze over and detach from our conversation. Maybe Julien knew that I was not buying in, or perhaps he realized that I would have given the "play the long game and be safe" speech if we were in a different setting. Ironically, I did not recognize the ease with which I had switched at that moment. Now, I played the loathsome role of the hypocrite and dream killer as the older referee had done to me. If I had more time, would I have said, "Life is a journey?" Ugh!

Still, it could have been that Julien didn't notice. Music, women, and spirits distracted him. The man had likely consumed enough alcohol for what he said to make sense to him and was probably too drunk to realize that I was dimming his light. I nodded my head from my proverbial high horse, too full of myself to buy into his vision. Time to move on. I didn't want to ruin his good time by being realistic, I thought sarcastically.

I shook his hand and wished him luck. Then, I finished his story under my breath as I walked away. "He ain't going nowhere," I said. My hope in him had died. That was the last time that I talked with Julien directly. I watched as commentators covered an NBA game two years later and spoke highly of a young rookie starter. This player averaged a crapload of points per game at a junior college and earned a one-year scholarship to play at a Division I university. They were talking about Julien.

Julien averaged enough points per game to prove NBA worthiness in his final year of college ball. Finally, the announcers said Julien had played his way onto an NBA team. I shook my head and laughed a proud laugh. I was happy for Julien. Again, he belonged in the league, and as much as he tried, Julien couldn't even mess up a dream meant for him. Nor could naysayers derail him from it. Shame on me.

We're All on Different Paths

Let's look at it another way. Visualize your route in life as a long, winding cart path like the ones designed for golf courses. Each person has such a course and direction; like a fingerprint, there are no two alike. Your paved road will take you through and around obstacles, varying in angle, location, size, shape, and difficulty, making the challenges uniquely designed for you. That's why some people can seemingly get away with things you may not. Their obstacles may not be yours, or some similar challenges occur at different times. Your story is not my story. You get my drift. Imagine that all cart paths have a cover above them, made of various materials and strengths.

When you step off your path, you forfeit your covering and leave yourself unprotected and vulnerable to hazards seen and unseen. Veering off the path is an unnecessary risk that may not harm some and can devastate others. For this reason, you can be off your path and still reach your destination, but not without getting pelted by storms, hail, rain, and extreme sun. Being off your path may land you in rough terrain, slowing your travel. You may land in life's (water) hazards and (sand) traps. Traveling off your path, you may get lost and risk getting turned around and unintentionally revisiting the most extended, most demanding locations on the course repeatedly.

However, staying on the path might make your travels smoother and more protective. Of course, there will still be curves, hills, and weather; that's life. However, you will progress with less turbulence if you stay in position. You may succeed sooner because God may order your steps, not as a command—more like arranging your stride in sequence and length. The confirmation comes when you say, "I don't know why I did that," or "It happened fast, and I didn't plan it," and whatever it was turned out for your good.

Nevertheless, the covering represents God's protection, where you may find rest and people to push and encourage you. Resources represent God's provision. Too much, and you can get too comfortable in one place. The covering in the spot above you may begin to wear or give way, which forces you to move along the path where there may be more substantial cover. How about that raggedy, unfulfilling job you can't believe you lost or the career-ending injury that forced a pivot? That may have been your covering giving way, forcing you to move.

That is an inspiring way to look at life because options are ripe. Anybody rolling their eyes like slot machines to the "patience" speech might be more open to changing behavior if told they are not competing against everybody. Instead, they are competing against how much and how fast they learn. Their learning curve dictates progress. In other words, the speed at which a person masters their course, or as we say these days, learns to "be the best version of themselves," will achieve their version of success. I saw a teenager wearing a t-shirt that read, "Built Different." I nodded, and to myself, I said, "We all are." Our readiness to meet moments is what we control, including activating resources to which we have access. Yes, I said it, "We all have resources." Now, I will show you a convenient way to access them and when to keep or discard them.

Progress May Be a Stone Thrown Away

Now that I've piqued your interest, let's discuss how to assign constructive meaning to the "life is a journey" metaphor. There's more. We will also learn how to apply individual resources when needed. Consider the following:

- You are your 25-year-old self.
- You are wearing an invisible backpack.
- Your backpack holds medium-sized stones, about the size of your fist, each weighing 2 pounds.

I chose this age for relative life experience, but you may imagine yourself at your current age. You will carry your backpack throughout your remaining life. Each stone you decide to take represents something you have learned or experienced that you may apply to your journey. If you need a new stone, create it in your mind, "act like you want it," and it will appear in your backpack.

For example, one of the stones in my backpack is to "control what I can and give zero energy to the rest." In my earlier referee example, that meant understanding the rule book like pastors know scripture. To cite, interpret and apply rules made me the expert on the court. I controlled my professional appearance and arrived two hours before the games. I ran hard on the court, hustling into a proper position to see action in my area, increasing my chances of correctly calling plays. My effort communicated my respect for coaches and their games, no matter the level. This stone also freed my mind. I didn't have to worry about whether I'd get positive evaluations from evaluators or coaches. I didn't agonize over my schedule, the number of game assignments, or high-profile game assignments, and I certainly didn't entertain conversations about the business of other referees. I did not control those things.

I remember speaking with coaches like they were my friends early in my career. When that backfired, I sought a new stone for my backpack: "effectively communicating with coaches." I created and rehearsed one-liners for tough plays and associated each with an official rule. For example, I had one for split-second blocking or charging plays. If I called a "block" and the coach yelled for an explanation, I would say, "The defensive player didn't beat him to the spot." That phrasing is straight out of the rule book for defining a blocking foul. End of conversation! To control what I can is still a stone in my backpack. I apply it to every area of my life.

In retrospect, one of Julien's stones may have read, "Ignore naysayers." As I said earlier, I never spoke to him again, and I would not blame him if his lack of communication was intentional. Time and again, people show their asses. I was no exception. Typical. Someone comfortable with negativity will always find a place to deliver it. Therefore, disengaging applies to family, friends, acquaintances, co-workers, social media, and even former teammates like me. I thought my relationship with dreams to that point in my life would have encouraged me to treat Julien's dreams with more respect—not as if dreams had to be linear, coherent, or without messiness.

Perhaps Julien embraced "discovery" as a stone in his backpack. This skill could have provided a framework for deciding who to ignore or let go of, such as naysayers. Deeper still, discovery may have helped him probe and better discern who to call a friend or foe. Continuing with this hypothetical discovery may have offered Julien ways to evaluate options, consider consequences, and improve decision-making. Finally, faith may be his cornerstone. Suppose that he grasped onto faith through all his trials, self-imposed or by chance. Faith destroys oppression and calms panic. Faith also produces, never consumes, and dares us to dream. There may not be a better resource to call upon that simultaneously dispenses with naysayers and obstacles and allows us to soar beyond our wildest dreams. The point is that using stones as a metaphor for skills provides a perceptible way to harness our power.

You may also discard stones that are no longer useful. Since each stone represents a life skill, experience, or tool and together can get heavy, it would be best to decide which to carry in your backpack. No matter what they represent in skills, more weight will weigh you down, which may determine the speed of your progress or complete stoppage.

For example, a student once remarked, "You must like sports cars," after seeing my new purchase.

At that moment, I said, "Yeah, I do."

However, after searching for the source of why I buy sports cars, I realized that I purchased vehicles with manual transmissions to have two ways to start them. I don't remember when I put the "car mistrust" stone in my backpack as a child. I only remember that my mom and five siblings were often stranded, sometimes on the side of freeways, because our car would stop. Extended family or good Samaritans often gave us rides home. My father, who worked multiple jobs, was the only person who could start our cheap, junky cars once stranded.

Therefore, I vowed always to know how to start my car when I grew up, as if being stranded was normal. Then at 16, I bought my first cheap junky car for $500. It was a vehicle with brilliant color, fat tires, a racing steering wheel, and a silver-holed gear shift resembling brass knuckles. Sounds fancy, but I was only interested in having a manual transmission. Again, a car with a stick shift presented two ways to start the engine: a traditional key start or rolling the car fast enough to pop the clutch. I learned to park my car on a slight hill. If the physical key start did not work, I didn't have to push the car and jump in to pop the clutch. Instead, I could take the car out of gear with the key in the "on" position and let the car roll while my foot pressed and held the clutch pedal against the floor. Then, I could shift into second gear, released the clutch pedal, and the car would magically run.

Popping the clutch was a sure thing. However, as an adult, I learned that my first car topped the list as the worst vehicle ever manufactured in the United States. Therefore, I got a lot of practice popping its clutch, which only perpetuated the need for my stone of "car mistrust" and, consequently, more cars with manual transmissions. Suppose I put aside my need for speed, typical for a young man. In that case, I would not consider a stick shift if starting my car was not a deciding factor. Then, I realized that the pain and frustration of being stranded as a child reinforced the notion that buying sports cars increased reliability. It was disturbing to learn that such negativity still informed my decisions, even though I had the means to afford a reliable vehicle as an adult. That revelation shocked me into declaring my next car an automatic. The days of junky cars and needing a stick shift to start them were long gone. God only knows why I was 40 years old before I bought my first automatic and removed the "car mistrust" stone from my backpack.

We have learned that stones may be behaviors or attitudes, which I call skills, short for coping skills. Whether positive or negative, your stones may appear in your career, friendships, intimate relationships, academic pursuits, or any facet of life. Moreover, to "act like you want it" means using your resources: research, mentors, family, friends, acquaintances, schools, tutors, employment agencies, or pastors. Remember that it is up to you to identify (or create) the skill, and then you must act (to get it).

Next, you may use a stone to anchor you. These stones may represent your faith, prayer, meditation, exercise, music, empathy, or any skill that may keep you positively connected. Finally, you may use them to access the high road. For example, one of my stones is to affirm others while driving. Suppose someone cuts me off in traffic or speeds like a maniac. In that case, I may say out loud, "I hope their emergency isn't life threatening and that they make it to their destination safely." I have found that it is impossible to bless someone sincerely and have simultaneous road rage.

Conversely, suppose you hold on to a skill that is no longer helpful. It may weigh you down by intentionally or unintentionally informing your decisions and behavior, such as mistrust, despair, intolerance, or prejudice. For example, I held on to the perceived need for a stick shift too long. Likewise, people who grow up poor may hoard money (poverty mentality). Someone left at the altar may need help to walk down the aisle again (mistrust). Someone who grew up listening to unfounded, negative opinions of others may act on judgment (prejudice). In other words, you are in control of what you carry through your life journey, and progress may be a stone created or a stone thrown away.

We have conceded that life is a journey. That our first reactions are rarely to say, "I'm going to play the long game," or "You can do it," depending on which side of the conversation you are on. Instead, we present counterarguments—playing devil's advocate—at best. At worst, we commit to the opposite ideas and offer discouragement. We are often blind to the juxtaposition of wanting others to believe in our audacious stretch goals and readily dim light on other people as they share theirs. Perhaps that is because human beings naturally suffer from constantly evaluating each other. Then, we often use our experiences as a barometer for what others can attain. For example, we may size up strangers based on size, looks, walk, or dress. Then, we may silently read into additional clues as we verbally author the rest of their stories. Likewise, we are equally critical of people we know. So, our advice is tainted as we encourage caution over risk-taking. As a result, we gravitate toward paths of least resistance, reinforced by familiar mantras like "Work smarter, not harder," "Patience is a virtue," or "You must be realistic."

However, if we are alive, we are on this journey, and we can reset or "course correct" as long as we have breath. In other words, we can decide to emerge by moving with an individual purpose, aligned with God's purpose for us and prosper, or we can give our power to naysayers and invite unnecessary struggles. Whichever path we choose, we have resources, which we call skills. To simplify it, we have assigned equal shape, size, and weight to our (coping) skills represented by stones. All stones exist to serve our desires and switch from inertia to dead weight when no longer in use. It makes sense then to choose which stones you will carry and which you will throw away.

Coping Strategies

Sometimes we choose without choosing. It may seem like you've blinked, and just like that, you're deeper into a circumstance than you could imagine. I'll describe this phenomenon within four coping skills (stones) that seem part of us, three of which we must discard to push past adversity. The problem is that you may not know which one you'd use until you face a challenge and that only one of them is positive:

1. Withdrawal
2. Separation
3. Assimilation
4. Self-Affirmation

Examples of these strategies are all over society—all walks of life. No age, class, or race escapes. But nowhere are the coping strategies more apparent, concentrated, and addressed than with college students. So, using campus examples to describe behaviors associated with each coping strategy seems fitting.

Coping Strategy 1: Withdrawal

At its most basic level, withdrawal conjures the visual depiction of an addict. Our understanding of withdrawal may also reflect on scenes from television and movies—a person in the fetal position, in tattered clothes, shaking, sweating, disoriented, and cringing in obvious pain. For all the empathy we can muster, we still factor in their effort and responsibility for getting to that place. We pronounce they did it in the name of fun, irresponsibility, and poor decision-making. However, withdrawal as a coping strategy is only similar because of the judgment of outsiders.

For example, a ride-share driver, making small talk, told me about his son, Tim, who is home from college after his first semester.

"My son said that he had a horrible time at school—that he didn't make friends, join organizations, or participate in school activities. But I know the truth, and I have the bills as proof. He spent all my money eating fast food because he refused to go the cafeteria, he received all Fs because he did not go to class, and it's all because he partied his way out of school."

"May I offer a different perspective?" I asked the driver. "To retreat may have been Tim's remedy for his discomfort. Rather than make new friends, Tim may have found sitting in his dorm room easier. Eating out versus a crowded dining hall may also be a cry for anonymity. For some, going to class can feel as traumatic as speaking in public. Therefore, it is more likely that Tim withdrew psychologically and had no fun flunking out of school."

Thus, the proverbial "sticking your head in the sand" or ignoring things, is an alternate definition of withdrawal. This common idiom conveys that an apparent problem isn't there, meaning withdrawal is a negative coping strategy. We must be sure that stone is not in our backpacks.

Coping Strategy 2: Separation

People who choose to separate themselves desire to limit contact with people who are different. They opt to stay within their comfort zones, or they cling to stereotypes to support their disdain for differences. Not their own, though, because protecting their ways makes perfect sense. Some may claim to want the well-rounded experiences inclusion offers, but only on their terms. For example, white people may favor protecting individualism. Some may support kinship (in thought) as long as hierarchy, privilege, or power for those with it continues. They shout, personal rights! Then, with a straight face, expect everyone to stand for the national anthem and its hyperbolic message.

Some non-white people confuse "sticking together" with only dealing with members of their racial group. Then, they balk at underrepresentation in areas traditionally dominated by white men, such as technology, banking, and finance. Their moral judgments and diminishing status serve as excuses for self-destructive behavior, or they claw to keep members of other minority groups and themselves in the fight for scraps. They might be surprised to discover that more significant opportunities come through networking and participation.

In other words, all who choose separation are short-changing themselves. By and large, disengagement undermines knowledge gains, and it increases volatility rather than breakthroughs. Thus, without cultural exchanges, all parties suffer. I hope this is familiar information and that we use it to denounce influential people who target specific groups and ban their cultural and historical conversations and books. The more significant point is that this country will not revert to the overtly racist and sexist practices of past eras. Why continue to support the conditions that cause disunity?

The breadth of reading and observing a wide range of life experiences assists in creating harmony because of differences, not despite them. For example, attending an unfamiliar cultural event for the first time may feel scary. However, the benefit of learning far outweighs the moments of discomfort. You may feel trepidation on the first day of a nonnative history class. That, too, is okay. Such devotion to dialogue and willingness to learn the points of view of others may prove enlightening and build bridges. Attending nonaffiliated religious services or events may offer contradictions and revelations. Just learn. Accept being vulnerable and feed curiosity through firsthand experiences. These practices serve as ways to expand open-mindedness as human beings and build friendships across traditional barriers—race, class, or beliefs. The salient point is that people with unbiased attitudes toward others (or different subjects) increase their growth, critical thinking, understanding, and love for humanity.

Moreover, where separation coincides with privilege, we also see hostility and resentment—even delusion. For example, on January 6, 2021, a mob of thousands attacked our nation's Capitol building. They injured and killed police, and they threatened to hang the Vice President of the United States and the Speaker of the House. Also, in 2021, a foiled plot to kidnap and kill the Governor of Michigan occurred. Those men are facing over a decade in prison. In addition, the Governor of Florida signed (into law) new guidelines limiting race-based discussions in businesses and schools. His rationale is that he doesn't want white people to feel bad about historical events. Other States have followed in a quest for cultural deprivation. Yes, I said it! States are outlawing the same conversations I mentioned earlier: the dialogues that we know leads to cultural understanding, new friendships, individual growth, and community growth.

Businesses and colleges are microcosms of American life. Therefore, employers, neighborhood leaders, and campuses offer a choice like the tales of Hercules and his crossroad, also known as Hercules' choice. This famous allegory simplifies a complex societal reality between vice and virtue. For us to choose separation is akin to young Hercules choosing vice: a life of pleasure, comfort, and entertainment. As the story goes, all pleasures, ease, and appetites might be satisfied before Hercules requests them. Extravagance would also oblige people to fawn over him. The obvious, more noble choice, however, is virtue. The latter option meant Hercules must earn respect, generate sincere friendships, and operate ethically in business. Doing these things would establish a reputation of integrity for posterity. In other words, sweat and growth must precede moral dissonance and pleasure for Hercules. The same is true for us. Thus, separation is a negative coping strategy and should not be a stone in our backpacks.

Coping Strategy 3: Assimilation

The third coping strategy sounds harmless enough. However, culturally speaking, some describe assimilation as the opposite of separation. Instead of wanting to be set apart, assimilators have absorbed so much that they may want to be something or somebody they are not. Consider the following short accounts of assimilation, each increasing in gravity.

Jill

Let's start with an exchange that happened a few weeks after the start of the school year. Jill sat down to dinner with her son, daughter, and husband. Her sixth-grader son had only known the rigidness of his private Catholic school until this year. He clearly picked up a habit from his new school when he inhaled a pull from a vape pen while the family said grace. His younger sister stared to her right; her eyes bugged, her jaw dropped, and her palms clamped in a praying position.

"Over my dead body! Give me that!" Jill admonished.

"All the cool kids at school vape. No need to get so excited, Jill."

"I'm not Jill to you, I'm your mother," she snapped.

"But all our teachers tell us kids to call them by their first names. It feels weird, but I'm getting used to it."

"Don't get used to it. In this family, we don't have vices, and as a show of respect to your elders, you will say Mr. or Ms. to your teachers, and you will never outgrow who I am to you. I'm Mom."

Jill was swimming upstream. She knew it, and so did her husband. It is hard to think of children who do not ignore home training, family tradition, and cultural norms in favor of what's trending with their friends. As a result, opting to follow their school culture manifests rude and offensive examples of assimilation. Jill admitted that things at home were tense for a stretch. However, once fully empowered with sound reasoning, her children complied.

Marisha

Another classic case of assimilation is the story of Marisha. Marisha's father died when she was 12. Her mom moved Marisha and her three younger brothers to Sioux City, Iowa, for a job opportunity and a lower cost of living than in the Bronx, New York.

Being the only Black girl in her grade level, Marisha faced pressures to conform to her all-white neighborhood and school. Then, searching for mutual interest that might attract and sustain friendships, she sacrificed family traditions and her cultural foundation by not sharing them. Right away, Marisha joined an established friend group of three girls. First, she introduced herself as Mari. She assumed that Marisha sounded too "Black" and might be another excuse for bullies.

Anyway, the girls instantly hit it off. But Marisha sensed a particular hierarchy. She was at the bottom, vulnerable, and at risk of being alone. Thus, Marisha became the quintessential "yes" person. "What do you guys think?" was the extent of Marisha's input. The young women accepted Marisha only when she followed along and did not show interest in anything apart from their group's interest.

The four of them did everything together. Still, unfortunately for Marisha, she felt obliged to eliminate everything about herself that would resemble being Black to show allegiance to her new friends. For example, instead of running track, she played field hockey. She also replaced listening to R&B with Hard Rock. One day Marisha's mom dropped her off at the hairdresser. "Can you straighten my curls to fall straight like white girls' hair," she asked the beautician. Marisha also laid out to tan when her friends lay in the sun. She wore Birkenstock sandals and Doc Martens boots to look like her friends. Her final assimilatory act was accepting the gift of blue contacts from the lead girl of the group. Marisha inserted them when she left home and popped them out when she returned and before entering her house. Suffice it to say that it takes a strong family unit to resist the lure of assimilation.

Sarah

Another unsettling story follows Sarah, a woman who was born in a small, affluent suburb of Atlanta, Georgia. Sarah was an enigma for her family as she embodied the stereotypical loner, competitive, and "woe is me" traits of a middle child. She clamored for attention. However, her spiraling esteem stemmed from her height and weight insecurities. Standing 4'11" and dressing in oversized, dowdy clothes to hide her mom's curvy genetics made most white guys consider her invisible. By contrast, only non-white people welcomed Sarah for friendship and sought her for dating. Indeed, her social groups, which involved different types of people, were another reason her peers pushed her further to the fringes. Sarah went along. It was a "like whomever likes you" kind of thing. Ultimately, Sarah sought further acceptance in other communities as she grew older to cope with belonging.

She did not realize how the experience of being an outsider in her community had affected her personally. I suspect that nobody wants to be in places they aren't wanted. Then, something in her thinking went awry during a study abroad trip to Ghana. She watched the Ghanaian children dressed neatly for school and moved orderly between periods (e.g., class, lunch, and recess). They donned matching uniforms and dress shoes and were well-groomed. I felt the need to defend the beautiful village where everybody felt purpose and inclusion, especially the school children.

Nevertheless, Sarah considered them needy because they didn't attend schools with air conditioning and technology-enhanced classrooms. The children did not take expensive field trips or carry individual tablets. "How sad is it that the poorest schools in America have more than these children?" she remarked.

Sarah should have considered that value systems vary by ethnicity. One size doesn't fit all. For example, the villagers may honor history, religion, and tradition as central academic themes. Ghanaians may qualify administrators by their hearts rather than meaningless credentials. They may require teachers to be villagers and parents, eliminating presumptions about children's competence or having less. Who knows! Now consider what an elder from a Ghanaian village may find about the conditions of American schools. First, children who walk to school fear violence or abduction. Here, we speak of coping strategies and practice active shooter drills. Curriculums include race and class bias. What's more disturbing is that students may not receive a healthy lunch or lunch at all. For the sake of this comparison, I'd insist that modernized or current doesn't mean better. As I tried to clarify, Sarah's experience should have been sobering and respectful, not critical.

Still, Sarah returned to the States with a skewed perspective from her trip. And then, she dropped a bombshell: "I am going for my Ph.D. in African Studies. My trip was a sign that I am supposed to teach Black children. They need saving," she said.

She also openly shared a hidden motive—that teaching poor Black American students their history would engender gratitude and undoubtedly mean a community would finally accept her. I had many questions, but to ask them would ignite an unresolvable debate. She lost her sense of self and thought she had found it.

A life of service deserves recognition. We can agree. However, the condescension in drawing biased conclusions about Black children and swooping to save them is consistent with old stereotypes. There are many ways that people can contribute to the well-being of others. But assimilating can be unhealthy and offensive. The lack of authenticity assigned to someone teaching your history who cannot feel it is one thing. Knowing that the teacher's ancestors created the inequities that motivated them to teach is another. That would be like white male teachers ascending onto Indian reservations to train Native Americans how to teach Native American history.

Rachel

I don't want to give much oxygen to the next story. Still, it is essential because it is an egregious example of assimilation. So, I will be brief.

Born into a white American family, Rachel grew up in Lincoln County, Montana. She shifted her perspective on race after her religious parents adopted four Black children. They eventually divorced, and Rachel decided to become Black publicly. For many years, she pretended to be a Black woman and eventually ascended to the presidency of an NAACP chapter. However, she and her family argued constantly. In time, Rachel's mom exposed Rachel as an impostor to the local news media, and the story garnered international attention. Still, Rachel doubled down on her racial claim to no avail. Senior officials eventually fired Rachel from the NAACP and from teaching African Studies at Eastern Washington University.

Since then, Rachel formally changed her name to Nkechi; it's of Nigerian origin and means "God's gift." She has moved on with marriage and family. Still, the lie survives. All lies do. For example, George Washington didn't cut down a cherry tree. Saddam Hussein did not have weapons of mass destruction; Bill Clinton had sex with that woman; nobody stole the 2020 presidential election. Furthermore, not everything is fine, you weren't late because of traffic, and Rachel is not a Black woman.

The central message of *Emerge: Be You!* is that you can achieve by being the best you. You are enough. You don't have to resort to nefarious behavior, put anybody down, pretend to be something you are not, lie, or assimilate. Thus, I caution anyone carrying the stone of assimilation in their backpack.

Coping Strategy 4: Self-Affirmation

Count me in as part of any strategy that utilizes our best aspects. Self-affirmation restores, enhances, builds, and agrees. But wait. I am not speaking of self-affirmation as phrases we repeat to ourselves to make us feel better. There's no denying that reciting such daily affirmations are valuable ways to maintain our self-worth. Therefore, I concede that role is helpful. Instead, I want to describe self-affirmation as a pathway to internal and external power. First, let's lean into nature for perspective.

Consider, for example, giraffes and how they give birth standing up. First, the baby giraffe drops six feet from his mother, walks within an hour, and runs with the herd that day. Otherwise, the baby calves are at greater risk of threats (e.g., starvation, dehydration, and predators). Next, the maleo is a humongous, colorful bird that can fly the moment it hatches. Then, without parents watching them, the baby birds fly directly from their eggshells to the forest; their colors serve as camouflage against the trees. Finally, of course, there are other animal species hardwired to protect themselves. Just as animals and birds have adaptations for survival, so do we. Self-affirmation is one adaptation that is unique to people.

We've all heard of hysterical strength activated in high-stress moments like the young woman who lifted a car off her unconscious dad or the firefighter who lifted a 4,700-pound truck one foot off the ground. I once saw a guy get shot five times at close range; three bullets in the chest, and two in the neck. Yet, not only did he beat the guy's ass who shot him, but he also got into the ambulance unassisted, looked at the crowd, laughed, and said, "Buckshot."

Those examples may sound like one-offs, but perhaps they're clues to our possibilities. Therefore, I won't turn 180 degrees and discuss our bland physiological adaptations, such as sweating and swelling. Suppose "That which does not kill us, makes us stronger," is valid for all and not only a catchy phrase adopted by some. Then, all people can release self-affirmation from within and activate power associated with victory over threats.

One way to begin is by identifying your triggers. Then, please describe how you are above reacting to any of them. Used this way, self-affirming is a powerful way to resolve incoming threats and negative behaviors. Moreover, self-affirming neutralizes messages influencing most people's self-image (e.g., family, school, social media, and television). Wherever we can draw comparisons or criticism, affirming ourselves can eliminate rapid reactivity. Suppose you are snapping at the idiot who posted manure on your social media page or flipping off the person who sat through a traffic light cycle, texting, no doubt. Your reaction is the threat that may lead you and the opposition to the symbolic escalator. Once on, opposing sides one-up each other until feelings get hurt or worse: someone dies. Instead of reacting, you can eliminate making situations personal by practicing self-affirming behaviors.

When students are self-affirming, they don't drink or smoke their way out of school. I'm not talking about cigarettes, either. Nor will students sex their way out of school. That would include risky behaviors such as unprotected sex, which may lead to disease, unwanted pregnancies, or the pressure of a promiscuous reputation.

For example, a young woman enrolled at my college the summer after high school. Let's call her Suzy. She wanted to acclimate to college more slowly than she could in the fall semester. That reasoning sounded right. It was still a guess because I did not know her. Lessening the fall class load was why I took summer classes between my first and second school years. One evening, I went across the hall to the room of two football teammates. One of them opened the door, and he pulled me in from our handshake before letting go. My mouth fell open at what I saw. Then, I said out loud, "I'm leaving before anybody can include me as part of this, but one day, I will tell this story." Before leaving, I counted eighteen men taking turns performing sexual acts with a willing Suzy. I knew she was consenting because she verbally said, "Next" to a guy in line while simultaneously ravaged by another group of guys also taking turns.

A few days later, I went to another friend's room on the floor housing the basketball team. When he opened the door, I counted eleven guys with Suzy. I did not go inside. The next day, I revisited the teammate who pulled me into his room, the home of the first act. I needed his explanation of the escapades of the previous days. I also wanted to warn about the legal ramifications of a white girl in Iowa potentially claiming rape once the sexual act(s) with primarily Black men finished. When he opened the door, I saw two women in the room. I recognized one of them as the main character from both incidents: Suzy. Both women were vigorously groping and kissing my teammate's roommate, John. I'm aware of the irony that John is his name. I did not make it up, nor did he pay them. So, he is John and not one. Regardless, they were getting heavy into another sexual moment, undeterred by my presence. It was as if they were alone. Coincidentally, John organized the encounters and escorted her to different rooms. Just as I was about to excuse myself, John stopped them and spoke to me.

"Yo man, you remember Suzy?" he asked.

I looked at Suzy and responded, "Uh, yes and no."

I wanted her to know that I did not participate. She couldn't have known otherwise.

Then, my friend offered the unthinkable: "Okay, this is Suzy, and this beautiful woman is Suzy's mother."

My mouth fell open again. Who would have thought?

In one week, Suzy's reputation suffered irreparable damage. She was the talk of the town in ways that did not allow her to return to school. Way out there, I know. Still, sexing your way out of school does not have to be extreme. Any sexual behavior that causes a student to fall short of earning a degree is what I mean when I say sexing their way out of school. Moreover, you should not have trouble applying "sexing your way out" to areas beyond school (e.g., employment, marriage, leadership, and politics).

Anybody could have joined those sex parties; however, self-affirming behavior strengthens us against our demons, whatever they are. Of course, there will still be days we say or do things that are beneath our standards. It will feel different when we do until we dislike the feeling more than the satisfaction of the act.

For example, when men self-affirm, they wouldn't refer to women as bitches and hoes. They would understand they are also talking about their cousins, sisters, mothers, grandmothers, and future wives. Nor do men mean-mugging each other passing by offer proof we are tough guys. Just ask, "Wassup?" and keep it moving. Likewise, self-affirming women do not refer to themselves as any "bitch." They do not use variations such as nasty bitch, bad bitch, boss bitch, or queen bitch, and they do not recite music that centers around dehumanizing them. Nor would women who self-affirm engage in conversations that view being like men or not needing men as empowering.

When Black people self-affirm, we will stop referring to ourselves as "nigger." I remember the mind-bending moment my father used the word "nigger" beyond educating us that we should not. He taught us that it is a vile, derogatory word that people use to denigrate Black people. My mother added that we could not make the word positive because of its origin. Thus, our family relegated the word profane, and my parents did not allow cursing. For those reasons, when my father yelled "nigger" at a man, I knew he was deliberately cutting low, making the moment personal. Simultaneously grabbing his machete also signaled he was ready for battle.

Moreover, what also made the moment memorable is that the man he called out was white. The man lost all aggression and stood stunned after hearing the word. My father continued, "That's right, the word means ignorant, and you are a nigger. Now what you gonna do about it?" The man was shocked more by being called the n-word than he was shaken by facing an angry man wielding a weapon. Finally, exasperated, the man turned around and left without saying a word. Let me be clear. I am not suggesting that people use that word as a synonym for ignorant. Instead, I strongly support that eliminating that word should be nonnegotiable.

Through his immigration process, Dad witnessed that people of all ethnicities chose white. How can that be possible for Asians, Cubans, Africans, and Brits? This practice taught him that "white" as a race was as fictional as the n-word. Dad saw himself as proudly West Indian. Still in protest, after verbally scolding the man, Dad marched into the DMV and asked them to put white on his driver's license. Then, he cornered people in conversation by illustrating the absurdity of race as a social construct by showing them his license. Brilliant!

We weren't allowed to use the word while growing up at home. In college, I heard the word used a lot. I tried accepting its use as a term of endearment when a rap group said, "N-I-G-G-A meant, never ignorant, getting goals accomplished." Recently, I saw an older man wearing a cap with those defining words on social media.

However, trying to justify a word with a hateful origin and hundreds of years of usage and intent did not make sense. Therefore, the alternate definition did not remove the sting I feel when the word lands, no matter who says it. My reaction from hearing the word and the visceral flinch that follows is my self-affirming spirit dealing with the n-word as a threat. A sobering presence tells me to trust what I feel—that I am a threat to myself if I allow or use it—simply by trying to normalize using language meant to destroy me the way this society has normalized lying, openly carrying guns, and mass shootings. In other words, self-affirming power tells us in precarious moments, "You're better than that." Then, it forces us to behave more fitting of our aspirational selves consistently.

Uh oh. I'm going down a rabbit hole. There are websites, position papers, and forums battling for who gets to use the n-word. Why do non-Black people ask, "Why can't I say the n-word" as if they are missing out on a privilege? I heard a biracial teen telling her white mom to stop using the word, and she posted the conversation on social media. Then, the mother said her child racially profiled her because she didn't want her to say the n-word. Let that sink in.

It seems that since industries can shut down programs and cancel the careers of people who use hate speech, they can do the same for all those using the n-word. Hypocritically, those industries promote and normalize the n-word, especially in movies and music. The reach and damage of such are significant. I remember walking down a long road in Mombasa, Kenya. A young adult spotted me from a distance. He repeatedly yelled the n-word until we were close enough to embrace. When he let me go, I told him my name and that I was not an n-word. He didn't understand and called me the n-word as he walked away.

Finally, we may develop to a stage where we can affirm others by supporting their beliefs. It only requires treating others the way we want others to treat us. Then, look for ways to respect people you contact (e.g., sales associates, store clerks, rideshare drivers, and mail carriers):

- Begin with an open mind.
- Look for common ground.
- Listen to understand.
- Don't get emotional.
- Seek understanding.

When you emerge, people around you should elevate too. Therefore, self-affirmative behavior supplies value clarification, strength, self-preservation, and opportunities to help others. Thus, self-affirmation is such a stone to keep in our backpacks.

CHAPTER FIFTEEN
THE STORY OF MARY ANN, PART 2

This chapter will continue the "stones" theme and wrap up Mary Ann's story. It was a tremendous victory for Mary Ann to overcome the naysayers and stick with her new program. To lose 45 pounds was more than she had lost and kept off during her many starts and stops in approximately 25 years. Every 5 pounds meant a new milestone to celebrate. Yet, she continued to declare never to regain the weight already lost. Therefore, down was the only direction Mary Ann would allow her weight to go. Every pound lost meant breathing easier, moving better, and incorporating various exercises into her training program. I'd feature unexpected challenges for her to perform independently of our training sessions to keep things fun and exciting. I would carefully create some of the challenges. Others I would grab from a colleague and modify. However, there was one I pulled out of thin air. I had no plan. I hadn't decided which muscle groups to focus on, the exercises, or whether she would begin with fewer reps per day and increase. I wasn't sure if incorporating a time frame would be the way to go as 30-day and 60-day challenges were prevalent.

Nevertheless, I knew that Mary Ann would do whatever I said without a fuss, eye roll, or questioning. She would say "okay" and determinedly do it. Before long, I figured that it was time to deliver the news. There was silence between us while Mary Ann finished the last exercise of our session—sit-ups.

"Eighteen, nineteen, twenty, and you're done," I said. "Members in this gym recognize that you are going harder, and your results are inspiring more people than you know. Even other trainers workout a little harder when they see you," I said.

"Uh oh. I feel a 'but' coming," Mary Ann responded. "This stream of consciousness sounds a lot like you are buttering me up for something because you're not the warm and fuzzy type," she said, chuckling nervously.

"A fair point," I conceded. "We are going to start a sit-up challenge, and to be clear, 'we' means you," I quipped.

"Knowing how extreme you are, you'll probably make me do 5,000 sit-ups," she said as her eyes searched my face for clues.

Rather than admit I had only an idea for a challenge with no plan, I doubled down on Mary Ann calling me extreme.

"Actually, you're going to do 20,000 sit-ups."

"Wow. Okay, when do I start?" she quickly responded, as if that would have been her response no matter what I said.

I was proud of myself when I blurted the scary, outrageous number. Somehow, the words fell from my mouth as my eyes prepared for Mary Ann's response. However, I could not find anything, not even a flinch. The speed of Mary Ann's reply was also gratifying. She did not need the usual rewards of gift cards, a t-shirt, or a training discount. Instead, Mary Ann enthusiastically subscribed to this and any prescribed activity contributing to forward motion. Her eagerness was not an anomaly. Mary Ann understands that attitude is an essential factor in the results equation if there is such a calculation. She has a knack for seeing the big picture by connecting present work to future results. For example, this challenge would develop her weak, squashy core and represent another step toward the healthier life she always wanted. In other words, this challenge could be a defining moment in her journey. Such moments appear in our lives; sometimes, we miss them, dismiss them, or are discouraged by their significance. Not Mary Ann; she embraced the effort and attitude necessary to push through plateaus that sometimes lasted for weeks. Mary Ann maintained the firm view that slowly losing weight was better. That way, once it was gone, it was gone for good.

Mary Ann went home that night and created a spreadsheet without any prompting. The document was her system for recording her daily sit-up total accurately. Organizing around progress motivated her doubly and complimented her type-A, personality-driven, hardworking, determined to succeed, highly organized, and goal(s) focused personality. Steadily, she increased her daily count from two sets of 15 in the morning to 100 sit-ups in the morning and 100 before bed. We didn't focus on 20,000 sit-ups, only on consistency. She never missed a day through the summer.

Early fall of 2015, I asked, "How many sit-ups have you completed?"

"I have no idea," she responded. "I just do them every morning and night like clockwork."

I confessed that I never expected her to complete 20,000 sit-ups as a goal. My only goal was to create a habit and focus on numbers other than weight, calories, and body fat percentage. It worked.

Mary Ann's capacity and proficiency with challenging exercises reached exceptional performance levels, and she could not get enough. Occasions like Mary Ann reaching another milestone were like watching the winner of those extreme sports shows conquer obstacle after obstacle. First, we cheer them away from hazards and into the victory circle. Then, when the cheering is over, we watch their final interview because there's satisfaction from knowing why they took on the challenge. Likewise, when I asked Mary Ann to describe her motivations for the ab challenge, she said, "I always dreamed that I would run because it seemed that everybody else was doing it. But my family discouraged runs, telling me that I would hurt myself. So, I thought they wouldn't feel that way if they could see what I could do at the gym."

By 2016, Mary Ann had lost over 112 pounds and ran a half-marathon nearly an hour faster than her first effort. She said, "I ran down the hill and made the turn completing mile 8, and to my surprise, dad was there to hand me granola bars and water. He said that I looked strong; it was my proudest moment."

Even more important than participating in the half-marathon, Mary Ann learned that her parents rooted for her and her new lifestyle that day. Her wealthy uncle and aunt supported Mary Ann's journey by paying for years of personal training. Mary Ann's sister, a self-proclaimed fitness nut, would join Mary Ann for active vacations and day hikes. You would be right if you sensed another "but" coming.

Mary Ann's boyfriend, who was morbidly obese, offered only negative motivation by centering his attention on himself. Imposing his need for her time over her medical need to progress toward healthy outcomes showed how little he supported her efforts. Mary Ann understood that she must soon deal with him as an obstacle. However, for the moment, medical procedures remained top of mind.

Mary Ann spent most of 2017 prepping for surgery, having surgery, or recovering. It proved to be the most challenging period of our training. Sure, we had overcome a few setbacks. Plantar Fasciitis required her to wear a boot. Cortisone shots were for knee pain. Occasional low back pain flared up from sitting too long, resulting from her sedentary job. Those were normal to Mary Ann, as were her seasonal ear infections, which required doctors to put tubes inside her ears in the past. We knew those trials would come. However, we did not anticipate the double-sided reality that morbidly obese people face. Maintaining excess fat is dangerous; when they lose excess fat, keeping the remaining skin is also life-threatening. So, Mary Ann's first surgery that year was a tummy tuck with muscle repair. Her surgeon said she could fit her fist into Mary Ann's diastasis—separated abdominal muscles. Before surgery, her surgeon said that she would perform liposuction as part of the surgery. She would only do it if necessary because the procedure would extend her recovery, which was already six weeks. After removing 15 pounds of skin, the surgeon said, "Many patients require liposuction after a surgery as involved as yours. No disrespect intended, Mary Ann, I was shocked to see the strength of your stomach muscles; and they're freaking flat."

The surgeon's words confirmed what Mary Ann and I had known for years. While losing the weight of an entire person was grueling, the sweat equity Mary Ann invested in developing core muscles would pay significant dividends later. Muscular abs and the fulfillment of earning them provided momentum, preparing her for trials. Unfortunately, Mary Ann's surgery was long and complicated. Recovery proved slow and painful, and one surgery led to another.

Bleeding rashes from her stomach hanging over her beltline forced Mary Ann to undergo her second procedure. Days into recovery and still in the hospital, Mary Ann nearly passed out from bleeding internally from a hematoma. Unfortunately, her doctor also learned that one of her drains was infected. As a result, Mary Ann developed Methicillin-resistant Staphylococcus Aureus (MRSA), a type of bacteria resistant to several antibiotics. Mary Ann was lucky to have remained in the hospital. However, she was extremely close to her body going into sepsis, a life-threatening complication of an infection that may cause multiple organs to shut down.

We can all recall coming to a moment of truth after making it through something risky or frightening. We may say, "I'm not doin' that no more." That's our inner defenses getting keener, which may give us a more significant concern for self-preservation. But Mary Ann was already scheduling the third and fourth surgeries she would have that year.

Mary Ann's third surgery was to remove an encapsulated seroma, an 11" x 13" capsule containing over a liter of fluid. Her fourth surgery was a thighplasty, also known as a thigh lift. The thigh lift is an invasive procedure performed on patients who have lost significant weight and have loose, sagging skin on their inner thighs. The surgeon removed 5 pounds of skin during the thigh lift procedure, bringing Mary Ann's total weight of skin removal to 19 pounds.

It is impossible to calculate Mary Ann's hardships from a distance. Mary Ann is practically half her original size to the casual observer, and an occasional "attagirl" seems appropriate. It's a nice gesture that earns an unemotional "thanks for noticing" smile from me if I hear it. Only people with similar experiences to Mary Ann's will have the mental framework for understanding and appreciating what she's accomplished and the mental strength necessary to press forward.

Let's return to our conversation about "Life is a journey" and the stones in our backpacks example. There are stones you may identify in Mary Ann's backpack that you will see in yours, some to add and others to remove. For instance, we can reason that weight loss is a significant part of Mary Ann's journey. Her bleak obesity prognosis in 2012 forecasted an early death or a more complex life because of an imminent heart attack or stroke. Mary Ann had decisions to make. Hiring a trainer and getting her uncle to pay for it are examples of resourcefulness, one of the stones Mary Ann still carries in her backpack. Of course, I understand that not everyone has a rich uncle. Still, we can agree that we can all uncover resources.

Please return to that piece of paper Mary Ann handed me during our initial conversation. It is called a physical activity readiness questionnaire (PAR-Q). A PAR-Q is a summary of information about a new client, essential for establishing a baseline to begin setting goals and moving forward in health and fitness. Mary Ann's PAR-Q read (in part): "Three hundred seventy pounds; 48% body fat; severe knee pain in both knees; back pain from a curved spine; stage two hypertension (diagnosed as stage four); flat feet, wears orthotics; medications for cholesterol and high blood pressure; moderate drinker; and weight loss as her single goal."

When I introduced you to Mary Ann, I hinted that success in her case would take exceptional imagination and creativity to adapt to any one of her concerns. So, our initial conversation was not an attempt to address her entire predicament. Dropping weight would do that. Nevertheless, this combination of data prompted Mary Ann and me to change her overall goal to a measurable metric. We chose 150 pounds as her goal weight, equating to 220 pounds of weight loss. You might think that setting a high weight loss goal was not what I was supposed to do during an initial conversation. But it was vital that she knew and understood that I was clear about the task and stakes of taking her as a client. Then, after a flinch from her and a deep sigh from me, we established smaller weight loss objectives attached to timelines and mini celebrations for every five-pound increment.

Before the COVID-19 pandemic, in December 2019, Mary Ann's body fat was under 30%, and any knee pain was from running marathons or half-marathons, playing on her tennis team, mountain biking, or hiking. She no longer experienced pain from carrying excess weight, and in what must be some modern medical miracle, Mary Ann's podiatrist looked at previous x-rays and told Mary Ann that her arches came back. There's no longer a need for stability shoes and orthotics. Her doctors confirmed that her spine is now straight, so there is no need for back support. Mary Ann lost and kept off 200 pounds. Whew! So, we must acknowledge resilience as another stone in her backpack with all of this.

By now, we can agree that lifestyle changes are complicated. Only driven people commit to the challenging grind specific to weight loss: frustration, discipline, depression, self-doubt, obstacles, and time commitment. Getting started is easy, though. Only because some people start programs like announcing New Year's resolutions. Only good intentions! Weight loss generates supportive reactions initially. It begins with insincere niceties such as, "That's so good. I wish I had the time for that," as if God didn't give us all the same 24 hours in a day and the free will to prioritize them.

Once you have demonstrated that you won't stop, there is no shortage of people telling you that you make them proud or that you're an inspiration. Positive information and messages may come from many sources, such as texts, emails, testimonials, or links to success stories. Everybody seems to have an opinion to share through their words or actions. Then, reality hits you in the face. We realize how much American life revolves around food and alcohol, such as work functions, happy hours, watching, or participating in sports. Then, support wanes. People do what they've always done. There will still be donuts in the breakroom, wings and beer while watching sporting events. You cannot expect acquaintances to change. However, a solid supportive step is when your fit spouse food preps with you rather than ordering pizza on your third day of eating chicken breasts.

In other words, substantial support for Mary Ann would have been her obese boyfriend not questioning her gym time or food choices but offering to join or give it a try. Sometimes, it only takes a modest amount of pessimism or unhelpfulness to drive goal-seekers off their path. They may easily break down and later vow to do their best. Their vulnerability helps explain why people grow frustrated and quit weight loss programs before reaching their goals.

Although Mary Ann resisted a few comments from her family early on, she has a history ripe with vulnerability. Mary Ann developed early. So, being 5'4" and overweight in the eighth grade, Mary Ann also had a D-cup breast size at that time. These differences fueled her classmates to bully her mercilessly. Thus, she doesn't have fond memories of school from K-12—no friends, sleepovers, birthday parties, or prom. There was only homework. Not even sports opened the door to friendships. This reality is the backdrop on which Mary Ann decides whether to dump her boyfriend. Her boyfriend filled her friendship and companionship needs, which had been scarce in her life. Thus, ending their relationship would be as challenging as keeping it. Everyone would understand Mary Ann clinging to her relationship of five years as an adult. Instead, she fought the easy path, and they parted ways. Mary Ann would have a better experience achieving her fitness goals without relationship conflict as a distraction. Knowing this, she chose herself; in doing so, she removed the stone of comfortability from her backpack.

In 2011, before I met Mary Ann, she signed up for a half marathon and didn't attempt it. She could only walk briskly for a few steps, which caused her heart rate to skyrocket and dizziness to set in. So, she watched. However, what drives Mary Ann now is knowing that she can do all of it. Belief makes someone like Mary Ann succeed, whereas unbelievers fail. Therefore, belief is another stone in her backpack. Mary Ann didn't allow failed attempts to lose weight to consume her, nor did she let always being heavy determine what she would become. Instead, she brought her strengths to the surface.

Recognize also that some of your stones may serve a temporary purpose and, if kept too long, convert from helpful to dead weight. In other words, just as important as the stones carried are the ones you discard. For Mary Ann, that was people whose support for her waned.

I likened discarding our temporary stones to my first science class in college. It was known as a weed-out class. On the first day, the professor said, "Everybody, look to your left. Now, look to your right. You have now seen the people who may fail my class." Some students immediately packed their belongings and left. Less than half of the original number attended his next class period. The professor knew the committed few remained. It is a stark reminder that those who start with us might not finish with us. Kudos to Mary Ann.

Section Five

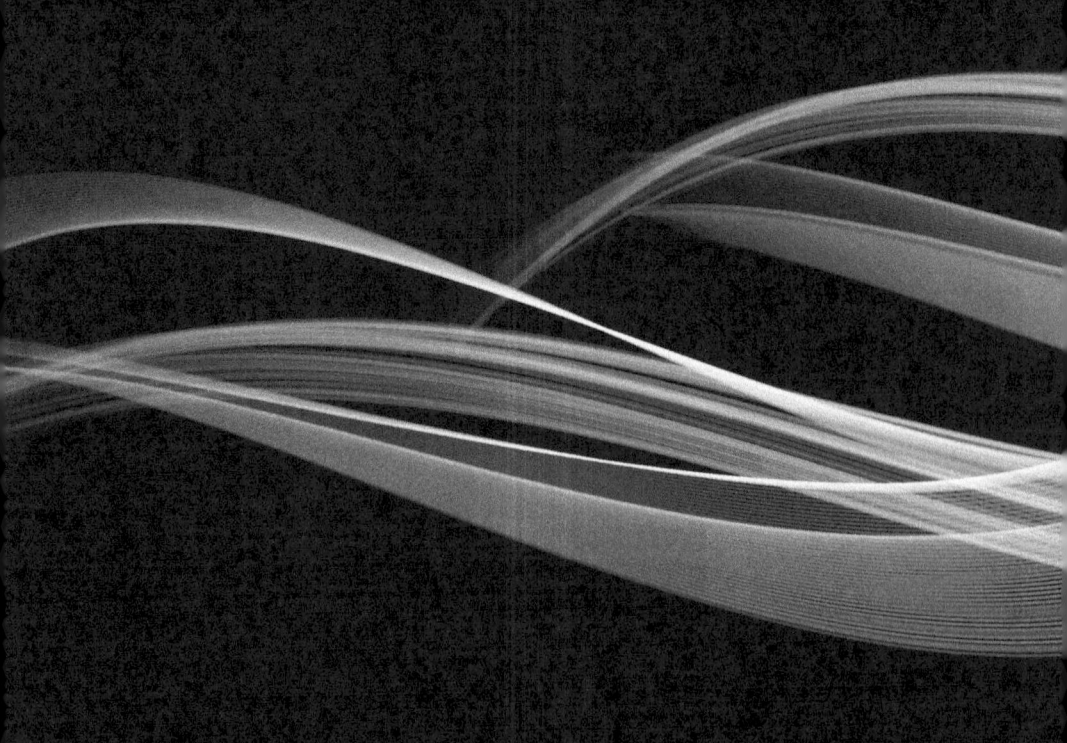

TRANSFORMATIVE INSIGHTS

Uplift!

What would be different about the experience of your peers if you weren't present?

Would they be better off or worse?
Are you a blessing or their curse,
And do strangers see you as darkness or light?

As you emerge, by being you,
It signals that others could too!
All ships rise with the tide.

Hughes Suffren

CHAPTER SIXTEEN
EMERGING

Emerging is like finding yourself trapped, recognizing you have the power to get out, and going for it. I usually support or explain my thoughts using nature or scripture in a place like this. This time, however, I will offer a different observation lest I become too predictable. Most of us have seen circus elephants and videos showing this beastly heavyweight stomping down city streets, battering the pavement, and bowling over cars while escaping from the circus. Producers have included similar imagery in television shows such as *When Animals Attack* or *Animals Gone Wild*.

However, we rarely are privy to how elephants become circus elephants. A trainer takes a baby elephant who knows nothing of its natural habitat. Then, they tie the young calf to a big tree secured by a thick chain tightly wrapped around one leg. As the elephant walks the chain length, it tugs and pulls until its leg gets bloody and sore. To avoid the pain, the young elephant walks back. It learns that tension against the chain equals pain. Walking back reduces pain and earns them treats like food and affection. As the elephant grows, the trainer replaces the big chain with smaller chains and trees. Then, a rope and a stake in the ground hold massive adult elephants. Literature also suggests that elephants have the largest brain and the most advanced memory of any animal. Plus, snapping the rope must be as easy for circus elephants as twirling and snatching a loose thread from clothing is for people. Still, the elephant remembers the pain of its youthful failures and consents to a rope and a small stake in the ground anchoring them. Circus tents have burned to the ground with elephants in them because they did not think they could free themselves. As you can see, allowing past pain or failures to dictate your future is illogical. Still, death by fire demonstrates the power of programming.

My example may be too far outside your human reality. Allow me to make emerging personal and closer to home. To emerge is a picture of being underwater, losing oxygen, and just short of panic. You can sense, see, or feel light, representing the direction you must travel for survival. You wind, twist, and push through obstacles and currents and burst through the resistance, teary-eyed and gasping for air. You made it!

You may have envisioned a diver cruising from the ocean depths and bursting past the surface. I see that too. I also know that we all have been through this process, and it's called birth. Our unconscious fights to survive the elements, breathe and beat the odds, and prepare us for what is to come in our lives. Once again, nature and scripture present guidance and critique applicable to human events. In this example, nature tells us that handling the obstacles to obtain the privilege of life prepares us to manage whatever life brings.

If you're nodding because you sense I'm on the right track, let me slam dunk the lob I tossed earlier. Suppose a circus elephant unintentionally pulls the stake out of the ground, or the meager rope snaps unexpectedly. A moment of freedom is all it takes. The elephant will never allow another object to restrict its movement. Many have tried and failed. Therefore, I caution anyone who tries to recapture an elephant who claimed its freedom. That same powerful memory delivers. If secured to a car, the mentally liberated elephant might pull it down the street because it recognizes newfound power. As a result, the elephant will never be a part of the circus again. That's right; an elephant must be an elephant. Nobody else can say otherwise.

Unfortunately, we give too much power to common proxies for living bound (e.g., fear, burnout, underemployment, and debt). Undoubtedly, any amount of debt can consume a person who will permit it. Therefore, the physical act of emerging begins with first becoming aware, which we have determined is an internal process. It sounds simple, but resolving what it means to "be you" might be problematic, depending on the depth of your programming (memory) and lack of study. However, when you answer your questions of purpose, you raise your expectations. Then, you burst through ceilings. You don't have to set out to change the world. Instead, emerge and be you, and the world and the people in it, will react accordingly.

CHAPTER SEVENTEEN
VALUABLE PERSPECTIVES

Dad waited as we turned into the driveway and moseyed toward the car as mom parked. Then, we jumped out while mom let out a lung full of air before opening her door. She must have needed a moment to summon inner calm. I never considered how defending something as right as attending church must have felt. Or the pent-up anxiety caused by the weekly dispute with my father, which always ended unpredictably.

"Where you been? It's 2:15."

"Church."

"All day? Every Sunday? That makes no sense at all! Every week, I'm here by myself."

"And every week, I hope you change your mind. But you choose not to come."

"That preacher ain't tellin' me nothing. I speak to God. I read my Bible. That's it. I'm not bound to go to church and give that man my money. Money, money, money. And for what? He's making you look like a joke."

"I read the Bible, too. Church is a chance to fellowship with other people."

Dad would dismiss her with a wave and the sucking spit sound. These gestures together meant no more talking. Only the Lord knew what might happen next because my parents' clash over church intensified irrationally, often based on dad's hunger.

For example, one Sunday, while we piled out of the car, dad came outside with his shotgun. There was no debate that day—only irrational intensity. Nobody paid much attention as my father walked toward the end of the driveway. Until BOOM! We didn't know whether to duck, run, laugh, or shake our heads. We only knew another emotional scab would form! Then, dad picked up the bird's carcass and prepared it for a quick meal.

The fact is, only the bird might have been surprised that dad would do something like shoot him in a neighborhood to prove a point. Well, if not for the being dead part of the story. It sounds nuts writing about it. Even so, our "normal" didn't seem extreme in those moments. Thick-skinned, we built high tolerance for the crazy stuff city living brought. Therefore, the bird was no big deal, which begs the question: What trauma have you excused, as being normal, that you must address? Let's be honest. Often, the event (or series of events) that comes to mind prevents you from standing, being you, or emerging as your best.

For example, my father went from zero to 100 at times. I presumed his triggers dated back to how people exploited him as an undocumented immigrant. My dad shared that he clung to his humanity through beatings and witnessed others beaten for not working hard enough. As a result, workers wore the consequences of manufactured disobedience as scars, limps, and missing teeth. Those who died were alligator food. Finally, one day, my father escaped the work compound as his employers searched to make him the next example. Strike one was refusing a command (to dismember a man). Dropping the machete and running was strike two, and there would not be a third strike for my dad. Thus, fleeing the compound and Florida was an extreme example of choosing himself. Marrying a random American woman for a green card and divorcing her came next. A green card gave him the right to work, but only for long hours and without rights. Like before, his new employers cheated and demeaned him routinely. He struggled with earning a few cents to a dollar per hour for someone else's benefit. In addition, his employers always spoke rudely to them. They constantly hinted at incarceration and deportation, and, to break the spirits of immigrant workers, employers reminded them, "You're a dime a dozen."

Dad spoke perfect Spanish and broken English while at work, even though English is his first language. "You'd be surprised by what those jack asses say when they think you don't speak their language," he said. My father spoke five languages fluently. So, he understood. He also trusted the naturalization process would change his circumstances from mistreated to respected. He studied and longed for the day he would cross citizenship off his list. Success came. Unfortunately, becoming a naturalized citizen did not produce his desired result. He was still a Black man in America with the wrong speaking accent—a second-class citizen. There are some things democracies cannot legislate and some wounds that time cannot heal.

Nevertheless, people react to trauma differently. For instance, men would gladly endure debilitating pain than have someone perceive them as weak. Although no man would call their motivation for that choice fear, this angst leads to various extreme behaviors. Case in point, some men refuse advice from other men. Perhaps receiving help symbolizes losing authority. Other men avoid medical doctors. "Nobody is gonna tell me what to do," they say. Next, we've all seen white guys argue with police officers and judges. They try to save face or assert authority when they have none. Then, there are people like my dad, who shot a bird to one-up our pastor.

It turns out that we all hold on to experiences that may keep us stuck. There can be many consequences to avoiding dealing with trauma. It can lead to persistent distress, such as anxiety and depression. It can also cause physical symptoms such as sleep problems and difficulty concentrating. Therefore, it is essential to address trauma in a healthy and supportive way, such as through therapy or other forms of support, to move past it and heal. Avoid dealing with it and stay stuck or lose your grip.

In other words, trauma is a typical emotional or psychological response to an event like nightmares from watching my mother almost drown. Traumatic events often breed debilitating reactions such as fear, shock, denial, unpredictable emotions, or the inability to move on. Let's continue the analogy. Arguing parents or a bird falling from the sky could be nothing. However, hypothetically, either incident could produce powerlessness and send me, the teenager, back to where the trauma occurred: childhood. Dad pushed mom, and she was drowning in the pool. I was unable to do a thing. Such cycles of stress have the power to undermine personal achievement. But gaining perspective can change all of that.

The men and women in my family approached life from opposite spectrums. My maternal grandfather and my father taught us practical wisdom—life lessons. The children could leave the house and use whatever they told us, which worked. For example, dealing with bullies, racism, and injustice were subjects for them. On the other hand, classroom matters, addressing teachers, future goals, and other more philosophical conversations were for my maternal grandmother and mother. There was a similar distribution of truths among my uncles and aunts. In other words, the men chiseled us into form with raw street knowledge, and the women buffed our rough edges into smooth, savvy finishes through teaching scripture. Thus, the significant difference was that men were more practical, and women were more biblical, which explains why mom only valued the application of biblical training as practical living.

Nevertheless, my sister and I didn't think about trauma or emerging from or to anything. Instead, "getting better at stuff" was the extent of our language and how we talked about our growth. However, my parents, grandparents, uncles, and aunts inspired us toward self-mastery intentionally. They helped us debrief learning moments from school, life, and activities so that we would eventually answer our questions of purpose independently. Who am I? What is my essence? What contributions will I make, and how will I know when I get there? What am I capable of achieving? What is important to me? What do I need to improve? What is my power? Digging deep for answers brought discovery and self-assurance: to bring our souls to everything we do fearlessly. My family gave us all the support we needed, and each of them offered valuable perspectives.

Mom always had a way of quickly interpreting situations and concisely saying the right thing at the right time to put all in earshot at ease. Cautious and measured, she was more like my grandmother, her mother, than her father. Her ability to see the big picture quickly and handle delicate details ushered in a calming presence that is royal, sincere, and disarming when she enters a room. While mom wasn't pushy and didn't rear us with a specific plan for our lives, she would not allow complacency from her six children. For example, when my older sister was seven years old, she took private lessons in piano and flute and danced jazz, ballet, and tap. I was five years old. I took piano lessons, flute lessons, and guitar lessons. Not long afterward, we added sports.

The arts and sports can be powerful tools for coping with and recovering from trauma. They can provide a sense of accomplishment, help people express their feelings, and distract from difficult experiences. Engaging in creative activities can also promote relaxation and reduce stress, which can be helpful for people who are dealing with trauma. Additionally, participating in a group activity, such as a sports team or a choir, can provide a sense of social connection and support, which can be especially beneficial for those who have experienced or might experience trauma.

We attended every free academic program Kansas City, Missouri, offered to city kids each summer. I refused to call us poor because our experiences were rich. We did everything we wanted, somehow. My sister and I even attended private school. Still, we qualified for government subsidies that my father refused. He would never take a handout but kept the schools guessing about tuition payments. It took school officials seven years to realize dad's verbal gymnastics was all the payment they would get. Finally, they put us out. Mom would make daily miracle meals. Sometimes, she stretched powdered milk for the babies, which was an acquired smell and taste, and we got used to both. When we ran low on condiments, mom poured water into the bottles. Weakened ketchup, mustard, or hot sauce tasted better than having none.

Money was in short supply. Still, when my five younger siblings came of age, my mother introduced them to academics, arts, and sports. I remember one of my younger siblings asking mom whether she could quit playing the piano. My mother said, "Yes, after you find something else you want to do. I won't allow you to sit around the house and do nothing." Mom saw that we made it to all our study sessions, practices, rehearsals, recitals, and games. We also always attended activities such as walk-a-thons, summer camps, birthday parties, and sleepovers. Fortunately, all those activities prevented us from having spare time. "Quiet time is the devil's time," church elders and Mom would say back then. Said in plain English, sitting idle was an invitation to traumatic events, and activity helped us move past life's challenges.

However, there were summer days when we didn't have scheduled activities. We spent those days at grandmama and granddaddy's house. They were our babysitters and assumed that role for my cousins as well. Therefore, it is not a stretch to say that my older sister and I, along with a few cousins, grew up more like siblings. We shared music, dances, and close birthdays. My male cousins were not more than a year apart, and my sister was two years older than the youngest. I even have a cousin one day older than me. We looked out for each other. We also shared things that we learned from our respective schools and neighborhoods. We participated in summer enrichment programs and went downtown to gaming arcades and movies together. There were too many of us in the same age group for any of us to be alone.

Growing up as latchkey kids, we walked to school in pairs. We also walked home together, checked in with mom at designated times, and stayed inside until a parent returned from work. When she called, we'd better answer before the third ring or have explaining to do. Fearlessly and frequently, we caught the bus to grandmama's house by ourselves, which required transferring to another bus and walking several blocks. We earned our parents' trust and increased responsibility by taking care of our business without being asked. We would follow their rules, such as not talking to strangers, never splitting up, and not breaking house rules or laws. When asked to summarize an outing, we had to respond without hesitation. We gave our parents our accounts, and everybody's version must match without sounding scripted. In other words, our parents didn't turn us loose in the city without accountability.

Our excursions began supervised, and our parents gave us a path to follow. There were times when our parents followed us incognito. They came clean by offering details that authenticated their presence. Since we gave them the truth, we never had to worry about anything. However, the feeling that someone was always watching encouraged us to think twice about getting into something questionable.

Being a like-minded group made our parents more comfortable with us experiencing the city without adult supervision. They taught us and reminded us to stick together. We learned how to respond to drug dealers, pimps, and police because all were severe threats to one of us but insignificant threats to all of us. We are a product of the grandaddy who rescued his parents from the evils of sharecropping—the same man who held the Klan and an Alabama sheriff at bay with a shotgun and a pistol while ordering my uncle out from the back seat of a patrol car in the early 1960s. So, if granddaddy's stories taught us anything, it was to be comfortable in our skin. They also taught us that predators and police were two sides of the same coin; we could handle either without fear.

However, we didn't think ourselves to be invincible. We knew our city was dangerous. When danger reared its ugly head, we dealt with it as best we could and let it roll. I recall sitting on the stoop in front of our house on Swope Parkway, a busy four-lane street, two lanes in each direction separated by a substantial grassy median. A disheveled woman, wearing enough makeup to make a circus clown cringe, stumbled past on the sidewalk in platform shoes that gave her 4-6 more inches in height. Focused on the spectacle, I was startled by the screeching tires of a Cadillac Sedan de Ville. The back door swung open, and a man jumped from the car before the woman could take another step. He grabbed her by her long wig and dragged her to the car. She was crying, screaming, and holding on to her hair and his wrists, trying to keep the wig from coming off. He pushed her into the backseat. He jumped in after her, and without closing the door, he started beating her with a wire hanger. As the driver sped off, a soft, still voice pierced through the woman's screams and the car's music and screeching tires. Standing at our front door, my mom said, "Come inside."

That's how fast things can change. In other words, traumatic moments unexpectedly occur when living in the city. I lived less than two blocks from my school. My mom could see the playground from our living room window. Since I played basketball daily, mom would check on me from the window by looking for my ball arching toward the hoop. If I took too long of a break, my dad might show up and tell me to come home because idle time in our neighborhood was dangerous. Keeping moving gave us a chance.

I recall being 10 or 11 when a friend and I casually walked home from school, laughing and just being kids. It was a typical day for all accounts until a Kansas City Police Department (KCPD) squad car swerved in front of us. Two right-side wheels bounced onto the grass near the sidewalk's edge, and the other two skidded to a stop in the street. One officer jumped out and barked, "Turn around. Hands on the wall," which was the brick part of a storefront adjacent to its door. Then, he shouted questions too fast for us to answer: "Where you boys coming from? Where are you going? Do you have any drugs or stolen items on you? Any weapons?"

While he questioned us, his partner sat on top of the patrol car's trunk, his shotgun pointed up, laughing. He laughed louder with each question. Then, while our hands stayed fixed to the building and our feet spread apart, they jumped in their car and sped away. This harassment was common in our neighborhood. The officers' approach, noticeable body language, and seemingly choreographed positioning made the stop look routine. Without another word, my friend and I parted ways. He ran home. I waited until I stopped shaking, thinking we were luckier than most. Still, they took something from me that day. I couldn't put my finger on what to call the theft. Whatever it was, they replaced it with a target. My Black skin was the X on my back. It made me wonder about all traffic stops and the guilt or innocence of Black men detained. I still wonder as a passerby.

Telling our parents about police harassment may have ended the freedom we enjoyed. So, my friend and I kept it secret. We didn't know the word trauma or its impact like we understood racism and harassment. Still, I accepted the incident as my story to tell, like granddaddy's.

The irony is that a police officer visited our school once a month and acted like they were our best friends. Their visits were part of a nationwide community relations program called Officer Friendly. The program's success was a mixed bag nationally, but remnants still operate in some police departments.

Police officers participated in classroom activities, played games with us during recess, and performed question-and-answer sessions at the end of each visit. However, it certainly did not work for our school. Too many kids had their own stories to lament and had visceral reactions when a uniformed officer entered our classroom. In addition, engaging with officers waned as the number of students who experienced police encounters outside of school grew. Therefore, kids would stop playing or excuse themselves when officer friendly tried to join activities. Eventually, the police stopped coming, which caused the program to end.

Nevertheless, understanding the power and experience of the adults in our lives meant using them as guides. Mom taught us scripture, and dad taught us principles. We needed both. Dad's teaching could have been more linear and comprehensive. Instead, he delivered the lessons when the spirit hit him, sometimes in barely comprehensible parables or when the moment required. For example, I remember when three neighborhood kids chased me home.

"What are you running for?"

"There's three of them!"

"I don't care. Get back outside and fight."

I went back outside without hesitation. Dad's words made me think I could take all of them as long as he was there. Fortunately, Dad was not far behind. He walked onto the porch as I scampered down the stairs and onto the sidewalk. Next, he ordered one-on-one fights, returned inside, and watched from the window.

The biggest boy was the older brother of one of the kids my age. He chose to go first by extending his foot to the long crack in the sidewalk. This overture meant I was supposed to extend one of mine to the other side of the line, and we would fight toe-to-toe. Then, he put a small, pencil-sized stick on his shoulder as a challenge. The act of me smacking the twig off his shoulder was "hood provocation," an act of war, and the official start to the arranged fights. I swiped the stick and took my foot off the sidewalk crack. Yeah, I broke the unofficial rule by moving, and that was the moment I officially lost. But there is a difference between an official loss and an actual loss. Besides, his size told me that fighting wasn't fair and how I won didn't matter. While he inched forward, I took two quick side hops, grabbed a brick, and threw it at his head, barely missing because he ducked. I startled him. I smelled his fear and saw it in his eyes. Before he could collect himself, I grabbed a bigger stone and cocked it back to throw. The three took off running, and I chased for more than a few strides.

Among many things I learned that day, I found that chasing was a natural response to someone running away. So, I must never invite a chase again. Meanwhile, with the tables turned, I ran after them and cussed them a bit. It felt good to be on offense. After a few bold and convincing strides, I stopped, tossed the brick to the side, and returned home. My father had words for me as I walked by the top of the stairs where he stood. At that point, his message was unnecessary, but I knew he had to say it anyway.

"You don't ever run from nobody," he said.

"I know," I said as I kept walking.

There was nothing else to say. I could never be a coward. That may have been the first of many life lessons that made sense.

Although my dad was not hands-off, he was not involved in the daily decisions of my rearing. There were things we were better off not sharing with him, such as low-level stuff, because whatever dad dealt with, he brought the thunder. For example, they addressed problems with our school differently. Don't get me wrong. When mom came to the school, we felt comfortable, and she took care of the issue 100 percent of the time. But when dad arrived, we felt powerful, as if the building shook and everybody knew that our dad had caused the rumble.

He worked multiple jobs. Sometimes, I joined him for odd jobs, such as cleaning building floors or hauling furniture or trash; it meant time that I could see him. Dad was all business. As the oldest boy, Dad ensured that I knew how to do things. He taught me how to perform tune-ups on our cars, change a tire, and jump dead car batteries. By sixth grade, I knew how to turn on the water if Kansas City Water and Power cut off our water for not paying past bills. I cannot remember how old I was when dad gave me the "protect the house" speech: "Son, you know where the guns are and how to use them. If someone tries to break into the house, shoot them. Never shoot to scare. Shoot to kill because a dead man can't testify." How's that for both trauma and perspective?

By ninth grade, this was happening. "You're the man of the house," dad often reminded me as he walked out the door for work. My parents worked nights, and both would be gone for a few hours. One night, I heard somebody pulling at the flimsy screen door at the back of our house. The would-be intruder yanked open the locked screen door as I grabbed the 12-gauge shotgun. First, I knelt on the other side with the gun pointed at what I considered waist high. Then, in an aggressive tone and trying to sound much older than 14, I asked, "Who is that?" I shook the main door and kept one finger on the trigger. Then, the screen door slammed shut. Next, I heard footsteps running away.

Once again, I broke the rules of engagement. I opened the door, chased the intruder, and shot once down the driveway. I was not supposed to go out or run after him. But remember, runners, invite chasers. So, I ran to the end of the driveway and fired again. The second time, I aimed down the block in the direction the perpetrator ran. Finally, holding the gun, I sat on the living room couch and waited for my father to come home at 2 AM.

"What happened?" he asked.

"Somebody tried to break in the house," I responded.

"Did you get him?"

"I dunno," I shrugged.

Dad grabbed the gun. He cracked open the barrel, checked for a spent shell, and loaded a live round. I handed over additional ammo from my pockets. Then, he walked outside to the end of the driveway, retracing my steps. Finally, to be sure there wasn't a wounded man or a dead body, he walked to the end of the block. Finding no sign of the intruder left my father flummoxed. When he returned, my father asked, "How did you miss?

I'll never forget childhood moments when my father counted on me to be him. I am sure we all have stories about learning lessons and valuable perspectives from adults who treated us like adults. If describing a hostile encounter, you lead with, "I'll never forget," what follows may have been traumatic.

My Father's Practical Wisdom for Powerful Living:

1. You don't ever run from nobody.
2. Beware of debt.
3. Don't talk too much.
4. You have no friends.
5. Drink at home.

Two things are clear from reading this list. Most of us have experienced trauma, shockingly, at young ages, and we must address trauma often. If an event has you searching your cabinets for milk and looking in the dishwasher for clean socks, you know what I mean. On its face, my dad's teachings came off as pessimistic warnings. However, this list gave me a personal ideology that enabled me to see stuff coming rather than rely on repressive measures.

You Don't Ever Run From Nobody

We never discussed running from people again after I confronted those boys. As I said earlier, rehashing it was unnecessary. However, my father mostly spoke to me in riddles and parables. There was always more to what he was saying. In this case, the whole meaning of "You don't ever run from nobody," for example, was that you don't ever run, period. That includes running from a work situation, a health concern, a past mistake, a debt collector, a demon, or your calling. To him, it didn't matter. Evasion was cowardly. Running still invites chasing, and you must face whatever is after you, sooner or later. Face your opposition toe-to-toe and do what it takes to win, like the start of the fight with those boys on my block. Along these same lines, "You don't ever run" also means that you should not chase things that are willing to leave, have already left, or were not intended for you, such as ex-partners, one-sided friendships, or danger.

Beware of Debt

My father taught me rudimentary principles regarding money, such as paying yourself first and saving from every dollar earned. He wasn't all talk either. I knew all about my father's finances. He periodically displayed his paycheck on the kitchen table, opened. Then, we would do the math together with the bills lying there. It didn't matter that we'd come up short every time. He first paid his savings account and investments and made partial payments on revolving bills, claiming they'd always be there. Sometimes, dad would prove his point by evenly positioning a stack of unopened bills, ripping the envelopes in half, and tossing them in the trash.

Furthermore, he made it clear to me that "Beware of debt" went beyond monetary responsibility. His lecture went like this: "Beware of debt. The worst thing in the world is to owe somebody, even if it's a favor. So, if you can do something yourself, do it. Don't depend on nobody. People are selfish. They will remember they did something for you and will want you to do something for them in return. So don't ask nobody for nothing. If somebody sees you in need and wants to help you, they will offer. Then, it's up to you if you need it. Never ask. Listen to your father." Then, he'd make me repeat the lecture verbatim.

Don't Talk Too Much

Dad said, "Don't talk too much. The more you talk, the more people will try to figure you out. So let them talk so you can figure them out. Because when people figure you out, they will try to take advantage of you."

You Have No Friends

"You have no friends," my father said. "All you have are acquaintances." One day, he asked, "Who are your friends?"

"Earl, Joe, Paul, David, and Barry," I quickly responded.

A few months later, my father asked again, "Who are your friends?"

Speaking much slower and less assured, I recited the names of four or five different people.

"But what happened to Earl, Joe, Paul, David, and Barry?" he asked rhetorically.

"They're not my friends anymore," I replied.

"They were never your friends."

Then, he switched to the third person. He did that often but only when sharing a life lesson.

"Listen to your father. You have no friends; all you have are acquaintances."

Drink at Home

My father didn't engage in much small talk, but he told stories so elaborate that we would have to look to mom for their veracity. She would not co-sign embellishments or tall tales, especially if my dad had been drinking. He drank rum, at times, whiskey; he also drank beer. When we were very young, he would offer us beer or wine to have with dinner. Of course, my mother would never let that happen. So, we knew to say "no." Besides, even I knew I was too young to drink. As we grew older, he continued to offer. I'm trying to say that we were always around alcohol; it wasn't foreign. Our garage was unattached to our house. That is where we stored a colossal refrigerator stocked with liquor.

In high school, my father offered wine and beer with dinner, and my cousins would come over. Sometimes my cousins accepted his offer. I never did. When we started going to clubs and bars, my father pulled us aside and said, "Now, you all are grown, and you been around alcohol all your lives. So, if you're going to drink, I prefer you drink at home. I do not want you guys out drinking in the streets."

It was a good talk, even though alcohol was not a big thing for us. We just wanted to be out in the streets having fun, and drinking wasn't part of the fun. We preferred talking to women, dancing with them, and collecting their phone numbers. We saw a lot of carnage due to alcohol, ranging from beatdowns to drunk driving accidents and death. Therefore, we saw drinking in the streets as trouble and knew how to avoid certain kinds of trouble. We understood that being alert could save your life and that being impaired may cost you your life. Those were the stakes. However, my mother was opposite my father concerning drinking.

"You know your grandfather used to drink."

"Yes mother, I know the story."

Mom would tell it anyway.

"He used to drive into Selma and go to a nightclub and come home drunk. Mama used to worry about him. I remember when he got a new car. That was an accomplishment in those days. When he brought it home, the kids ran around the house screaming, happy. We didn't have it long. One day we found your grandfather on the side of road after a night of drinking. The car was a total loss."

Retelling the story was her setup.

Then she would say, "That's why I always say, if you never take your first drink, you'll never be an alcoholic."

Of course, we had a few functioning alcoholics in our family, and I knew their stories from mom. Therefore, I was scared because I thought if I liked alcohol, I might succumb to the disease.

Therefore, I embraced Mom's line. If anyone offered me a drink or asked why I never drank, I'd say, "My mother said if you never take your first drink, you'll never be an alcoholic. That's good enough for my mother. So it's good enough for me."

I mean, really, what could anybody say to that? That message is clear and concise and disarms any rebuttal. Only once did anybody offer a comeback other than an apology.

Some fool said, "I don't know if I can trust a man that doesn't drink."

"I know I can't trust anybody who thinks I must drink," I said.

He remained a distant acquaintance for sure.

With so much parental focus on making good decisions, drinking surfaced as a blip on my radar. Physical safety and performing optimally at everything eclipsed alcohol altogether. That's how I moved. Therefore, I never peddled anti-alcohol sentiments or pro-sober agendas. But unbeknownst to me, my peers drank less around me. For example, a teammate with whom I rarely interacted said, "Yo man, I've watched you go to the same parties and clubs as me. It looked like you had as much fun at the parties not drinking as I was drinking. So, a few of us decided to try it your way. I'll speak for myself. I don't drink when I go out anymore and I want to thank you because you saved me a whole lot of money."

My father taught us that taking charge of our lives doesn't mean everything will go smoothly. Instead, it allows us to deal with circumstances within our control from a position of strength. Still, random stuff will happen. For example, a friend and I walked from a college party to a nightclub. A police car pulled up, and an officer jumped out of the car and asked us to stand still and face his patrol car. I admit that I flashed back to my adolescence and froze. To relive the moment the police officers harassed and ridiculed me at age 10 corroborated my trauma. I "came to" when I noticed a white kid in the back seat shaking his head at the officer. The cop returned to his car and sped away without saying another word. "Oh my God," I thought. I was just in a makeshift lineup.

Everything about that stop was problematic. It was the dead of winter in Ames, Iowa. It was dark outside and snowing. We wore oversized puffy coats, skull caps, and hoodies. The guy in the back seat may have had a few drinks, been woozy from an assault, or otherwise impaired. He could have been high on adrenaline or hellbent on choosing somebody. Who knows? I would not have been surprised if someone were misidentified that night, and it could have been one of us. I learned that taking charge may slip to someone else and back again from one moment to the next. That's life happening.

When I shared our incident with friends and several volunteered their cop harassment stories that were much like mine as a 10-year-old, I thought they copied it. The only problem is that I hadn't shared my experience with anyone. Nevertheless, the three other Black guys with similar stories of harassment at young ages were from Los Angeles, Chicago, and New York, respectively. Events so identical can't be, I thought.

Then, another common encounter discussed by our larger group occurred during traffic stops. Those stopped while driving alone reported having their driver's licenses in hand before the officer arrived at our windows. Still, we had to endure jabs to the temple with the police officer's gun barrel. Or the officers asked for our driver's licenses while simultaneously mushing our faces with their gun butts, even though our driver's licenses were in our hands—part of our training as we all had received similar lectures about the dos and don'ts of police stops.

Because of these experiences, I cringe when people listen to such encounters and respond with, "Police just need more training." Of course, all cops know such stops are unacceptable for their children. So then, the question becomes, what do young non-white drivers need to counteract the viscerally disturbing feeling caused by hearing a siren or seeing a patrol car? More counseling?

In a 2016 article entitled, "I'm a black ex-cop, and this is the real truth about race and policing," the author writes the following words of a former police officer:

> *On any given day, in any police department in the nation, 15 percent of officers will do the right thing no matter what is happening. Fifteen percent of officers will abuse their authority at every opportunity. The remaining 70 percent could go either way depending on whom they are working with.*[4]

That's one of my burdens. What are some of yours? Some people may experience trauma because of a natural disaster. Others may experience trauma due to physical

---

[4] Hudson, R. (2016, July 7). I'm a black ex-cop, and this is the truth about policing. The Guardian. https://www.theguardian.com/commentisfree/2016/jul/07/philando-castile-alton-sterling-police-racism.

or emotional abuse, severe injury, or other events. It is essential to recognize that everyone's experiences are unique. What may be traumatic for one person may not be traumatic for another. Nevertheless, if you have experienced trauma, seeking support from a mental health professional is crucial. In addition, a trusted loved one can help you cope with the experience and its aftermath.

Not everyone has experienced trauma, but everybody has something that makes them feel vulnerable. If that thing returns you to a place and time, otherwise slowing or preventing progress, you must address it. Finally, discussing your challenges doesn't make you weak. Metaphorically, seeking help is to stand (in the waist-high water of your pool), which we have acknowledged as the first step toward emerging and being you.

Section Six

CONTROL WHAT YOU CAN

Trouble Won't Last

The world is many neighborhoods, and (in my hood)
They say 9-1-1 is a joke.
I want answers to my emergency.
Emerging is our prophecy
Before our lives go up in smoke.

The devil is our advocate,
Ear hustling our godly pleas.
Adding noise, we know his ploy.
It is to steal, kill, and destroy.

Even Jesus asked trouble to let up.
He said if it's necessary, let it be.
Got 99 problems but only need the One,
Who in His image created me.

But what good is an image
When Satan stirs evil inside our souls,
Skews making our decisions,
Right thinking with revisions,
Underestimating his demonic hold?

Hold up. Wait a minute.
Return to the prophecy.
You'll be the head, not the tail.
God don't lie,
And trouble won't last always.

Hughes Suffren

CHAPTER EIGHTEEN
CONTROL WHAT YOU CAN

Never let your emotions overpower your intelligence.
—Anonymous

I would choose Miss Underwood as my most impactful teacher 10 times out of 10. Why? Because she expected a lot from us, which guaranteed that we would learn more. Incredible as it may seem, we felt more seen and valued because she looked like us. In addition, her teaching practices helped us feel more connected to our identities and cultures. Therefore, I will begin this chapter with a concluding question that should motivate Black and Brown communities to flood academia with teachers. What possibilities exist for students of color with at least one Black teacher in elementary school, middle school, high school, and college?

Two weeks into my first English composition class, I remained in awe of my first Black teacher, Miss Underwood. It is impossible to communicate what it meant to see her in charge. However, it meant different assumptions for our class. Suddenly, we were capable of learning. There were no smart kids and dumb kids. There were also fewer detentions and poor conduct reports. I never had the opportunity to ask Miss Underwood about her teaching style. But I got the impression that teaching our mostly Black and Brown class was personal. Instinctively, our culturally informed relationship produced reverence, trust, and understanding at a glance, as if we were her children. Miss Underwood's high expectations for learning and behavior surpassed mere competence and proved infectious. Even our regular class clowns relented, and their focus resembled our usual A-student crowd. After so many years, I utilized what most stuck with me from Miss Underwood and her class—a simple theorem. How people learn and behave are personal choices, and each decision to act produces intended and unintended consequences.

Miss Underwood's mission since the first day of class had been to help students become strong writers. So, before assigning graded work, she bombarded us with sentence structure exercises as well as tips and tricks for perfect grammar. Then, Miss Underwood corrected our assignments using a green pen for good writing and a red pen for missteps, which she required us to fix. Miss Underwood thought this would be a positive way for us to learn, and by default, we would create study guides for future work.

We spent weeks moving through the basics and then to intermediate lessons. Miss Underwood thoroughly tested our proficiency before allowing anyone to move on. She encouraged us to move at our own pace, which did not include holding still for the less confident or slowing down those more advanced. I tested two grade levels beyond my classification and showed perceptible improvement from week one. Miss Underwood taught us to write with considerable thought and expression accuracy and to strive for our distinct literary voices. To do this:

1. She harped on errors and frequently asked, "Why should anybody read your work if you are too lazy to proofread?"
2. She taught us techniques, such as reading our text aloud, to catch careless errors, common mistakes, and misspellings.
3. She taught English composition to resonate with our recent experiences.

For instance, she charged us with our first assignment, to write a persuasive paper about something unique to America. "Keep it simple," she said. "A personal observation, perhaps." Then, of course, we had to move or convert her while demonstrating command of basic writing: central idea, organization, support, word choice, and grammar. "Simple" was great advice.

I will never forget my thesis sentence: "If Americans do something illegal long enough, sooner or later, it will be legalized." I cited examples such as "ain't" becoming a dictionary word and alcohol and prostitution becoming legal to support my idea. My paper practically wrote itself.

When Monday came, anticipation filled the room as we waited for Miss Underwood to start class. Students masked their doubts and nervous tension with unusual silence. Instead, they made the most audible sounds of kids' feet tapping, pinching spring-loaded ink pens open and closed, and the clock's secondhand ticking. Some students questioned the degree to which their paper sucked and whether they passed. Never mind the grade for others. It simply felt good to care. Finally, this left a girl named Leanne and me expecting the A we earned in every class.

Miss Underwood had a reputation. Former students touted her as a tough grader but a fair teacher. They emphasized that ours was no ordinary composition class. Miss Underwood expected next-level ideas, advanced sentence structure to communicate those ideas, and error-free work. She described the course's vigor as moving at a high school pace from day one. She didn't disappoint. I appreciated how Miss Underwood pushed us through intense writing exercises. It did not matter that we were only sixth graders.

Then, the second bell rang, signaling the beginning of class and time for Miss Underwood to return our first graded assignment—a 500-word essay. Miss Underwood asked us not to look at our papers, walked up and down the rows, and placed each student's paper face down on their desks. Then, she told us what to look for when we reviewed our essays: "There is a lined notecard stapled to the back of each paper. It includes my summary feedback at the top and your temporary letter grade at the bottom. You will have until Friday to correct all mistakes for which I will award partial credit. Failure to correct your errors will reduce your temporary grade to an "F" as your final grade. I only assign final grades to completed assignments. Any questions?"

After delivering the instructions, Miss Underwood gave the okay by rotating her palm down to up. Then, we flipped over our papers simultaneously. In the margins of my essay, she had jotted down favorable comments such as, "Great idea, nice thought, and well done." Then, I excitedly flipped up the page to read the notecard.

At the top of my card, she wrote, "Best Paper!" So naturally, my jaw dropped when I glanced at the bottom and saw a big fat D. I flipped over my paper again, this time for clues that would explain her double-talk. Without a doubt, the "best paper" should not earn a D. Unfortunately, there were three red marks within the text of my essay. The first was an "sp" abbreviation identifying a misspelled word, another underlined a comma splice, and the last circled an incorrect verb tense. I was angry because some of my classmates made higher grades for what seemed like remedial work compared to the complexity of my composition.

After class, I made a beeline to Miss Underwood's desk. Indeed, she made a mistake with my grade, I thought. I laid my paper on her desk calendar, stood with crossed arms, and waited for an explanation.

When she looked up, I said, "You graded my paper wrong."

Then, she politely explained: "You have an excellent grasp of mechanics and storytelling style, but the mistakes you made were tacky for someone with your ability."

I felt no pride in what felt like a backhanded compliment. Miss Underwood had much more to say as I stood there wanting to take the damned D and be on my way.

"I do not tolerate misspelled words, grammar errors, and sloppy tense changes. The cost of each inaccuracy was a letter grade. However, poor behavior is another matter. First, you started pouting when you saw your grade; then, you stopped paying attention. Some teachers won't care like I do. So I'm going to help you with that."

"I apologize, Miss Underwood, and I don't need help."

"It's too late. You have earned an additional writing assignment for acting on a short fuse.

Write, 'I must always control my attitude, effort, and actions' 1000 times. You may turn it in with your corrections."

That day, Miss Underwood delivered harsh truths by affirming my strengths and condemning my shortcomings with equal intensity. There was nothing subtle about what Miss Underwood meant to convey. She would not accept mediocrity, not trying, or disrespect. Lesson learned. My conduct mattered.

Indeed, raising the bar proved pivotal. I learned to control what I could in her class, which transferred to my other classes. Essentially, Miss Underwood's criticism of my behavior expressed a sentiment in class that I only got from my family outside of class—tough love. It was unprecedented, and I did not experience it or another Black teacher throughout my academic career.

Finally, our writing class reinforced another principle I learned two years earlier in athletics: Repetition develops skill. I preferred that mantra over the cliché "practice makes perfect" because I saw the former as a champion's approach and the latter as unattainable. In other words, I would seek skill rather than perfection, and I could apply skill development to everything. From writing to sports and cleaning my room, I wanted to be the best at whatever I started. This serendipitous revelation to control what was in my authority I owe to Miss Underwood. So then, as I grew older, I expanded that philosophy of control to include the following: First, never give decision-making power to someone else because of my actions. It does not matter if they are teachers, law enforcement officers, doctors, dentists, judges, et cetera. Second, if I want better rewards, I must produce better actions.

I am unsure when I first declared, "If you stay ready, you don't have to get ready," as one of my mantras. But it worked for me. I even tried to control my karma by amassing good deeds, which I admit is doing good for the wrong reasons. That was before adulthood. I had a pious view of individual behavior, thinking I had an edge if God owed me, especially when I wanted something to go my way. So, I would be sure to be right in how I acted, spoke, and made decisions during basketball season or near a big exam, confident that God would deliver.

Don't dare get super holy on me and act like you have never bargained with God. Most everyone leans into that conversation, whether religious or not. For example, some of you have pleaded for safety. "God, I will never do this again if you get me off this roller coaster (or a plane experiencing turbulence)!" Until, of course, you do it again. Other people may have brokered a deal: "God, if you get me into school, I will study every day." Raise your hand if you have said, "God, if you give me this significant other, I will treat them the way you would want me to." I suspect that we have all been there.

A friend named Ken described a similar experience of control and tough love. As a young staffer, he submitted his first report to a newly elected congresswoman in Washington, DC. He wanted to communicate that he was on top of his responsibilities by submitting the document early. She promptly emailed, "Is this the best you can do?" Slightly embarrassed and fearing that his work was inferior, Ken revised and resubmitted the report. Again, the congresswoman quickly responded, "Ken, is this the best you can do?" Frustrated and worried, Ken stayed up all night, expanded on details, and emailed the report just before the start of business. He admitted to himself that he improved the brief with each iteration. Then, when the congresswoman questioned him a third time, Ken scheduled a meeting with her the same day. Ken needed his job and felt he wouldn't get many more opportunities to prove his value in the role. Therefore, Ken wanted to find out first-hand what needed to improve. He entered the congresswoman's office with the confidence of a student sitting for a midterm, unprepared, after realizing they studied the wrong chapters.

The congresswoman introduced herself and said, "It is nice to meet you Ken, how can I help you?"

"Well, I have been busting my butt on this report and you keep asking whether it is my best. Of course, I want this job. I don't know what else you want."

"I want to know if what you submitted is your best."

"Yes, it is my best," Ken said sharply.

"Okay. I guess I will read it now," she said.

Shock and disbelief shot through Ken, mixed with relief. "You mean you haven't read any of my reports?"

"No," she said. "When I sit down to read your report, I want to know that I have your best."

Ken learned a valuable lesson about excellence despite potentially losing his job if he did not take control of his effort. Beyond that, the congresswoman taught Ken not to fear outcomes when he gives his best and to look unblinkingly at the unknown when he does.

In other words, taking charge of yourself is a no-brainer, with apparent limits being all that exists outside our control. There is no reward for shrinking in fear. Because one of the most constant facets of life is that unfavorable events happen, even when you control all you can. Therefore, it is up to us to prepare for them. How do we do that?

As previous chapters suggest, we can answer our questions of purpose. Those answers guide our thoughts, daydreams, interpersonal relationships, employment, and other behaviors that keep us on our path. Do all you know how to do. For example, Ken trusted his abilities and did all he could, and when that did not seem enough, he did not shrink. He acted. Likewise, we may act in faith, which also provides breakthroughs. Still, some painful struggle will force its way as a priority in its own time. When it does, we may use the tools we have and learn new ones to help us persist. In other words, life teaches us that to be alive means facing challenges. So, there is no sense in crying, "Not fair," or asking, "Why me?" Complaining has never done any good, anyway. Instead, learn, accept, and believe that struggle and challenges are standard and that you can appropriately handle whatever comes. So then, how we deal with setbacks using the tools we carry in our backpacks is essential.

Too often, we mismanage disappointments in ways that cause blowbacks or repercussions. For example, many years ago, my overly protective younger brother walked through the halls as a senior in high school. Coincidentally, he saw my sister, 11 months his junior, running to the bathroom crying. "What's wrong with you?" he asked emphatically. Then, through tears and sniffles, my sister mentioned the band teacher's name. That was all my brother needed to spring into action. He ran down the hall and burst into the band room while class was in session with a frown and a squinty-eyed stare. Then, he threatened the band teacher with clenched fists in front of 50 students. Alternatively, my brother could have comforted my sister and gotten more information. Instead, his actions set a series of unintended outcomes in motion, which he could have avoided.

We can derive some sense of the quickness of repercussions and their lessons from my poor behavior in my English class, my brother's hot-tempered reaction in the name of protecting our sister, or from Grady, my high school teammate who cursed at my coach in a previous chapter. You may recall that his behavior also launched a series of events with their momentum. Ultimately, Coach Taylor had the final say, and Grady caught a humiliating beatdown for his reckless remarks. Try to hold on to these three examples of acting without thinking as we explore the following two avoidable events, which vary in degree and gravity.

A taxi driver suddenly stopped his car to avoid an object on the road. The impatient driver, who followed too closely, rear-ended the taxi. The taxi driver sprung from his car and raced to its rear to assess the damage to his rear bumper. Still incensed because the taxi driver swerved, the car's driver floored the gas pedal to scare the man. Unfortunately, the driver smashed the man between the two vehicles. The car driver also injured the taxi's passenger, who began stepping out of the car during the second collision. In this example, all three people involved responded to their initial misfortune in a way that caused a series of additional adversities. Our training to respond to an accident instructs us to call 9-1-1 to report it immediately. Then, call our insurance company. Furthermore, imagine if the passenger also called for another means of transportation before jumping out of the car. The time between the initial collision and the duration of their phone calls may have prevented the reactive, heat-of-the-moment second collision and the ripple of disasters that followed.

The second example involves a situation with a more common motivation—distracted driving. A friend was driving his motorcycle with his fiancé as his passenger. The portion of highway they traveled is known for its abrupt stop-and-roll traffic on a particular curve. As they slowed considerably with the pace of traffic, something else happened beyond their control. A cell phone rang in the car that followed. The woman inside the vehicle faced a tempting question. Should she answer the phone? She chose to reach for the phone and answer the call. In those seconds, lives changed forever. She hadn't noticed that traffic suddenly slowed to half the posted speed. When she rear-ended the motorcycle, the crash's impact sent its passenger airborne. My friend's fiancé flew over the bike and the car they followed. Unable to stop, the car ran over my friend's fiancé and killed her instantly. Along with losing his fiancé, my friend suffered broken bones, job loss, grief, and depression. The driver who caused the accident was charged and convicted of vehicular homicide and spent eight years in prison.

These developments vary in scope and significance and boil down to an urgent message. People who do not take the few extra seconds needed to properly make decisions involuntarily fill up principal's offices, unemployment lines, jails, hospitals, and cemeteries. These outcomes apply to perpetrators and victims. Situations may worsen when you don't follow your training and sometimes when you do. In other words, sometimes stuff happens. The causes often take time to discern. Crap will hit you in your blind spot like the most dangerous punch in boxing—the one the boxer doesn't see. All it takes is one questionable decision to set off an adverse chain reaction. It turns out, though, that from the standpoint of each person, not reacting would have been a helpful way to deal with the initial incident. Let's rewind. Suppose the driver doesn't answer the ringing phone, the driver who hit the taxi takes a moment to think through his next steps, Grady doesn't react to Coach Taylor, my brother decides to listen to our sister more, and I do not exhibit poor behavior by demanding an explanation from my teacher for giving me a D. That shows us that "all people can control is their attitude, effort, and actions." Miss Underwood was right.

Today, most people are open about experiencing more stress, racial tension, anxiety, social discomfort, and anger. One reason is Covid-19 and its variants. It is no longer the fear of infection or death at the forefront of our collective thinking. Instead, the ongoing threat of disruption the disease or new variants places on our rhythm is more pressing. For example, more people are managing changes in employment, income, housing, education, daycare, and perceived losses of freedoms than before the pandemic. This describes only one element. Another significant outcome is heated politics and political figures encouraging anger to be our tool. Now drivers are more aggressive. Mass shootings have increased along with gun sales. You can feel an unsettled tension during in-person shopping. Then, as people look for scapegoats, minority groups lead as usual targets, causing a significant rise in racial animus and hate crimes.

Fundamentally, any behavioral professional would agree that building our emotional and psychological strength would help prevent emotional outbursts. One way is to acknowledge vulnerability and deal with it directly. That may be anything from getting more restful sleep to exercising, practicing yoga, or doing anything that restores your rhythm.

Another strategy could be to involve other people. Reconnect with people and activities that have traditionally brought you joy. In other words, it's easy for our anger level to reach 100 if we walk around in an angered state of 50. Dial your agitation back to a nonexistent zero, and there may be space to think through an event that knocks you for a loop.

Still, the heat of an emotional moment requires a handy mechanism that grants us our pause, leaving room for a better next step. For example, if you recall that I said, "This isn't real," aloud in my childhood nightmares. Then, I would wake up. With more practice, I developed the skill of rewinding bad dreams and creating new endings. Unfortunately, we cannot reverse time to avoid unfavorable incidents. However, we can predetermine calming words, such as "Chill" or "I have the power to be happy no matter the circumstance." Any meaningful word or phrase that will reduce the intensity of a moment will do. "If this happens, I will do that." You may use breathing or close your eyes and count to three. Anything that helps maintain your natural rhythm creates the best headspace for your next decision.

Predetermined strategies deliver no matter how explosive, emotional, or negatively charged the situation. That's important. Sure, like any advice, it's easier said than done. However, I will demonstrate in the following chapters how quickly situations may spiral out of control when emotions rule, even when you think them through.

CHAPTER NINETEEN
MY VIDEO WON'T GO VIRAL

One of my most treasured childhood memories is watching television as a family. We cheered Olympians, learned from mini-series programs, and discovered the world of science and nature through documentaries. However, the best time was cracking up at our favorite skits while watching situation comedies. My favorite skit was a buddy cop duo: Smitty (Officer Smith) and Hoppy (Officer Hopkins) from the television show *Sanford and Son*, set in a poor neighborhood in Watts, California. Back then, Smitty and Hoppy appeared when Fred Sanford and his son, Lamont, called the police. Hoppy, the white officer, tried hard to fit in. Naturally, the audience wanted Hoppy to succeed. Even so, his formal speech was off-putting, confusing. Still, to everyone's dismay, he took the lead in answering questions. Then, silence falls over the room once Hoppy starts his long-winded answer to a police question. Next, comes a dramatic pause. Finally, everybody present would look at the Black officer for clarification, and his breakdown would be hilarious. One classic example was a neighborhood child appearing scared to speak with the officers.

Then, Hoppy said, "Sonny, you know in the lawman–juvenile relationship, the primary consideration is the establishment of an atmosphere of mutual trust between the official and the minor in question."

At that point, the child turned and looked at Fred and Lamont. Then, all three turned their confused gaze toward Smitty for the layperson's breakdown:

"Be cool little brother; the fuzz is your cuz."

Everybody inhaled with wide open mouths and nodded their heads to show they understood. Then, the live studio audience erupted into laughter. Finally, Hoppy always left the Sanford house mixing up some form of cultural expression when saying goodbye. For example, Hoppy routinely said "right off" instead of "right on," or when he said, "peace and soul," he would mix up the hand gestures by giving a fist for peace and two fingers for soul. After an exasperated breath, Smitty would push Hoppy out the door while correcting his embarrassing gaffe.

Meanwhile, when I was no more than six or seven years old and watching those reruns, we lived in the Kansas City, Missouri, neighborhood of 43rd and Wabash, a part of town every bit as dangerous as Watts. For instance, someone broke into our home on Tuesday, Wednesday, and Thursday of the same week. On Thursday, they left a note that read, "We'll be back." After approximately two weeks, a real-life version of Smitty and Hoppy arrived to take our report of the burglaries. They weren't as goofy as the sitcom portrayed, but they were every bit as unhelpful.

Before leaving, the white cop offered my father some bizarre parting advice: "The best thing to do is buy a gun," he said. "To avoid trouble, make sure the perpetrators are deceased and inside when the police arrive. Otherwise, the wheels of justice may turn in their favor and leave you robbed yet again."

In classic *Sanford and Son* fashion, my parents looked to the Black officer who clarified, "Shoot to kill, drag them inside if you have to, and the law will be on your side."

The practice of life imitating art was in plain sight that day, minus a funny punchline. Nevertheless, that was one of those moments that stayed with me. Luckily, my father moved us away from that neighborhood and avoided potentially becoming a murderer. However, reflecting on that moment made me wonder about adverse chain reactions from bad decisions and how sometimes it is better to be lucky than good. As luck would have it, there was never a break-in while someone was home. Therefore, our family avoided the consequences of a future lousy decision. Unfortunately, long after that, I would have a few knucklehead moments.

It was the spring semester of my first year in college. The receiver core of the college football team decided to form a squad and play intramural basketball. During one game, I was guarding a white guy much bigger than me. He stood approximately 6'6" tall and weighed about 240 pounds. Although much older, he was sculpted more like a bodybuilder than a hooper. Anyway, he drove through the lane, and I fouled him. Unfortunately, we only had referees for intramural basketball in the playoffs. Therefore, it was left to players to call fouls and violations. I conceded the foul: "I got you, your ball."

"Get the fuck outta here," he said as he threw the ball at me hard, intentionally hitting me square in the face. He'd soon learn that speaking to me that way, and throwing the ball, constituted his first and second mistakes. Standing there without fear was his third lousy decision. I closed the distance between us with two quick strides. There was no time for talking. The smirk on his face let me know he didn't think much of me or my slight 6'2", 180-pound frame coming toward him. That would be his last mistake. When my second stride hit the floor, I threw a stiff left-hand punch into his right cheekbone. The guy must've had a glass jaw because his eyes rolled to the whites, and the right side of his face went flat from shattered bones. Then, like a chopped tree, he slowly fell the other way. Since I knocked him unconscious where he stood, his left cheekbone broke his fall. I didn't know much about reciting calming words or minimizing my temperature during an emotional moment. I only knew he missed a lesson or two growing up, and it was my duty to teach, not talk.

Proving that his heart pumped mouse piss, he filed assault charges, even though he started the fight. Months passed, and I faced our court date. Finally, he arrived at court, testified, and submitted his evidence. There were no witnesses, only time-stamped pictures of his jaw wired shut and snapshots of his recovery—drinking his food from straws for six to eight weeks. The rest of his treatment plan included plastic surgery and speech therapy. It sucks to suck, summed up my thoughts exactly. He was a heavyweight boxing type, meaning without displaying the streetball bravado that got him knocked out, he could not hide his physically imposing stature. His age, revealed in his filings, also showed that he was a man in his 30s who tried to punk a teenager.

Next, the judge asked me to give the court my version of the incident. I gave the judge the details of what happened. The judge lay the side of his head on one hand as if bored or trying to stay awake. I knew I had already lost. So, I finished by saying, "My father always told me that if someone hits me, hit them back." However, this judge, a balding, middle-aged white man, showed no mercy. He bore a striking resemblance to former Alabama Governor George Wallace, down to a cantankerous, fiery attitude.

Still, it was the reason he gave before ruling that was so disturbing: "Look at you," he said. "You are violent by nature. Therefore, I find you guilty of simple assault," and he slammed his gavel.

I didn't physically move, but my thoughts raced. His words cut deep, and I wondered how many judges thought like him. I guess independence and freedom are to white America what violence and guilt are to Black men.

"What do you mean violent by nature?" I said as I returned from my thoughts.

The judge slowed his walk, acknowledging that he heard my question. Then, he continued through the back door, presumably to his chambers, without looking back. I figured he wanted to respond nastily, or he wished he had handed me a stiffer penalty for not kissing his ring.

Two years later, I was listening to music in my apartment when another imitation of the Smitty and Hoppy duo came by unannounced. I recognized them as officers who picked up extra shifts; they worked undercover security at campus parties and security detail for home football games. After they knocked, I spoke through the screen door.

"What's up fellas?"

"We were in the neighborhood and wanted to follow up on an anonymous tip."

"Okaaaay, what does that have to do with me?"

"The tipster alleged that you have stolen property on the premises."

I laughed until I noticed they remained stone-faced. Then, as the moment turned awkward, they appeared to have run out of small talk. They had not come with a search warrant. Plus, I knew that I would never have anything illegal. Then, unfortunately, I took their bait. I played the role of crash test dummy by treating those familiar faces as friendly people. I asked them inside.

"Come in and look around," I said.

I held the door open. They practically leaped inside. They stayed only for a few seconds, though.

"Look, we'd better go. Nothing to see here," one officer said. "Yeah, we've wasted enough of your time," said the other.

"No problem, I'm sure I'll see you guys around," I said as they walked out the door.

The following week, after they left my apartment, I saw them just before the start of football practice, which was too soon even for them. The two officers, who posed as my friends, stood on the receiving end of a tirade from my head coach. He threw down his hat and pointed his finger in their faces. The tongue-lashing lasted less than a minute. Whatever the coach said to them, he meant. Then, our offensive coaches briefly huddled. When my receiver coach searched the field and locked his gaze on me, he confirmed what I already knew. So, I took off my helmet and laid it on the ground. Then, I took a knee, placed a hand on my helmet, and waited. A few minutes later, my receiver coach stood in front of me. I did not look up. Therefore, I could only see his shoes. Then, he took a knee and started talking once he reached my eye level. "The police have a warrant for your arrest. Get dressed. You have two hours to turn yourself in. I'm sure this is a misunderstanding," he said. And I nodded.

I wondered what had happened between the officers and my head coach as I walked freely toward the fieldhouse. Maybe he convinced the officers not to cuff me. On the other hand, he could have emphasized that I was not a flight risk and that the media was hanging around practice. Or I'm in less trouble than I thought. I was only sure of one thing: This bogus Smitty and Hoppy duo played me.

I showered and drove to the police station, where I felt like a pariah. It was like entering the wrong neighborhood, surrounded by enemies, and wishing your boys were close by and had your back. This feeling was a taste of things to come. First, an officer officially charged and booked me, barking typical law enforcement terminology. "Any tattoos or marks? Look into the camera without expression." Click. "Turn right." Click. Then, on to fingerprinting.

Afterward, the booking officer led me to a holding cell, handed me a file, and introduced me to the waiting public defender. The file contained a charge sheet that read:

Incident: Theft of television (and the address of the theft—a laundromat)
Incident: Possession of stolen property

Coincidentally, my TV was the only thing I owned and did not purchase. A former teammate and student gave me the TV to settle a debt. He told me it was a gift from his grandmother, which seemed plausible. It never occurred to me that someone would lie about their grandmother.

Liar and thief were moot points as my public defender rambled: "You should consider making a deal" was enough for me to stop listening.

I spoke loudly over the public defender, who suggested I plead to a lesser possession charge. Each time he opened his mouth, I interrupted, "I will take my chances in court," until he left.

I did the same when he called. Finally, he stopped calling. I'm from the city. I know rackets. They were in this together: the police, the prosecutor, and the public defender. The district attorney or a judge finally got my message that I would never admit to something I did not do. We had reached a legal impasse with no evidence I committed a crime and a defendant unwilling to confess falsely.

Several weeks after the district attorney dismissed the case, I saw the two police officers at an event. I approached them to hear what those fakers had to say.

Without a greeting, the white officer spoke out of guilt first and said, "Hey man, we were doing our job. Nobody thinks you stole the television. We felt you had to know it was stolen. Therefore, we left your apartment to obtain two warrants: a search warrant to legally re-enter your premises to recover the stolen item and an arrest warrant."

Still, without saying a word, I looked at the Black officer. He dropped his head and broke it down as plainly as the television Smitty would: "You shouldn't have let us in."

A flash childhood image of the cops giving my father advice popped into my head. Then, I had a fleeting thought of my father following their recommendation—shooting and dragging a burglar inside. My final thought was the same two officers suggesting my father shoot intruders would come to arrest him for the shooting. In other words, I thought the cops in my childhood would have also played my father. When I snapped back to the present, I called those deceitful pigs "punk bitches" to their faces and walked away. I knew my remark could draw more unwanted attention from the cops. I peeked over my shoulder to see if this Smitty and Hoppy were coming for me. Then, I made a note to my future self: never give anybody a reason to assert authority over you, and that words from my mouth can make bad situations worse.

Merging Schooling and Education

Never be ashamed of a scar. It simply means
you were stronger than whatever tried to hurt you.
— Unknown

I felt powerless as a 10-year-old when police pranked me at gunpoint. Indeed, there is more to the code: serve and protect. Likewise, I realized I was defenseless when police lured me into police custody on bogus charges. There is no shame in tricking an 18-year-old into a false confession or a makeshift lineup. Lastly, I felt vulnerable when a judge demeaned me in his courtroom. Calling me violent by nature was a reality check if I ever thought fair and impartial had meaning. The remark also reminded me of what I could face if I failed to apply what Miss Underwood taught me in the sixth grade: Control what I can control.

Still, my feelings crystallized into full-blown hatred, real and warranted. I left the world of "ignorance is bliss." Never would I return. Representations of so-called American justice caught my wrath. I wondered what else I didn't know that could hurt me. One of the few scriptures I could recite from memory back then was Hosea

4:6: "My people are destroyed for lack of knowledge" (KJV). I took that scripture literally and became a history buff.

I studied the system of racism that operates locally and globally. I learned about America's ill-gotten gains and populations in chains, a system broken distinctly in two. Never to be equal. But what I hadn't learned about was unresolved trauma. I carried a large stack of it. That's right, trauma builds. For example, suppose someone doesn't adequately deal with trauma. In that case, the person may find it more difficult to cope with future challenges or stressors and may be more likely to experience additional traumatic events. This progression may lead to repeated trauma, increased suffering, and feeling stuck and incapable of emerging.

Then, five years and two degrees later, I had become an educator. I had to wrestle with history and hope for my sanity. Either could lead to self-destructive behavior. So, I moved to Southern California to start fresh. Unfortunately, something happened before the end of my first year on the job—an uprising.

Breaking Point

My first awareness that Black people and Brown people were protesting was from the sound of sirens from fire trucks and police vehicles. Then, a student ran into my office and said his younger brother was missing. I asked him to call his family and sit in my office until I returned. Next, we heard a warning from a loudspeaker saying, "Stay inside for your safety."

"Stay here and call your family," I reiterated to the student, and I walked out. Since I worked on campus as a resident director, my apartment was in the building. I hurried there to catch breaking news highlights from the local news stations and to grab a radio for my office. When I returned, the student gave me a thumbs-up as he quickly removed his feet from on top of my desk while he spoke with a family member.

Los Angeles was on fire, and tensions between whites and non-whites were life-threatening. In addition, there were reports of random assaults on people and property. So, I grabbed my walkie-talkie, a bullhorn, and a clipboard and headed outside in real crisis and protection modes. I wanted to appear official to off-campus authorities as I directed curious students inside for their safety. Therefore, I also wore a reflective, bright yellow safety parka that I thought I'd only use for evacuations.

Outside smelled of ash and tear gas. I didn't venture far from my building because the police patrolled in groups. The mayor and governor also deployed the national guard to enforce a city-wide curfew and protect property. Police officers made occasional arrests when they had the upper hand. Otherwise, they sat in their cars and watched as looters pillaged and burned the poorer parts of the city. Conversely, other patrols formed human shields around affluent parts of town, such as Beverly Hills and Bel Air. From that, I reasoned that decision-makers valued protecting and serving other communities more.

Black and Mexican people finally reached their limits with police brutality after seeing a video of officers beating Rodney King. The year was 1991, and the feeling that police brutality frequently happened to Black men spawned spontaneous protests in major cities throughout the United States. However, this time, someone recorded the brutal act. This recording marked the first viral video that exposed two specific policing standards: protecting and serving white and wealthy people but assaulting and apprehending Black, Brown, or low-income people.

This year in my life was low and emotionally draining but not in terms of what I thought about myself. My self-esteem and confidence were riding high. Instead, I felt less of America and my place in it because of what its institutions thought about me. Every American who truly believes in the Constitution also believes it should protect all of us and make us feel safe and equal. It's not like I asked for world peace. I just wanted things to be different than they were. For me, though, history taught me at least two things. First, freedom in America has always been illegal for Black people. Why else are Black people still fighting for rights that are supposed to be accessible to all citizens? Second, replacement players would always be in this played-out race game.

Through what mechanisms are the universal racial codes shared? The undiscussable ritual, for example, compels people to follow me in stores, hike my security deposit, or lower my appraisal. The demonstration of bias is clear, systemic, and global. Or so it seems. "Oh, we didn't know you were Black" should not be the first words from a search committee when I arrive for an interview though it has happened. One employer notified the chief of police of my hiring and submitted my car information and current address to prevent officers from profiling me. My supervisor suspected sharing those actions with me would have brought more comfort. Instead, I found the University's perceived need to notify the city unsettling and reprehensible.

I understood that there was racism, but not the point of racism. Indeed, the racist white person hiding under a white sheet, behind a badge, or in Congress must know that returning to slavery is impossible. Gone are the days when water hoses, police dogs, and police batons intimidated us. Freedom and courage are equalizers. Besides, the general public now has everything at their disposal that white racists have always had access to. Guns do the same damage no matter who is firing them. I don't know how we move the needle further and faster, just that coexisting requires decency as a first step. Still, ramping up rhetoric that supports a second civil war is disconcerting, especially when it seeps deeper into mainstream conversations and surfaces as random acts of aggression. Perhaps cruelty is the point of it all.

Up to this point, the Rodney King story sounds a lot like the murder of George Floyd approximately 30 years later. George Floyd was an unarmed Black man subdued and killed by Derek Chauvin, a veteran police officer kneeling on his neck for nine minutes and 29 seconds. After a bystander's video spawned global protests, Chauvin was arrested, convicted, and sentenced to 22.5 years in prison. However, this story sounds more like the murder of Tyre Nichols, a young man beaten to death by five Black police officers after they manufactured a traffic stop.

Nevertheless, in the following months, police violence continued, and the beating of Rodney King still fed the news cycle, daytime talk show scripts, and late-night television. Finally, when the LAPD shot a gang member execution-style, the Crips and Bloods agreed to a ceasefire. Then, they negotiated a peace treaty with other LA gangs.

Almost immediately, there was a drop in street crime and collective relief around the city. Rappers produced upbeat songs about brotherhood, getting along, and a productive future. Fortunately, the truce and the cultural and political shifts that followed proved to be more than lip service. I attended a celebration of the reconciliation held at a large park. I listened intently to the attendees, ear-hustling as many gang conversations as possible. As best I could tell, their interactions mimicked a gigantic family reunion.

Non-gang members and members of the Crips and Bloods intermingled, ate, and, most of all, talked. Black and Mexican gang members chopped it up. Some played games such as dominoes and chess. At the same time, others discussed future meetups and building alliances. However, the police attended in force and spoke to known gang members with an unexpected tone and intent. Instead of supporting them, they baited them one against another openly and unashamedly. I didn't know why the police might be against the truce. I recall a group of uniformed officers who spoke to a gang member in a loud whisper,

"Blue is dead," one officer said.

"Your cousin's killer is here and y'all wanna be friends?"

"This ain't gonna last anyway," offered another cop.

"This is a new breed of gangster," another officer said, causing all four in their group to laugh loudly.

My friend, who also heard the whole thing, said, "These cops been doing gang members dirty for a long time. Now, they're worried that if gangs all get along, they will turn on them."

I mulled over his statement and tried to brainstorm other reasons cops spoke that way at such an event. He was right. The cops needed division, bickering, and escalation, and instigating a brawl might accomplish that. I scoped a scene that was becoming more dangerous. We left.

I had family who lived in all the hot spots: Los Angeles, Compton, and Watts. Yet, I had none outside the raging city, where I needed to go to clear my head. Now, I cannot say how I reconnected with a former teammate from college. However, the timing was perfect. His name is Danny, and he lives in Moreno Valley, California, located approximately an hour east of Los Angeles. He asked if I wanted to join his basketball team that played in a recreation league there. Coincidentally, Danny had also organized my intramural squad in the past. Remember the one I exited with a knockout?

Moreno Valley was quite a drive for basketball games. Still, I needed a mental outlet and camaraderie to escape my tension-filled city. The drive to Moreno Valley was less scenic compared to other California areas. There were few exits if I was tired from a long day and needed to stop. When I arrived, I noticed a city with charm. There was farmland on the outskirts of town, mountains within view of the city, and open spaces that gave it a small-town vibe. Still, the low crime rate did not make Moreno Valley safe.

Nevertheless, I started making the weekly drive. One night, I was returning home from a game and noticed a police car gaining on me fast. As he passed, the officer looked inside my car, slowed down, and changed lanes. Once he was in my lane and directly behind me, he slowed to allow approximately forty yards of distance between us. However, whenever I changed lanes, he changed lanes. He was following me.

With Rodney King's beating fresh on my mind, I began visualizing my part in potential scenarios if he were to pull me over. First, I considered whether I would pull over or continue a low-speed chase to a police station. I wouldn't say I liked the latter because there were too many unknowns. For example, they could set up a roadblock or spike strips. He could employ the PIT Maneuver, a pursuit intervention technique by which a pursuing car forces the fleeing vehicle to skid sideways abruptly. He could also call for backup. Those scenarios might result in evading police and gun charges for the 9mm pistol resting in my lap. There was so much to consider. Then again, Rodney King's beating began with a police chase. That was out. Then, there was the option of calling 9-1-1 or complying altogether. Again, I wouldn't say I liked any of the scenarios I was coming up with because each left too much to chance. Other events relied on someone to save me or the civility of the police officer who racially profiled me. I was disturbed more by the threat of brutality and death than by arrest. I was not taking a beat down. My family built me differently. A video of me taking a beating won't be my viral recording.

I told myself that I would stop if the officer turned on his lights to pull me over. First, I would go through my learned routine from years of training. I would gather my driver's license, registration, and proof of insurance before stopping. I would also have my window down before he arrived at my car. Then, I would position my hands on the steering wheel at 10 and 2 o'clock with the items I retrieved in them. My father quizzed me many times on this routine. Still, my heart was pounding fast.

The officer sped up and started closing the gap between us. I had to think fast. After a quick prayer, I decided to go along with the stop unless he said the magic words, "step out of the car." To utter those words would constitute a threat that would cost our lives. I had chosen self-defense over passivity and visualized the scene. I was going to shoot him with every bullet in the gun. Then, I'd call my family for a final conversation before dying in a hail of gunfire when his cavalry came. There would be no other way for an alleged cop-killer. Isn't it incredible how your mind races when multiple options exist? Yet, when I settled on one option, my spirit, which stirred moments earlier, quieted and became still. I turned on my left blinker and changed lanes. Seconds later, he changed lanes. I drove approximately one mile and turned on my right blinker. This time, when I changed lanes, he changed lanes simultaneously.

My eyes glossed over like I was driving in a fog. All I saw was a vision of the officer stumbling back from the impact of fifteen hollow point bullets rupturing his body. I thought about how my parents and siblings would get the news. What story would the police give the press to tell? Would the official narrative be that I was a bandit, a gun-wielding drug dealer, and a gang-affiliated man on the run?

The scene was a dreamy, slow-motion fog different from other slow-motion experiences. This one felt more like a chaotic daydream I snapped out of as I settled on my choice, like coming out of hypnosis. Then miraculously, I saw something that I had never seen before. An exit that I don't remember came out of nowhere. I figured this was God giving me a way out. The ramp snuck up on me so fast that there was no time for a blinker. I swerved through the shoulder's loose gravel, down the ramp, and turned right into a gas station. I pulled up to a pump and turned off my car's engine. My hands were shaking, and my mind couldn't will them to stop. After a few deep breaths, I looked in my driver's side mirror.

The police officer had exited behind me. He entered the gas station and stopped in front of the vacuum/air machine. I got out of the car, filled with more adrenaline than reason. With my arms outstretched into a Y position, I walked toward his car, yelling, "What do you want? What? What?" He waited until I was about a car length away and still approaching. Then, he turned his steering wheel in my direction, stepped on the gas, causing his tires to squeal, and drove past me. He didn't slam into me because I jumped sideways off two feet and sprang further off one. He came so close to taking me out! I watched as he drove away.

The highway patrolman seemed to lose the thrill of tailing me for 'driving while Black' because he turned onto the onramp in the opposite direction of my destination. That happens. Sometimes the thrill of harassment wanes. Perhaps didn't stop me because there was no legal reason to back it up. That's not it. I gave him an excuse when I exited without using my blinker. Maybe this officer was returning to where he started, looking to profile another person racially and then another. We have learned that monsters reset their traps to manufacture horror, like Frankenstein's monster in the haunted house. Alternatively, he was pleased with himself and had enough. Regardless of his reason for starting and stopping his harassment, the most important thing for us was that he didn't pull me over and ask me to get out of my car.

The chase took less than five minutes. Still, I learned a few things about myself. First, I realized I had reached my breaking point. Everybody has one. Mom's break was in the pool, and dad's was executing a bird. Mine was the decision to kill a cop if he "cornered" me. It is in that mental space where training and reason no longer matter. A breaking point is the only way I would have stooped as low as someone else's poor behavior and been okay with it.

Our minds in crisis can justify and accept the consequences of poor judgment that would otherwise be out of character. This experience gave new meaning to my Uncle Eddie's words: "Don't mess with people because you never know who you are messin' with or what they are going through. Some people aren't in their right minds.

So just leave people alone."

The cop nearly learned the significance of my uncle's message. There is a reason to suspect that I'm not too fond of the police. Well, you got that right! It remains a sensitive issue. Nevertheless, the theme of this chapter is not about police officers or the judicial system. Although the fictional and real characters provide excellent examples of an organization mired in ineptitude and hostility, this chapter screams, "Control you!" Like I did, you may need help regaining such control. What seemed rational at the time was foolish and extreme. This chapter also demonstrates that unfortunate circumstances have no respect for people. Nobody is exempt. Hardships impact everyone. Unfortunately, for some people, communicating power over you is their message. Therefore, you may have defined yourself, arranged perfect stones in your backpack, and controlled all you could, only for life to still find a way to hand you adversity. How you deal with those difficulties influences whether you emerge or plunge.

Even though my examples varied in classification and seriousness, I made decisions that could have tragically changed the course of my life. I indeed made matters worse because I hadn't dealt with past trauma. Therefore, a secondary moral is that we do a pretty good job of being thankful for what we think we deserve—the good that happens. On the other hand, we may also want to be grateful for what doesn't happen.

Growing older and much wiser, I recognized that my chronic trauma regarding the police influenced how I moved in society. In other words, I had unwittingly hauled many stones in my backpack. Each connects to past interactions with the US justice system. Suppose those rocks represent distrust, hatred, fear, anxiety, intense feelings, and resentment. That's a lot of weight to carry. The risk of keeping them was burdensome. The danger of discarding them, I thought, underestimated an everyday threat. As it turns out, I replaced some of the stones. I substituted distrust, hatred, fear, and anxiety for caution. Caution was a practical choice, given the onslaught of viral videos 30-plus years later: George Floyd, Daunte Wright, Ahmad Aubrey, Tyre Nichols, and many others. Lastly, I discarded resentment and intense feelings as unhelpful, further lightening my load.

As I noted earlier, connecting to who we are is an ongoing process toward bringing our lives into their natural rhythm. This cadence regulates the energy required to act and react with the judgment that propels motion. Not surprisingly, your rhythm will sort behaviors that lead to setbacks as distractions, ultimately rendering them expendable. Therefore, when we change as individuals, everything around us also changes. Unfortunately, my rhythm could have been better. I saw how distractions or mishandling mishaps resulted in wasted energy only in hindsight.

Nevertheless, there is something about knowing who you are that no longer requires actively searching to answer our questions of purpose. Instead, you move, elevating instinctively. Think of how bloodhounds sniff for remnants of the scent. That's us searching for meaning. Once the dogs pick up the smell, their attention, energy, focus, and behavior drive them in specific directions. They no longer wander sporadically. Likewise, we generate fuel from learning how we tick. The more we know, the more we want to learn. Like that bloodhound, we confidently move in a distinct direction and pace, discovering parts of ourselves never imagined. Meanwhile, people who live their lives consumed by hate and resentment, masked as purpose, must also live hating and resenting: a well-earned epithet indeed.

CHAPTER TWENTY
CROSS-COUNTRY TRIP

The year was 1994, and I was in Hollywood, California, clubbing into the wee hours during Dr. Martin Luther King, Jr.'s holiday weekend. I had just left a club and walked into a hotel lobby. Then suddenly, the ground started shaking, and windows shattered. People were screaming and running as I tried to maintain my balance by taking steps to the right and left, like being on a rolling ship tossed by raging waters. I had experienced mild earthquakes before. This quake was mighty, destructive, and deadly.

This quake was named the Northridge earthquake because the quake's epicenter was in Northridge, California, just a few minutes from where I was. Southern California sustained considerable damage, and Los Angeles got the worst. Buildings crumbled. Gas lines broke. Power lines snapped, making it dangerous to drive on the streets, especially in neighborhoods. No matter how straight the drivers steered, their cars veered toward other vehicles because the ground moved beneath them. Seeing yourself driving within lanes and running into oncoming traffic was an optical distortion that caused many accidents. There was also significant damage to bridges and roads, sudden sinkholes, and puckering overpasses. A freeway exit ramp collapsed, and a motorcycle officer drove off it and died.

I'm not a native Californian, but I wasn't concerned about earthquakes until then. The damage an earthquake could do to a city within approximately 20 seconds was mind-boggling. The aftershocks were strong as well. The morning after the quake, I started looking for a job out of state. It was understandable. Living in a city where experts could forecast natural disasters was best. Within a few weeks, I accepted a position in North Carolina.

At that time, I had a co-worker and friend named Jean Williams. She was an older woman, a senior citizen, whom I greatly respected. Sometimes we would spend our lunch breaks together, and she would tell me about her activism in the 60s. I loved her stories. When I told Jean I would leave California, she took it hard and even got emotional. One day, we passed each other in a hallway, and she asked me to step into a conference room.

"Have a seat," she said.

This approach seemed different from other moments of coming together; it felt more formal and rehearsed.

She said, "I'm in the process of getting you a going away present and I need your blessing. I want you to have something to remember me."

"I don't need anything to remember you. I would never forget you, Jean. I have our conversations as memories," I said.

"Just hear me out," she snapped back. "I've applied for personalized license plates for your

new car. I know it's a personal thing, so I would like to get your permission, after having done it."

"Oh no, you don't have to do that," I said. My mind wandered briefly to something cheesy. The last thing I wanted was a license plate that did not represent me. That would be like somebody hanging art in your house that you didn't like. That mess would throw you off. You would be dissatisfied with every room you entered that displayed the pieces and wouldn't rest until you replaced them.

"There you go again," she said. "Just hear me out. The license plate would read, 18K-BLK. You see, 18 karats refer to the strongest gold you can get before it starts turning soft, and I think you are a strong Black man. So, your plate would read 18 karats Black. It sounds very masculine and strong; it's you," she said.

I needed a few moments to collect my thoughts, which Jean may have taken as rejection.

"I thought you'd like it," she added.

I gestured with both hands, the nonthreatening, universal motion for stopping or slowing down, and I said, "I love it. I am flattered and deeply honored by the gesture. You clearly put a lot of thought into my gift. It symbolizes strength and purpose, and I believe it would represent me well. Above all that, this license plate is a conversation piece. Every time somebody asks about my plate, I will tell them the story about us. I accept your gift. Thank you."

She teared up as we hugged, and we went back to work.

I planned my cross-country trip to go through Nevada, a small portion of Utah, and then across the mind-numbingly flat Interstate 70, which included passing through Colorado and Kansas. Jean told me I should time my trip. So I crossed Utah early in the morning. She said an officer would stop a Black man driving a new sports car.

The day came, and I left California. As planned, I timed my trip to include a brief 90-minute stop in Las Vegas. I couldn't resist gambling, winning a little gas money playing blackjack, and maybe collecting a big enough haul to offset my moving costs. There was another reason. I was driving while Black, and that warrants contingency plans. I might win money to cover sham legal fees. Once again, "If you stay ready, you don't have to get ready." I also allowed enough wait time to see a judge should the worst happen and a rogue cop decides to throw me in jail after a bogus traffic stop.

I left Santa Barbara, California, and made my stop in Vegas. I was too nervous about gambling. If I were to go inside, I'd spend every moment in the casino thinking someone was burglarizing my car. I couldn't go for that. For one thing, I only considered that my personal belongings would be visible after I planned to stop. I was sure that if I thought about my stuff more than I thought about blackjack, I would surely lose money because gambling demands focus. Besides, I was on a tight schedule. I had to collect my possessions, which I shipped via ground transportation. So, after thinking for a few minutes, I continued driving. I sank into my bucket seat, resetting my cruise control each time the speed limit changed. Finally, after going through the night, I reached the Utah border.

When I drove past the sign, "Welcome to Utah," it was just after 6 AM. The speed limit dropped from 70 mph to 65 mph. A change in speed limit was standard approaching city boundaries. At the same time, wide-open highways posted much higher speed limits—something like that. However, my logic for the changes in the rate of speed was pure speculation.

Nevertheless, slowing down became a habit that might prevent encounters with the police. Understanding the moment, I set my cruise control to 55 mph, 10 miles per hour below the posted maximum. A vast grassy median separated three lanes going in each direction. Minutes would pass before I would see a car traveling in either direction. So far, so good; my trek through Utah might be uneventful. I continued straight ahead and noticed a state trooper driving toward me in the opposite direction. Judging from how he turned his head and strained to see me, I knew he would turn around. He watched me for a few seconds, rubbernecking toward the median. I watched in my rearview mirror. Turning to look might communicate guilt, and looking straight ahead was normal. "Damn," I thought. He couldn't help himself. Crossing over the median took a lot of work. Still, he barreled through the mud and craters. After catching up, he kept pace behind my car for approximately 3 miles. I'm sure he had run my license plates and knew everything about me before he turned on his lights. Finally, I could see the kaleidoscope of color cascading throughout my car without looking into my rearview mirror.

As I pulled over, I reached into my glove compartment. I retrieved my car's registration, insurance card, and driver's license. As my father and grandfather taught me, I positioned my left hand at 10 o'clock on the steering will, and in it was my driver's license. I placed my right hand at 2 o'clock on the steering wheel, and in it were my registration and proof of insurance. I let down my window as I slowed to stop.

Before asking for my driver's license, the state trooper stuck his head inside the driver's window, past my head, and into the backseat. There, he saw boxes and small items from my apartment that I decided not to ship, such as stereo equipment, mirrors, and lamps. Then, in the most abrasive tone, he hurled accusations in the form of questions.

"Are you sure all these things in here are yours and none of it is stolen? Do you have receipts for this stuff?"

"Sir, I assume you would like to see my driver's license and tell me why you stopped me."

"Do you have any stolen merchandise in your car?" he asked harshly.

Unmoved, I replied, "Feel free to handcuff me, sit me on the curb, and search through every serial number for stolen items. I thought this might happen. So I planned to come early, and I have all day. It is about to snow. I have a lot in my car. You should get started. However, before you do, I would appreciate you telling why you stopped me."

"I stopped you for speeding," he said, snatching the driver's license from my hand.

His snatching move was so demonstrative that he dropped my insurance card. Having to reach for the ground made him angrier. He returned to his squad car for what must have been an extended donut break, but I'm sure it was an effort to annoy me.

Finally, after approximately 20 minutes, he returned and asked, "Does your license plate refer to a gang set in California? You one of them Crips or Bloods?"

He accepted my slow, shaking head as an answer and handed me a speeding ticket. The citation read 75 miles per hour in a 65—representing the ubiquitous pettiness when non-white civilians don't bow down to the badge. I tried to mask my anger with a sly smile that communicated what I could not say: "This ain't my last couple of hundred bucks, you crooked-ass cop."

His continued presence let me know he got my message loud and clear. Most officers leave once they issue the ticket. Instead, he stood at my window until I returned my items and watched as I tossed the citation on the floor with the empty water bottles and candy wrappers. Bravado and pridefulness aside, I was relieved to be cited. Alternative endings could have been far worse. Depending on Utah laws, a crooked judge could pile on charges, including traveling with loaded firearms. Therefore, there was no sense in arguing that I had set my cruise control to 55 mph. He knew that I knew the fallacy of what he'd done. I considered the ticket amount a toll for crossing through Utah and a small price I'd pay for my dignity. I would never kiss the badge.

My adrenaline was high as I drove away. I wasn't thinking about where to stop, but it wouldn't be in Utah. After driving for many more hours, I was well into Colorado. I passed Denver and every other city with name recognition. As my adrenaline faded, I started to get tired. I didn't need gas. Instead, I needed caffeine and sugar. So, I decided to pull over at the next gas station or truck stop to get my customary driving food. It consisted of NoDoz, a familiar pill college students took to stay awake when cramming for exams. A bottle of Mountain Dew was on the list, also for its caffeine and not the taste. To supply my sugar high, I could not deny a family-sized bag of Doritos, a package of strawberry Twizzlers, and two giant rolls of SweeTARTS.

I pulled into a gas station and parked. Then, I grabbed my guns and placed the 9mm inside my waistband and the .22 semi-automatic in my jacket pocket. Everybody stopped and looked at me when I opened the door and walked in. This moment was reminiscent of a scene in a movie. Like the "oh crap" moment when a fleeing criminal realizes he ran into a police bar varnishing a weapon, and 50 officers aim with theirs. I mentally noted the scene and walked hurriedly to the restroom. When I withhold the urge to urinate for too long, my body seems to know when I'm close to one, and then I feel like I might pee myself any second. When I reached the bathroom door, I read, "Kill all the niggers." Someone with perfect penmanship had drawn the comment in permanent marker on the bathroom door. Therefore, I entered the bathroom and kept one hand on my gun as I relieved myself. Management should have had the decency to erase or paint over the slur. So, to piss' in that building was all they would get from me. I had my pride. I couldn't stand at the counter, be insulted, and hand over hard-earned money. Once again, I hit the road filled with adrenaline, hoping to find friendlier vibes at my next stop.

I drove until my gas gauge read a quarter tank. I pulled into the next gas station, put the nozzle into the tank, and went inside for caffeine and snacks. I noticed a different sign on the door when I went to the bathroom. The words were the same. However, this time someone posted a raggedy wooden sign with the words carved into it. There was no shock value this time, and wisdom outweighed my protest. I bought the items I needed and made it a point to get a bag and a receipt. The cashier offered neither. My uncle Sherman said always ask for a bag and a receipt. That way, proof of purchase would disprove petty shoplifting accusations. By then, my gas had finished pumping. Unaware of whether I was in or near a sundown town,[5] I called my mother and gave her my estimated arrival time. Somebody had to know where I was and that I was driving straight through. It felt good to make it home without further incident. After seeing everyone, my brother convinced me to play basketball at the playground. After 29 1/2 hours of driving, only the adrenaline of seeing him kept me going.

During the final leg of my drive, Andre, my college roommate, started his four-and-a-half-hour trek to my parent's house. We hadn't seen each other in over four years. Yet seamlessly, we picked up where we left off without missing a beat. We talked for about an hour before Andre took a brief nap. My father woke him after 45 minutes. Then, Andre returned to Iowa for the start of his second job. As Andre drove away, my father looked at me and said, "That's your friend," in a tone that suggested I only have one.

After a good night's sleep, I drove the remaining 18 hours to Raleigh, North Carolina, without incident. On that trip across the country, the significance of elders in my family praying for traveling mercies was never more evident. Before anybody was about to leave town, we prayed, in person or by phone, for the traveler's safe passage and protection from unseen dangers. In other words, prayer covered me from known or foreseeable threats. I was even spiritually protected from myself as I verbally sparred with a state trooper or slept behind the wheel. You may be sitting and thinking, "What's the big deal?" First, I could have lost money at the blackjack table. Lord knows I didn't have it to lose. Second, driving alone through Utah could easily have landed me in a small-town jail for being Black. As we know,

---

[5] A sundown town or city in the United States excludes non-white residents, particularly African Americans, through discriminatory laws, intimidation, and violence. The name "sundown town" refers to warning African Americans and other minorities to leave by sunset.

SECTION SIX • CONTROL WHAT YOU CAN

there were many dangers in that, many that could have cost me my life. There was also the threat of organized hate, known and unknown. That threat level rose when I stopped and dropped when I was moving. On top of that, I suffered from exhaustion, which meant that sometimes God had hold of my steering wheel. It is the only explanation for waking up after dozing off, finding myself centered perfectly in my lane, and maintaining the speed limit.

I did not take for granted the feeling of safety, relief, and thankfulness when I parked in front of my new apartment in Raleigh. It was time for a quick walk-through because UPS would deliver my belongings in a few hours. I arrived on time, filled with expectations. Fundamentally, there's nothing like starting fresh—strange roads to travel, new surroundings to frequent, new faces to learn, a change in pace, and even acclimating to different air and pollen. Even though I was 2,000 miles away, telling and retelling the story of Jean and my license plate made me feel connected. As a piece of California, my friendship with Jean was still with me. Through the years, Jean, and sometimes my colleagues, asked me whether I still had the plate. Five years later, I moved back to Southern California, and many more years passed. Jean had died. I may have officially given up the plate. However, since Georgia only requires a rear plate, 18K-BLK is fastened to my front bumper. I miss my friend, turned angel and ancestor. May Jean rest in peace.

CHAPTER TWENTY-ONE
CROSS-COUNTRY TRIP

<u>Scene 0</u>

A person speaks, and two figures sit on opposite shoulders, ready to inform.

PERSON
    I'm thinking of cheating.

ANGEL
    Don't do it. Cheating is not who you are.

DEVIL
    He doesn't appreciate you. You should be sick of his crap. He doesn't even take you out anymore and you deserve better.

PERSON
    Cheating would be wrong. But he's not even trying.

ANGEL
    Communicate how you feel and work together to find a solution.

DEVIL
    Why bother? Your new friend appreciates you. Being with him will be exciting, and your husband will never know.

We know this scene all too well. The angel displays wings, a halo, and a kind expression, offering positive, moral advice. On the other hand, the devil dons horns, a pitchfork, and a mischievous face, offering tempting, harmful advice. This metaphor represents our internal battle between right and wrong, good versus evil. Whatever names you wish to give, the energy remains the restraint or the nudge tailormade for the decisions we face in our lives. Your headspace is the battleground.

I chose duplicitous dialogue and opposing motivations, each with entirely different and often mutually exclusive ideas about what makes life fulfilling. Cheating is also a relatable quandary. Thus, my thoughts here are simple. We must discuss our competing impulses to be 100% honest about getting unstuck. Unfortunately, the cheating phenomenon in the United States thrives in every community. Therefore, we can reasonably say that cheating is rampant and takes place on both sides of partnerships. More married women have propositioned me or hinted at illicit entanglements than I remember. In addition, I've been part of conversations where men have normalized their infidelity. Even so, I will say such moral dilemmas are preventable.

Fortunately, adultery was never my issue. I knew I was a natural flirt and was good at that game until someone flirted back. Then, escape was also intuitive. The more I thought about it, I was playing the immature game of chicken. I recall staying ready to pivot as I'd turn and run if women showed me any rhythm. I knew all along that I didn't want to be bothered. The flirt was my fix. However, to linger while flirting meant I was interested, and she was 100% available. The alternative would involve sneaking around or looking over my shoulder, which I viewed as unnecessary, dangerous, and against my values.

Now and again, I'd reflect on my role in a messy entanglement many years ago. As you remember, Evelyn wasn't my proudest moment. I will never know whether she deliberately withheld being married and not wearing her wedding ring. Either way, the incident taught me the relationship between suppressing moral voices and getting caught up in a mess. Both are linked to people becoming the philanderer or trollop the devil uses to tempt conflicted spouses.

The goal of the demon spirit is to hollow you from the inside, destroy you, and outwardly keep you stuck by coaxing you toward what you like. To fess up all the way, cravings are hard to stop because most people are not fully ready to do without them. For example, we know the dieter who hides cookies, the smoker who bums cigarettes, and the gambler who "only plays the lottery." Let's add that I'm the wellness professional and admitted cereal-head who buys single servings of Frosted

Flakes despite wanting to shed a few pounds. Unfortunately, every person in the examples above is stuck if we don't control our cravings. Thus, a vice doesn't have to be perverse, only something you repeatedly do that you know holds you back. It makes you less productive. Perhaps it serves as an unwanted distraction. But trust and believe your demon knows how to engage your triggers and cravings.

Now, imagine that you listened to the tempting spirit and drank despite your recovery, ogled the beautiful woman walking with her husband, bet on the big game, played poker, or blew a wad of cash on a shopping spree. Whatever vice provides sudden, brief satisfaction also keeps you on the proverbial hamster wheel. Therefore, the gatekeeper of our breakthroughs is our mind and our ability to overcome the only three things the world can offer: the desires of the flesh, the lusts of the eyes, or the pride of life. So, as we subject ourselves to wild goose chases to satisfy what feels good, looks good, and brings accolades, we are going nowhere. Thus, if I've learned anything about chasing worldly desires, it epitomizes what it means to be moving and still be stuck.

Some people try very hard and still blow off their principled voices. Then, they wonder why they cannot stay off the websites that make them run everywhere 10 to 15 minutes late because porn is a priority. Others make deals with the truth because lying is their vice. Then, they will justify succumbing to their comforts because they "deserve it" or "God has a plan." Picking an excuse is easy because any will do. If you find yourself stuck in a vice, remember that all limiting behaviors embody the desires of the flesh, the lusts of the eyes, or the pride of life. That's biblical (1 John 2:16 NIV).

The negative spirit resorts to trickery—allowing you to subdue your vice at times—to make you think you have it under control. Then, the urge returns with a vengeance and makes everything sacrificial (e.g., work, exercise, relationships, and social commitments). Before you realize that the menacing thing keeping you stuck is not on individual shoulders, it comes to you in the voices of friends, in social media posts, and in your head, using comfort cravings to hold you stuck. To reiterate, we want to keep some behaviors despite their damage. Yes, I said "damage."

For example, there was a student who was flunking out of college.

While concluding a long strategy session on time management and study skills, I asked her, "Are you easily distracted?"

That would be a logical question for a student falling behind in school. I expected her to rattle off the usual suspects: social media, friends, television, recreation, and family drama.

Instead, she dropped her head and said bashfully, "I'm easily distracted by guys, sexually."

I sat in a brief moment of stunned silence but managed my facial expressions as she continued: "It doesn't matter if I have a midterm exam to study for or a paper due the following day. If somebody calls me and wants to have sex, I'm going."

"Somebody?" I asked as I felt my look turn from blank-faced to fatherly disbelief.

"Yes. I know what you're going to say. I will still flunk out of school for sex. It can be from anybody with the right vibe. Sex is not always on my mind. But I will never turn it down."

She body-slammed all reason. That was a conversation I shall never forget. It shook me into understanding that "out of sight, out of mind" is another lie we tell ourselves to feign control. Therefore, as the student battled hypersexuality, she mistakenly thought she'd be fine if her phone didn't ring. Little did she know that subconsciously fixating manifested her strongest desires. Suppose you recall the dreams section of this book. We agreed that the things we crave become the content of our thoughts and dreams. Then, the Bible confirmed the power of our thoughts and dreams and admonished us to hold them captive. In other words, we create images and manifest futures through our thoughts, dreams, and daydreams. Therefore, it would behoove us to seek desires and habits that support our uplift.

Thus, we cannot run and hide from our vices. Deny them if you will. Meanwhile, there's no hiding place from yourself. That nudge is especially yours. It may let you think you have the upper hand, as your nemesis waits to catch you when you need a fix. Then, when you approve, it delivers. Overcome by guilt and despair, you face starting all over, sobered by the reality that battles for our minds are continuous.

However, always on time, God's voice rises above the shoulder dwellers who stand in as our conscience. When heard, God's message reveals a sobering clarity. For example, think about the times you prepared to go somewhere and maybe even been excited about going. Then, it suddenly dawned on you that you should stay home. Through conversations later, you found out that you avoided an accident or some other drama by staying home.

I walked home alone after school one day because my coach canceled basketball practice. Otherwise, I would have been on the activity bus with my sister going to the gym. When I climbed the stairs, I noticed our front door ajar. Something told me not to burst in like I usually would. Instead, I tiptoed across the edges of the wooden porch, not to make a sound, and peeked inside. Someone had smashed a mustard jar against our television screen, and they ransacked our living room. Next,

I heard a noise. That same something that told me to be cautious told me to run. I ran back to school to call my dad at work. A burglary in progress qualified as a situation in need of his thunder. Then, I called Mom for my next steps as Dad instructed. One of the items stolen by the intruders was my father's handgun, a Smith & Wesson .38 special with a hair trigger. That gun could shoot an unsuspecting round if you shook it. Thus, walking in on the assailants could have cost me my life even if they pointed the gun intending only to scare me.

A few months later, my father and I were visiting our next-door neighbor, who was also the father of one of the three boys my father had made me fight before. Everything was light and fun until my father leaned against the mantle and saw his stolen .38 hidden behind a picture frame. He grabbed the gun and held it up to check for familiar markings. Someone had filed off part of the serial number. Then, my father flipped open the cylinder and confirmed it was fully loaded. With his gun in his hand, my father ordered me to go home. I only heard one booming voice as I ran home to tell mom. Dad was bringing the thunder. When dad finally returned, he had a box of recovered items; some may have been "replacement" items. He also shared the story of his street justice.

In another example of divine communication, one of my uncles was on assignment at the Hyatt Regency Hotel. There was a large party that night. My uncle said he stood under the skywalks watching the festivities, not necessarily participating in them. Suddenly, he had to go to the restroom. How many times do we choose to fight the urge when something exciting or enjoyable is happening? He could have decided to wait. But he said God physically and audibly urged him to go immediately.

My uncle walked quickly because of God's command and having to answer nature's call. Then, loud gasps compelled him to look toward where he once stood. His jaw fell open as the fourth-floor walkway had dropped several inches. Next, one skywalk fell onto another, causing both to collapse onto a crowded lobby floor, killing 114 people and injuring 216.

Is the phenomenon of hearing from God real? At the time, I didn't think so. Nevertheless, my uncle said God's voice was real and that the voice of God told him to move. More than that, my uncle listened. Listening is active and can be interactive. In other words, hearing from God does not have to be one-sided, nor does it have to be by chance.

We may bear more responsibility for communicating with God than we want to admit. However, communication from God does not have to be a seismic event by which something unique happens. Therefore, our speaking and listening work both ways.

When I didn't know what to say, I said, "Thanks, God." We all have something for which to thank God. When I became more comfortable speaking with God, I thanked him for a list of things, starting with waking me up that day. As our relationship grew, my conversations increased in frequency, depth, and scope. Eventually, all formalities were gone. Now, talking to God may sound like I am speaking with another human being on a phone call.

From the start, there was no need to worry about how God felt about me. God's certainty was different from the uncertainty involved with approaching strangers. Indeed, there would be some who may reject my overture. However, the Bible says God loved us first. Therefore, we could never be strangers to Him. In other words, if our relationship doesn't happen, we are responsible for rejecting Him. With God, we don't need a phone number, email address, teleconference invite, or date. All we must do is start talking. Talk to God about anything and everything—big or small, profound or mundane. Remember, like in any relationship, ongoing communication strengthens bonds, and thorough communication builds trust and increases both parties' faith in one another. A direct line to God is powerful.

If you're anything like me, the next logical question is how does God communicate with us, or how do we even know He's listening? Again, I am no theologian. Still, I have found many scriptures that speak to God being the same and His word never changing. For example, Malachi 3:6 (Amplified Bible) says, "For I am The Lord, I do not change." This truth means that God's word, will, and attributes are the same today. There is no need to change what is perfect. Therefore, God still communicates with us in the ways He has always shared.

God speaks through an audible voice, and that's one voice I'd love to hear. Some people report hearing the actual voice of God, like my uncle, who responded by moving from underneath the hotel's skywalks that collapsed moments later. God also communicates by sending messengers. For example, a theme may be repeated in a sermon or random conversations you may have, which may serve as confirmation to go one way or another. Occasionally, God uses signs, the Bible, and mass media to communicate with us. For example, God reveals much to me when I'm taking showers. I know when the message is from Him; He makes it evident by making the complex simple.

I would love to say that I know God is speaking because his presence heats my blood, my skin may get a prickly sensation, or an electric feeling precedes mental calmness and emotional stillness, which feels different from the stress-reducing effects of the sound of water. However, no cosmic or cognitive power surge ushers into my mind the voice of God. Instead, while my mind focuses on soaping and rinsing, the most precise, most straight-up messages divert my attention to whatever was my problem. I'm stunned, present, and suddenly full of answers, which He gives so effortlessly. Sometimes, I jump out of the shower to jot down God's revelations. I usually say, "Thanks God," a couple of times while typing or scribbling enough of the message to revisit it more accurately later.

For this reason, I shower with my cell phone on the bathroom sink. Sometimes, I put a notepad and pen next to my toothbrush. Then, when I need to decide on the next step, or if something stumps me, I head to the shower expecting answers. Even though I figure out a lot in the shower, God communicates primarily through my dreams. Thus, there must be a correlation between our quieted mind and God's presence. This is quietness in the sense that soaping and rinsing do not require thinking and hardly qualify as overload. Or perhaps our minds are too inefficient to get what God has for us in a 15-20-minute shower. Maybe in those cases, God uses sleep and osmosis learning. All I know is that God still speaks through visions and dreams.

In other words, how God communicates to us is as old as the earth itself. God appeared in the burning bush. He told Abraham that He was his shield. God directed Joseph to flee Egypt, granted Solomon his request for wisdom, and instructed my uncle to move from under the collapsing skywalks. You get the point. Therefore, I presume that just because we may have stopped listening doesn't mean God isn't speaking and using His traditional communication methods. The good news is that God still speaks to you if you are alive. The question now becomes, are you willing to listen?

My relationship with God evolved, but not always on good terms. Sure, there were times when we were smoothly in step, and it was easy for me to trust Him. I remember those moments when my life seemed without challenges. I had no debt, held an excellent job, had great friends, was in optimal health, and enjoyed frequent travel. It was easy to trust God. I remember describing those periods as heaven on earth, at times losing sight that this is still earth and that everyday life is supposed to include struggle. Like many well-intentioned Christians, I sought fewer conversations with God during good times. Human beings are fickle and ungrateful. It is counterintuitive and commonplace to seek God less when we perceive that we need less. Then, we opt for anger and unbelief when God doesn't come to our beck and call as life turns hard. I am no different.

The Lord and I debated; sometimes, I got mad at Him, and resentment grew as trust waned. How dare God stand by and not be my fixer. Don't be too alarmed. God would know how I felt regardless of whether I kept my feelings to myself. Airing feelings and concerns in a relationship is honest and builds stronger bonds for all involved. In other words, parties in any real relationship will overcome conflict. Like my competitions with mom, my debates with God were one-sided. I lost them 100 percent of the time, and often I discovered clarity and understanding after time passed. God's wisdom doesn't come with every shower. I sometimes wait a long time for answers, and sometimes His response is for me to wait. That's frustrating. Remember though, Jesus told us that asking, and waiting are not punitive, and that timing is everything. For example, in John 13: 7 (NIV), Jesus replied, "You do not realize now what I'm doing, but later you will understand." Thus, if His response was sufficient for His disciples, I, too, should use His words to mitigate worry and doubt. Indeed, relationships are a process. God has pulled me from death's door many times. I've fallen asleep on the freeway and awakened in my driveway. Both hoodlums and cops have held me at gunpoint. I have swerved to avoid deer and other head-on collisions. Near misses while riding my motorcycles were routine. The situations were so big that I knew surviving had to be God. Yet, even after all of that, I was ungrateful.

One day, I was sitting in my car after visiting a friend at Loyola Marymount in Los Angeles. I was frustrated and questioning everything about my life and God's role. I took sole credit for all that God had done for me. My words were sharp, questioning, and disrespectful, and God did not ignore them. My verbal rant went like this: "Why am I trying to live right? Rappers, thugs, racists, swindlers, and dirty politicians are all making money and living a good life. All these religions are out there, some older than Christianity. I don't know what makes Christianity right. I'm at the point where I can handle whatever life sends my way. I'm going to start doing what I want to do. Maybe God ain't real."

God must have taken my last four words as a challenge, like when a teenage boy tests the physical strength of his father. Suddenly, my heartbeat was noticeably audible. I checked my stereo for sound, but my car wasn't running. I could hear my heartbeat slow down, and the sound was fading, like moments before the flatline buzz. Simultaneously, my body weakened. I fumbled with the door handle and managed to open it. I didn't have the arm strength to push it open. Then, I used my foot. Once the door opened and my left foot hit the pavement, I sat slumped and powerless. Falling out of the car, I had the presence of mind to call out, "Lord, I know you are real, and I believe."

With that, my heartbeat picked up, and I could hear when it reached its average pace. After that, I never again questioned God's power or whether he could contact me, steer me from the desires of the flesh, lust of the eyes, or pride of life.

Nevertheless, those of us who want to win, and overcome our vices, also feel awful when we give in to our temptations. Guilt, shame, and the feeling of getting older without defeating our offense can be depressing. However, the truth is, seeing the difference between a great "no" and a bad "yes" can be challenging; discernment is a real thing. So is questioning our strengths at our low points. Please stop it. Instead, embrace the reality that this battle for our minds is ongoing.

Giving in to a different way of thinking can be as challenging as changing your walk or run. However, as a preteen, my sister corrected her stride by thinking about it all the time. All of us can get there! Then, we'll be free to manifest different outcomes from new habits formed with gratitude rather than shame, lack, or feelings of inadequacy. Here, I would like to emphasize the significance of gratitude on our path to emergence.

When practicing gratitude, your focus shifts from what you don't have to what you do have. You acknowledge the abundance that is already present in your life. This mindset can help you cultivate a sense of contentment and joy, which can, in turn, help you attract more positive experiences and blessings and neutralize the voices of divisive spirits.

Additionally, when you express gratitude for the things you desire, you acknowledge that they are already present in your life, even if you haven't experienced them physically. This belief can help you align your thoughts and emotions with the energy of abundance and manifestation, which can help bring your desires into reality.

However, it is important to note that speaking gratitude alone is not enough to manifest your desires. It is also essential to take inspired action, trust in God's plan, and remain open to receiving your blessings in the ways and timing that align with His will.

CHAPTER TWENTY-TWO
ACCEPTING DOES NOT MEAN GIVING UP

Have you ever been so sure of something until you weren't? For example, your candidate is a clear favorite but loses the election. You could have trusted a financial investment was safe until the market crashed or the company went bankrupt. Or a company may have discontinued your perfect room or cologne fragrance. Sometimes life's sucker punch can be jarring, like one of mine.

I met the sweetest woman at a party many years ago; let's call her Janay. As I recall, Janay's girlfriends influenced her to go out for a good time, and with any luck, they hoped she would meet a great guy. Ahem, I'm the great guy in this story. Janay was open to a night on the town. It was a celebratory evening commemorating Janay's final exit from an abusive relationship. She had also completed her move into a new apartment. She felt lucky and free to no longer live with her abuser, even though clubs and parties were outlets outside her comfort zone.

Like me, Janay was a content people watcher. We even caught each other staring at one another several times. However, each time, her eyes darted to the ceiling. Then, she faked moving to the beat and mouthing lyrics. Neither move matched, and she knew it; they were just two reactions intended to deflect my attention. Instantly, I felt no pressure to ask her to dance. Thank goodness. I had two left feet, and her awkwardness was authentic. Therefore, I threw caution to the wind without anything for her to judge except for my appearance and approach.

I moved toward her through the crowd. Even as she turned away, her energy drew me. I busted her, trying to look at me peripherally, letting me know she felt my approach. I gave the appropriate number of "excuse me's" while interrupting the conversations amongst her group and asked to speak with her. She gave a wide-eyed glance in the direction of her friends. In return, they encouraged her by shouting over the music, "Go on girl," "All right now," and "You better handle your business."

She paused long enough to infect me with her uncertainty. Then, just when I thought she'd leave me hanging, she said, "Uh sure." I knew her response was for me because she moved toward me while eyeballing her friends. We stepped aside and talked for hours.

After that night, our phone conversations ended, with neither of us wanting to be the first to hang up.

"Hang up."

"No, you hang up."

"Okay, we'll hang up at the same time, on the count of three: 1, 2, 3."

"You were supposed to hang up."

"Okay, okay. Let's do it again. 1, 2, 3, click."

Adorable, I know. We got along great and dated long-distance during the summer months. I was a rising college junior, and she was a registered nurse, working and living in a small city two-and-a-half hours away. But once fall classes and my football season recommenced, we agreed that the distance between us and our mismatched schedules were formidable barriers to relationship building. So, we decided to call it quits with no hard feelings. Ending this dating relationship was like other breakups. I never severed ties on bad terms. It was always civil. Besides, when we met, we agreed that we would always respect each other, even if our dating ended.

We knew that breaking up was the right thing to do. Even so, I thought about Janay more often than I should. I had vivid flashbacks of our laughs, our hugs, and our spirited conversations. We did everything with all our might. However, for a good reason back then, I had a policy to never get back together with someone after a breakup; unfortunately, circumstances that lead to divisions don't change.

Some may need to debate my unwritten policy. However, without reading ahead, you know I broke it if I am writing about it. One spring day, without motive or hidden agenda, I called Janay. While our conversation was light, our feelings seemed substantial, measured in visceral terms. Thus, putting aside our tight schedules and the physical distance between us, I drove two and a half hours to see her the following day. If my interpretation of our conversation was correct, she might also be happy to see me. Still, positive self-talk did little to quell my nerves as I drove to the small city's hospital and parked. I guessed her work schedule from clues gleaned from our conversation. I knew that she'd soon head home. By the way, my trip was endearing, not stalkerish. Flip our schedules, and she would have done the same thing because, yeah, I gave clues too. I drove at warp speed and arrived with minutes to spare.

Soon afterward, Janay walked through the exit doors and toward her car. I exited my car and stood silhouetted in front of an illuminating parking lot light overhead. As Janay slowed, she changed her expression from tired and worn to beaming as she began recognizing me.

Finally, with outstretched arms, I yelled, "Janay!"

"What are you doing here, she asked, covering her mouth with both hands.

Once her shock passed, we ran toward each other and hugged like old friends. We talked for about an hour enthusiastically and charmed one another like the night we met. Then, reality returned. She must be tired. Wanting to respect her time and that she had just finished a 12-hour shift, I offered the typical closing statement:

"It was nice to see you. I'd better go."

I told her which nearby hotel I'd chosen. It was important to convey that I was unassuming about where I might spend the night. I also added that a quick "hi" and "bye" in the morning would be cool, as she goes to work and before I drive back to campus.

"I have an early shift tomorrow, but we'll see," Janay said softly. Her tone was melancholy, and her eyes were sad. "It was good to see you, too," she added.

While this goodbye seemed different from before, the conditions that led to our breakup had not changed. Our lives were divergent in ways beyond physical distance. For example, I had school and sports, while Janay had an exhausting full-time job with an unpredictable schedule. Janay also found comfort in living near or in her small town. Not me. After college, I was heading back to an actual city. For those reasons, I was leaving forever, knowing what I needed was in front of me. Walking away felt like wandering, and this time, I didn't see healing as a matter of time like before. Instead, this parting of ways could produce regret for what might have been.

We gave each other a long stare followed by sheepish smiles, communicating a mutual understanding—that our worlds were about to disappear. Again. Yeah, our puzzled looks feared closure. So, we slowly parted ways, plainly feeling we were leaving part of ourselves behind. That could have been the last time I would see Janay. Then, she called the following day and announced her estimated time of arrival. I lived by the motto, "If you stay ready, you don't have to get ready." I was mentally and prophylactically prepared for our eventual morning intimacy, even though I hadn't expected it. That morning marked a new beginning for Janay and me.

When I told my college roommate, Andre, that I had gone to see Janay, he shook his head and never looked up from his homework.

"I thought you'd be excited for me,"

"There's a reason you don't go back. But thanks to you, I have something to write in my journal."

He was taking a class that required him to keep a daily journal.

Janay and I began regular conversations, and the next month, she drove up for a weekend visit. Andre saw Janay as she got out of the car.

"Hey man, Janay is wearing those jeans," he said. We both understood him to mean that her tight jeans looked good on her. Then, he further clarified what he meant: "Janay has put on a few pounds and looks great," he said.

Indeed, both things can be true. The following month before we'd reunite again, Janay called.

"I'm two weeks late with my cycle, and I have thrown up every morning; I might be pregnant," she said.

"Not a chance, and stressing about it may prolong its arrival. Give it a few days," I said.

A few days later, she called crying and with unexpected news: "I'm so sorry. So sorry. I wanted to tell you."

"Tell me what?"

"After you and I broke up, I moved back in with my ex-boyfriend. We had a complicated history. Still, it made sense for us to get back together. I know a relationship won't work with him, and yes, we still live together. I am looking for a place of my own again. Anyway, I went to one of the doctors at my hospital and took a pregnancy test. The doctor left a voicemail that said, 'Hi Janay, your test is positive. Congratulations, you're pregnant.' My boyfriend got the message. He was smoking a darn cigar when I got home. Then, he replayed the voicemail to me. I don't know how he thinks the baby could be his. We haven't been together like that in a while. I don't know what to do."

She continued to sob.

"I gotta think, I said. "You've told me a lot." Then, a few seconds passed. "I didn't know you had a boyfriend. You should have told me."

We agreed to speak again in a couple of days and hung up. When we talked again, I could barely make out her words.

She was crying and trying to speak through her quivering voice: "I had a miscarriage," she said.

After a long breath, I spat some garbage about it being best if we returned to the lives we had before my surprise visit. Janay remained silent. We both knew what would happen the moment we ended the call. We'd never look back. Trying to console her, even with such a loss, would have felt strange. I showed as much empathy as I could muster. Still, that was a job for her boyfriend. After a few minutes, I wished her luck and hung up. Phoning this breakup was no problem at all. I could only be mad at myself for going back on my rule. Still, I felt shamefully disrespected.

For there is nothing covered, that shall not be revealed; neither hid, that shall not be known.
— Luke 12:2 King James Version

I graduated a year later and continued in a graduate program at the same school. I also secured a job as a counselor for the Student Support Services program. Then, during the week of Thanksgiving, I asked one of my student workers and good friend, Danielle, about her holiday plans.

"I'm going home," she said.

"Oh, I forgot you're from the Quad Cities. "By any chance, do you know a woman named Janay?" I gave Janay's first and last name.

"Of course, I know Janay. My sister and Janay's sister are best friends."

"Does Janay have a child?" I leaned forward and listened hard for the answer.

"Yes, I think she has a little girl, why?"

I gasped, leaned back in my chair, and told Danielle the whole story. By the end, Danielle and I came to the same conclusion—Janay probably lied to get me out of the picture. It was as if hearing the story aloud caused me to upgrade Janay's potential deceit from unlikely to probable. Indeed, everybody must be a sucker once, and that was my one for believing her so completely about miscarrying. I'm not sure why I gave a confessed cheater so much credibility. She lied about boyfriends and weekends away. Therefore, Janay might lie about a miscarriage. I heard Janay's probable lie for the first time when I retold the story. At that point, I questioned everything she told me. Was he ever an abusive boyfriend? Was he ever out of the picture? Bothered by the prospect that Janay could have lied about her miscarriage and had my child, Danielle offered to investigate over the holiday.

When Danielle returned from her holiday break, we reviewed the information she discovered against what I had. We determined with 100% certainty that Janay's baby could not be mine. That was about the time when I started having a particular recurring dream. The dream always stopped short, with me waking up startled and shaken. I wasn't sure if the dream finished when I woke up or if the vibration of my stressful feelings triggered my superpower, which interrupted the dream when I would not. I only knew that I could not create an ending the way I could with others.

In the dream, I hosted a bangin' house party. I made my way through the dancing crowd, refreshing drinks, telling jokes, and doing whatever it took to keep the party going. Then, I heard a soft, gentle knock on the door that I should not have heard over the blaring music. I walked to the door, reached out, and turned the knob. When I swung the door open, the music stopped, and the chatter quieted to only the drone of lights suddenly brightness. Everyone looked toward the door in unison, rotating their heads like spectators of a tennis match. Finally, standing in the doorway was a teenage girl. She looked up and said, "Hi. I think you are my father." At that moment, I woke up sweating each time.

I had this dream multiple times per year for over 20 years. Finally, one year, I was so disturbed by the vision that I tried to locate Janay, who had remarried, moved, and disconnected from anybody I knew. This period was before the reach of social media. So, I eventually gave up. Then, a few years ago, an ice storm threatened Atlanta, a city ill-prepared to handle inclement weather. Everything shut down. Finally, my friend, Cynthia, and I found a little Mexican restaurant open for business. As we sat, a woman walked by, and I turned my head and checked her out.

"You better leave that woman alone, as many kids as you probably have running around," Cynthia joked.

"Whoa! Think whatever you want. One thing I can say for sure is I don't have any kids."

We laughed. "But let me tell you a story about a woman named Janay."

Only two people knew the story: Andre, my college roommate, and Danielle, my college friend from Janay's hometown. I have always been private, and this was not something to brag about if bragging were my thing. As I reached the part of the story about Danielle going home as my spy, my phone rang. I looked at the caller identification, and Danielle's name sent a chill through me, accompanied by goosebumps.

"OMG, Cynthia, it's Danielle. I haven't spoken with Danielle in years, and she's calling while I tell this story."

"Aren't you going to answer it?"

"No, I am creeped out. I'm going to finish telling you this story. But now I'm beginning to think that Danielle lied to me. I will call her tomorrow."

The next day, I called Danielle. Genuinely happy to hear each other's voices, we spoke loudly and laughed after only saying each other's names.

Then, I broke the laughter with an accusatory question: "Did you lie to me about

Janay and whether she had my child?"

"I would never lie to you," she quickly replied.

I told her about my recurring dreams, my interaction with Cynthia, and the timing of her phone call.

"That's weird," she admitted. "Did you get the email I sent you last year? I sent you an obituary last April."

"I didn't open an email from you."

After a quick search, I found the email and opened the attached obituary. Unfortunately, Janay's mom had passed away.

"I knew that you dated Janay. So, I thought you might want to know that she lost her mom."

"Thanks. Now let's go back through what you told me. You said that your sister and Janay's sister were best friends, that Janay had a little girl, and because the baby was born prematurely, the timeline did not match."

"Uh-uh. I didn't say that. First, my mom and Janay's mom were best friends, joined at the hip, and second, Janay didn't have a girl. She had a boy."

Those are not the kinds of details any man would confuse, I thought. I was willing to concede only because moving on was more important.

"We have the obituary, which means names and lineage of living relatives. We also have social media," she said.

With these new clues, it took seconds to identify the young man as Jalen and find his social media profiles. He is my mirror image. Jalen's photos looked like photos of me when I was his age, although he looked a little more like my younger brother looked at his age, who is also my carbon copy. They share similar skin tones and have a slimmer build.

Danielle initiated a 3-way call by calling her mom after sending her a photo of me. Her mom answered, sighed, and said, "Oh my God. Somebody has explaining to do." Their conversation lowered in volume and faded into background noise as the volume of my intrusive thoughts muted them. So many emotions reverberated through me: self-blame, confusion, shame, humiliation, emptiness, and other painful and conflicting intensities, each fighting for prominence and powerful enough to consume me.

I began to think of the type of man I must have been to allow this to happen. For one thing, I must not be the man I thought I was, or I would not have accepted Janay's lame miscarriage excuse. It was too convenient for her unless convenience was also what I wanted. I looked closely for clues supporting the latter claim and quickly rejected that assertion. I would never knowingly let my child go. Therefore, I searched for other alternatives. For example, I wondered if this was God's way of teaching me a lesson or if this was karma for who I am or something I had done. But God does not lie or manipulate, and He has always favored me. I concluded that this mess was mine, my creation, or that I was at least a co-conspirator. My conclusion did not help. I resorted to soul-searching because I've always owned my behavior; still, I found only pain and heartbreak for a life I never had the chance to know. Jalen was my child. The realization of having an adult son sunk in. The gut-punching clarity stopped me from taking the deep breath I needed. I was finally sensing emotions besides blaming myself. Then, Danielle's mom hung up.

"How are you doing?" Danielle asked.

Danielle is a practicing children's psychologist trained to diagnose complicated matters. Since I did not want her to diagnose me, I chose my tone and words carefully because anger was the expected emotion for the moment.

"I'm alright. Being mad, after so many years, is wasted energy. I need to focus on my next steps."

"You're surprisingly calm. I'd be mad as hell. What are you gonna do?"

"I am going to send Janay a social media message in the morning. Skipping all niceties, I am going to ask if Jalen is my son?"

We hung up.

After all these years of dreaming and wondering, I was instantly aware of being a sucker for Janay's deceit. Anger began to fill me faster than optimism. I was a confused mess and was deteriorating quickly. On the one hand, this revelation excited me and provided relief, which seemed normal enough. On the other hand, this was anything but normal.

I paced in my living room, walked onto my balcony for the brisk night air, and stress-ate M&Ms and microwave popcorn. Nothing worked. I even looked toward the ceiling, where God is supposed to be, and asked obvious questions: Why now? What am I supposed to do?

There were so many potential actions popping into my head. My ego wanted me to show up—intense, loud, and wild—in Janay's city. I preferred everyone involved feeling something uncomfortable: Janay, her ex-husband, and her current husband. However, I could not choose who would hurt. Jalen could suffer in the middle, and I could not do that. In other words, left to my own devices, I might recklessly hurt people, even if that outcome were unintentional. Besides, I wanted confirmation and conversations, not revenge.

I decided to call Andre and then my brother. Both lost their words when they saw Jalen's photo. Then, my brother added details that connect us through family traits: Jalen's hairline, cheekbones, long chin, and the small gap in his front teeth. "That trick lied," my brother fumed. There were questions I wanted to ask Andre. To see what he remembered. First, I had to speak with Janay. I pulled up her Facebook profile and began to draft a message. I wrote my name.

"Hi Janay, give me a call."

Keep in mind that she can view my public profile, complete with a timeline and photos. I can also view hers.

"Hi, I think you accidentally sent me a Facebook request. Do I know you?"

"You would know me if Gordon were your maiden name, if you are or were at one time a registered nurse, and if you are from _____(city). I have a pressing question for this Janay. If I have the wrong Janay, I offer my sincerest apology and I thank you for your time, which now means a trip to the Midwest is in order."

"At first, I thought this was some kind of joke. Glad you verified. I am not a big Facebook user. Nice to hear from you, I hope you are doing well. Curious, what is so pressing? LOL"

"I will be direct. First, I want to know whether I am Jalen's biological father. It is eerie how Jalen can look like everybody in my family (me at his age, my mother, and he is a spitting image of my brother and his son). He even looks weird in caps like the men in my family because of our narrow heads, and the timeline of his birth fits. Second, I want you to know that I am not stalking you. Rather, you and I have mutual friends, actually acquaintances for you, from your hometown. One recent conversation led to another, and another led to social media. Soooooooo?"

"Oh my! I will try to ring you. This is not the sort of discussion one has online. Very inappropriate. I am very sorry, you are mistaken. This is very unsettling. I do not wish to continue this on this form. I will try to ring you tomorrow to put your concerns to rest."

"I agree with you about typing on this platform. That is why my initial message includes my number and a call request."

"I am very annoyed/upset with all of this. Try to ring you again. Unfortunately, I am only available in the a.m. 0730 to 1100."

Janay's assertion of repeatedly calling was insincere and cunning. Empty rhetoric. Indeed, she only called when I said I would not be available, and she failed to answer during the times she said she could talk. Janay's ways were to conceal, avoid, and mislead. There's more. No self-respecting woman, with nothing to hide, would whisper her voicemails when she left them. If Jalen is not my child, her need for ambiguity, sidestepping, and secrecy disappears.

"We have very different ways of handling situations. You are a worrier, and I deal with facts—truth. The truth is never annoying or upsetting, always freeing. To that end, I reached out to you as a courtesy. Yet you have returned my gesture with denying that you know me. You have threatened to shut off communication with me, all while speaking of your busy family life. I would have preferred that we agree upon a time to talk. Perhaps a weekend time would work. Let me be clear, my respect for you is the only reason I have not reached out directly to either your ex-husband or Jalen— a reckless plan-B for sure. At least your calls prove that you are willing to talk. We will find the time."

"I am not worried. I just want to set the record straight as quickly as possible so you can move on and crawl back under the rock you slithered out from under. Furthermore, your veiled threats are annoying and stupid. You have not been respectful at all. Get a life! What kind of person are you? I had only intended to talk to you by phone to set you straight. I already told you that you are mistaken. Consider yourself set."

"I will not engage in belligerent dialogue with you. It is unnecessary and unproductive.

Unfortunately, my question regarding paternity is a legitimate one, and a simple one that warrants a satisfactory answer. Whether you are the one who provides that answer is immaterial. That is not a threat and addressing this is annoying and upsetting for me as well. For so many reasons, I would like nothing more than for the answer to be "no." On that we agree. "Who am I?" you asked. I am not the man whom you said, "slithered" from under a rock, but one who will not leave a stone unturned for answers. I do not see how I am wrong for that."

I read and reread her messages and relistened to her tirades. In one voicemail, she used so much profanity that it was clear that we would not be able to discuss this matter civilly. Why the aggressive drama? In both breakups, we managed to maintain courtesy. We parted the first time civilly. Even after Janay lied and hid cheating on her live-in boyfriend to be with me, we parted a second time respectfully. Thus, her rage did not make sense. I did nothing for her to hate me. Only hate could produce her angry rants. On second thought, however, guilt is also a compelling trigger for her to lie and get emotional spontaneously. It would not surprise me if she felt a new case of guilt when she saw Jalen again because she must see me in him.

Just the same, she left me no choice but to contact Jalen directly. I sent him a carefully constructed, professional email. The first part introduces who I am, a little about his mom, and how I know I am his biological father. The second part of the email included composite photos of him and me at similar ages. Then, I concluded with what I hoped to be his next steps.

Jalen had grown well into his late 20s, an ample stretch to have had failed relationships and perhaps experienced unfaithfulness. Therefore, the discovery that he may be the result of his mother cheating could shatter Jalen's foundational paradigms: Who is his family? What are his roots? What is the connection between his mother and the strange man writing him? I felt guilty about being hopeful because the more disrupted he felt, the better for me. What man wouldn't want answers? That makes two of us. Indeed, there would be a 100% chance that he would riddle me with questions about questioning paternity. Therefore, to contain this lousy situation, I encouraged him not to reply to my email until after he spoke with his mom.

He responded the following day with a smidgen of anger expressed as a curiosity: "I spoke with my mom, and what she said doesn't add up. This doesn't make sense. You need to give me answers."

Then, he let loose a barrage of what, who, why, how, and when questions. I answered them as best I could. Next, I told him not to blame his mom for being fuzzy with the facts.

Then, I jumped ahead of more follow-up questions and said, "Rather than rely on two people's memories from so many years ago, a paternity test would answer your questions. Say the word, and I will be there within 24 hours. I don't wish to complicate your life, but only add to it. Knowing me would put a finer point on who you are inside, and I could be a resource for you in future endeavors. You also have a cool family on my side, and your grandmother prays for you every day, without knowing you exist, because she prays for all of us."

The following day, I received an email from Jalen written in the style, tone, and sentence structure of Janay. It read, "I don't wish to pursue this. Please do not contact me again. Blah, blah, blah."

Wisdom made accepting what was in front of me optional. Jalen is a man, an adult, not a minor. Therefore, I agreed to respect his wishes. However, accepting does not mean giving up. I provided my contact information and assured him it had stayed the same for almost 30 years. I reiterated that if he changed his mind, I would always look forward to his call. Meanwhile, I am hopeful that, in time, he may understand that rejecting me ignores his past and disregards a part of his identity.

When I called Andre, he presented more than emotional lip service regarding what he would do and how. Andre, a self-proclaimed pack rat, never possessed anything he thought was worth disposing of. The things he kept were almost random to those who didn't know him well. He didn't just keep some things; he kept everything. Jalen had asked me questions regarding conception that I could not answer. Andre could. Remember? Andre recorded notes in a journal for a class, which he still had in a box labeled college assignments. With Andre's recollections in his journal and Jalen's birthdate, I could narrow the date of conception to days. However, it was too late to give that to Jalen. Besides, Jalen's final response—"I don't wish to pursue this"—let me know that Janay told him the truth. Like I said, what man wouldn't want the truth?

More than enough time has passed for my recurring dream to return many times. Nevertheless, there have been no more house party fantasies and random children knocking on my door to wake me. Now and again, the blues douse me. Sometimes a young boy walking with his father sends me into deep thought and smarts a bit. Then, a realization that he may reach out follows. I no longer imagine how meeting him might happen. I only know it will happen. There would be no other reason for my recurring dream to dispirit and pursue me all these years.

Every man I've told wants to know why I haven't jumped in my car or on a plane. A few others spoke of men who have either been in my situation or, on the other side, men who learned that a child they fathered was not theirs biologically. Women friends have split down the middle on whether I should force a meeting or let it go. Again, I've accepted that with 99% certainty, Jalen is the son I've never met. I have also reconciled that Jalen is a grown man who made an adult decision not to have anything to do with me. I must accept that, but I don't have to like it. Because fighting the truth introduces baggage that may keep me stuck. I'm all about emerging. Thus, acceptance freed me from the dead weight of anguish.

CHAPTER TWENTY-THREE
WHAT IS YOUR LEGACY?

We never know what gesture, small or large, might be the tipping point in helping somebody emerge or what may trigger emergence for you. Still, it's fascinating how the magic of a moment may strike you—so individual, impactful, and internal.

A ripening force fuels us to pursue more insight and new aspirations. This phenomenon validates that the whole stories of our past serve as significant building blocks: no shame or regret, only stages in our maturation process. Each event is distracting or motivating. Some are paralyzing. Yet again, through faith, we emancipate ourselves from fear, our past reckless actions, the opinions of others, or any restriction. Too often, we identify a single transformative event in hindsight. When that happens, we've underestimated the lessons of strength used to power us through our challenges. Whether we snatch our deliverance depends on how strongly we crave the best in us.

Therefore, we must stay in the moment and remain open to cultivating the nerve for change. There is a common theme that runs through the process of emerging. Find your path. Let courage be your instrument of progress and give distance to negative people. "They will try to bring you down," said my father and grandfather. Indeed, a handful of people in my life spoke of my limitless abilities, including my father, grandfather, uncles, and coaches. They wanted me to know the power needed to soar was within me. It is within you too, and because growth lessons accumulate, one will eventually serve as a definitive moment of truth. We'll point to it as the sobering moment when Muhammad Ali stood in round 15, defeating Joe Frazier or the moment the commotion of the potential drowning stopped as my mom stood in the swimming pool. Nevertheless, we must not discount rounds one through fourteen or my mom's struggle to catch her breath before she stood.

Ultimately then, emerging occurs when the individual makes it happen. Then, self-doubt disappears, and the force of habit follows. Therefore, figuring out things and overcoming challenges embody the meaning of self-reliance. For example, my father urged me to search for answers as a child. When I would ask my father a question, he often responded, "You're in school; figure it out." He was right back then, and I knew it after he followed up to ensure I found the answer. Years later, Kobe Bryant added more context to my father's quips. An interviewer remarked, "It's either you have it, or you don't." Kobe responded:

That sounds like excuses to me. You gotta figure it out. Right. If you really have an obsession to figure it out, you will figure it out. And every puzzle is constructed differently. A. I.'s (Allen Iverson's) situation when he came into the league was different than mine; Mike's (Michael Jordan's) situation in Chicago was different than mine. Everybody has a different puzzle, man. You just gotta figure out your own puzzle.[6]

Thus, emerging is figuring out your puzzle and stepping decisively into your future. Learning that I had command over my thoughts and the authority to rewrite my nightmares was a corner piece to my puzzle. However, there's a 100% chance that your story differs from mine. What is your plan to become unstoppable?

I have provided a list of developmental precepts that will usher you through the emerging process by helping you answer your questions of purpose. In other words, you've emerged when you allow the answers to your questions of purpose to guide you. Those precepts are:

1. Self-acceptance
2. Self-help (creativity and using resources)
3. Self-discovery
4. Self-affirmation

We discussed wearing a figurative backpack in chapter 17. In that backpack, we will carry 2-pound rocks. We will label each rock as a skill that we may use to either protect us from something or to move us forward. What you carry is personal. Then, because of the weight of each stone, we must only take what we need.

Katz, D., & Rodriguez, A. (Producers). (2018, December 31). Alex Rodriguez and Big Cat interview Kobe Bryant - The Corp [Video]. The Corp With A-Rod and Big Cat. https://YouTu.be/ndGZU2BwAVY

Of course, I would never tell anybody what should be in their backpacks. But since the backpack is my metaphor, I've decided that it comes preloaded with four stones, each of which will help you answer your questions of purpose.

Stone 1: Self-Acceptance

Self-acceptance is the basis for all positive human interaction. Accepting yourself equips you to know your needs. Accepting who you are will also make you feel comfortable interacting with everyone, regardless of differences, because it only requires being yourself. That means not getting hung up on fitting in, such as wearing name brands to impress people. A college buddy used to say, "A raggedy car beats a dressed-up walk any day of the week." So, he saved money and bought a car with money others might have used for their wardrobe. Other questionable assimilation behaviors include withholding blessing a meal in front of mixed company. Some lie, brag, laugh, or compete, deliberately trying to impress. In other words, what other people might think carries weight for so many Americans. Yet, it carries no weight for you once you've accepted who you are. Accepting who you are alleviates insecurities.

To be clear, saying that accepting who you are doesn't mean being okay with being a mess. For example, people who "accept" always being late, not finishing what they start, or merely passing instead of pursuing A grades are pretenders, ultimately insecure. Picking up yourself and demanding excellence is power.

Some disturbing social trends in the United States include:

- Increasing political polarization and division
- Rising hate crimes and discrimination against marginalized groups
- Declining trust in institutions and the media
- Growing economic inequality

However, a more controversial trend is body positivity. On the one hand, the idea that all bodies are worthy of respect and should be celebrated, regardless of their size or shape, is not controversial. However, respecting your body shouldn't mean mistreating it is okay. Therefore, a 400-pound person wearing a half-shirt is not a celebratory event, and my saying that is not an example of body shaming. Newsflash: Nobody is perfect as they are. Finally, we should not celebrate mediocrity, no matter the category. Instead, celebrate success.

That was the case with Mary Ann, my client who lost over 200 pounds. Mary Ann embraced who she was early in life. Accepting herself did not mean it was okay to live a less-than-optimal life. Knowing that morbid obesity was an invitation to chronic illnesses and an arduous road to early death, she attempted to change. One afternoon, I was speaking with Mary Ann, and she said, "This is the first time I haven't failed at losing weight. I assumed I would fail this time too. I believed that I'd do a few sessions, decide it was too hard, and quit."

Mary Ann figured out things about herself along the way—her power. Then, she dispensed permanent goodbyes to self-doubt, helplessness, and underachieving. When she hit her stride, nothing could stop her.

Some people have Kobe Bryant's "obsession to figure it out." Another example may be my friend Keith's approach to learning to skate (in chapter one). It was as if he knew he'd be a great skater after 200 falls, so he rushed through the first 199. In other words, he embraced completing as many falls as it would take to become his best. That "obsession" is also what drove him to pursue medicine. I caught up with Keith while completing this book. He ultimately became a respected trauma surgeon.

Before coaching Mary Ann, she must have failed at weight loss programs as many times as Keith fell while learning to skate. Neither of them knew which attempt would bring success until it did. Still, each failure or fall led to their victories. In other words, each setback was growth for them, increasing their understanding of their capabilities. As a result, they healed from past failures and deliberately stayed clear of pessimism and pessimists. In such a context, *Emerge, Be You!* means battling and defeating the bully in your mind or any presence acting against your best interests.

Stone 2: Self-Help

Self-help means that you will seek independence and interdependence. One of the earliest messages of self-reliance I embraced was the lyrics of "God Bless the Child," a song co-written and sung by Billie Holiday: "God bless the child that's got his own."

The song describes a range of independence a child should seek, such as strength, education, money, and basic needs. Moreover, the lyrics emphasize that even God blesses those who show up for themselves. Pause here because you may miss that promise if you move too fast. The song presents a clear message and promises that if you get your own, God will bless you. "Bless me with what?" you may ask. Blessings are limitless.

Unlearning "can't" may be the most challenging part of the emerging process. But as "I think I can" evolves into a can-do mentality, limitless potential demands high achievement. Eventually, you will feel like a complete instrument needing an orchestra. In other words, God will bless you with like-minded people to form working alliances once you carry your weight. We don't have to rely on the words of a song.

Let's look at self-help in nature. One male lion, out on his own, is not a weak link. He can hunt, fight, and do what it takes to survive. He is independent, solitary, fearsome, and dangerous. However, when male lions meet, and they are without a pride, they always form coalitions. The lions know their interdependent force is exponentially more menacing, making it easier to defend themselves, hunt, and intimidate other animals. Therefore, teamwork sharply increases the quality of their survival.

Humans are social beings. We thrive from each other's input. An African proverb says, "When spiderwebs unite, they can tie up a lion." How apropos. That same deadly cat, the king of the jungle, can be subdued by spiders working together. Now think about what we can do when we bring 100% of ourselves to our endeavors.

Therefore, the critical components of self-help are creativity and using your resources. Unlike animals in the wild, people aren't born knowing their power. Instead, we recognize what it takes when forced into dilemmas, and the conquering strength is there for us, repeatedly.

Kudos to granddaddy, then. Accepting his rank as his parent's least favorite child is not typical. Then again, most parents would deny liking some children more than others. Yet, there was no lump in his throat or chip on his shoulder. Instead, my grandfather adapted to turn a little something into something more—the way an only child creates worlds out of thin air, with them at the center. In such a context, granddaddy emerged long before he orchestrated his family's escape from sharecropping. Therefore, his preceding "be you" moment was when he decided to devise an escape plan years earlier. In other words, he evolved, learned, and developed the necessary business acumen years before the culminating event. Essentially, creating the world he wanted was part of who he was.

Achieving freedom and a mind for business were granddaddy's rewards. He became a wealthy landowner, successful businessman, husband, and father. Some years later, sending his children to college was another of my grandfather's achievements. One after another, his children pursued higher education until one of my uncle's sit-in protests would eventually threaten my family's lives and livelihood. I must add that when my uncle protested injustice, he was emerging and being him. It was something he learned from his dad. However, at home, his family endured death threats. The Klan ordered vendors not to deliver goods to my grandfather's store and gas station, and the sheriff threatened to arrest anybody who patronized my grandfather's businesses.

Still, some of the town's racist leadership, the Ku Klux Klan, and sheriff's officers granted my grandfather a way to remain safe and prosperous in Alabama. As the spokesperson, the sheriff assured our family's safety and that he could restore vendor relationships. Unfortunately, the news was a *quid pro quo* for granddaddy to confidentially provide the names of families who held secret meetings to discuss Black rights and who participated in those meetings. If granddaddy did that, he would be "free."

My grandfather vehemently and disrespectfully refused to be their spy. Then, the sheriff and his goons went to great lengths to change his mind. Tensions continued to grow. Teams of hooded men took turns ransacking granddaddy's house. They even pulled the foam out of pillows and couch cushions. Under different circumstances, I could imagine granddaddy doing more than wielding a gun to keep his family safe. But somehow, the mischief always happened when granddaddy was away, and the Klan threatening our pillows did not warrant payback. Finally, after all the posturing ended, granddaddy was going broke, the sheriff had plans for additional raids, and my grandmother urged my grandfather to move the family.

I said that Muhammad Ali emerged when he stood for his final round and that my mom emerged from her fear of drowning when she stood in the water. Both were physical acts. However, my grandfather proved that sometimes emerging is standing on a principle. He added values to my definition of self-help. Anybody willing to "help" themselves at the expense of others is no better than Klansmen, lousy police, biased teachers, or manipulative current or ex-partners. Undoubtedly, the most satisfying trajectory is uplifting others as you grow.

Let's take a more comprehensive look at the first three questions of purpose as they relate to self-help.

1. Who Am I?
2. What is my essence?
3. What contributions will I make?

The "me" driven direction of these questions, which I admit to having been pointing, might easily be understood as a call to work on yourself solely. However, the answers to those questions bear more responsibility than that. Indeed, we do not live, learn, and move in a vacuum. No matter how much we investigate internally and project our futures, we are not alone. As we develop, our exchanges with the environment and people test and verify our growth naturally. Human, social, and political ethics are involved.

As a college administrator and instructor, I would ask students, "What would be different about the experience of your peers if you weren't present?"

Some sighed, and others nodded, indicating an epiphanic moment.

"I did not ask the question rhetorically," I would admonish. "There should be something distinctive or significant about your presence."

I followed up with the following rhetorical questions because it took a lot of work to get an oral response:

1. Would your peers pursue better grades because you encourage or model the concept that academic excellence is essential?
2. Based on your influence, would your peers seek genuine friendships and serious relationships or have fewer bad habits?
3. Based on your influence, would your peers be less likely to hold grudges, seek retribution, or form addictions?

As you may recall, I have never drunk alcohol. Still, my college friends and teammates believed I would eventually succumb to peer pressure. That never happened. Instead, some stopped drinking, and others no longer saw the value in getting drunk because I was present. The bottom line is that your presence should serve as leadership. Whether it is passive or active, it is still leadership. Simply put, other people should be better off when you are around.

Monday morning pundits surmise that it's best to measure greatness and leadership in sports by whether an athlete improves those around them. I suspect that's why one of my coaches withheld our statistics until the end of each season. He would not allow individual performances to diminish team accomplishments. For instance, I only played during the last few seconds of blowout games as a fourth grader on the combined fourth and fifth-grade team. Still, I felt as much a part of our wins as any starter because of my coach's structure. I also had an off-the-court event, which proved my coach's commitment to our team.

A grown man said, "Imma kill y'all," as he routinely chased us kids who got off the activity bus that took us to practice. I believed his threat because he swung the large buckle end of his belt while yelling it. He often plunked us in the back or the back of our heads if we dipped and dodged the wrong way when we scattered. Then one day, my coach caught me sneaking into practice late again. He hinted that the activity bus always arrived early. My evasive answers would have worked for anyone who would accept surface answers. But his concern was genuine, and his questions were direct. Eventually, his skillful probing broke through, and I revealed my embarrassing secret: A bully had me shaken. He appeared mortified when I shared bullying as my reason for sneaking into practice late. Then, I told him the entire story. When he looked me in the eye and said, "Don't worry, son, I'll take care of it," I believed him more than the bully's threats. Coach Graves' word was his bond.

I wonder why he did it. You know, coach us kids. He was a young guy who stood 6'2", not counting his enormous and perfectly round afro, and indeed, anybody who taught discipline the way he did had more going on than volunteering to coach other people's hardheaded children. No other coach impacted my growth and development more than Walter Graves. Expecting that we play without ego, Coach collected the scorebook after each game and gave us our season's statistics at our end-of-the-year banquet. He taught us more than selfless play and XX's and O's by connecting the figurative dots between consistent effort and excellence. We were lucky to have him.

I walked to the gym from the bus without fear of villainous antics before the following practice. My calm was as intense as looking over my shoulders for random flying belt buckles days earlier. As I said, I believed my coach when he said he would take care of the tyrant problem. When I opened the gym door and saw the bully standing in the dimly lit corner, my gasp was a quick, breathy inhale. He was approximately 3 feet from me at the top of the stairs. However, the look in the eyes of so many children who ran for their lives was now in our tormentor's eyes. Two men stood in front of him. One man wielded a large knife. I watched as he retrieved the blade from his big-brimmed gangster hat, which donned a long, colorful feather. The other man pointed a practice headshot with a snub-nosed .38 revolver. I knew the gun as a "Saturday night special" because actors referred to it on sitcoms such as *Good Times*. Plus, my father had one.

Nobody looked at me. I just stood there quiet and motionless, watching the men handle my business and that of my teammates. Then, finally, my coach's voice broke my concentration. "Come to practice, son," he said from the bottom of the stairs. So, as I walked through the three men and down the stairs, I emerged to a higher stage of development. From that day forward, bullies would not choose me as their target. They knew I wouldn't go for it because I carried myself that way. I also challenged bullies by not allowing bullying on my watch. "Hey, you wouldn't do that to me. So, leave them alone," I'd say to them until three bullies chased me home a year later. With my dad's help, I learned from that too. Don't run. Never run from anyone.

To thousands of Kansas City residents, Walter Graves was their city bus driver; to others, he was a fantastic man and inspirational coach. However, looking past the knife and gun remedy, he was also a dynamic leader who taught us that a regular guy could positively change people's lives. That's right. I was learning lessons about emerging and being me back then. And there is always time to apply such lessons.

In those days, the most compelling aspect of what the men in my life taught me was situational acceptance and that "accepting" must be combined with problem-solving as the next step because that's hugely important to what it means to be a man. In other words, I had to admit that my problems were my problems and then do something about them.

Continuing to reflect, I learned that what goes into young developing minds will manifest into the people they will become. Positive and negative. Good and bad. You see this sentiment supported in nature and scripture. For example, in Proverbs 22:6 (NIV), the Bible says, "Start children off on the way they should go, and even when they are old, they will not turn from it." Proverbs 22:8 (NIV) says, "Whoever sows injustice reaps calamity, and the rod they wield in fury will be broken." Therefore, the karmic nature of self-help demands that leaders have integrity—"Soundness; Incorruptibility; Firm adherence to a code of morals." We must do the right things without considering personal gains—like the heart of a city bus driver who ensured that young boys and girls could dare to dream and not have their best dream be to survive.

I believe that learning those lessons so early and having someone commit to me the way coach Graves did is why basketball was so important to me. I had something to prove and to give back. As an athlete, student, referee, and mentor, basketball was the vehicle I used to reach people. For example, I got through to gang members and ex-convicts by refereeing their basketball leagues. The trust we built led to facilitating off-the-court life skill development sessions. I did this as part of a gang prevention program in Los Angeles. Then, coaching the basketball team in the youth ministry at my church built a bridge for us to discuss manhood and scholarship. Finally, when I mentored young people individually, basketball was my way to help them dream more and worry less about surviving.

From the outside looking in, learning and applying lessons should be manageable. Yeah, I know how you feel. Unfortunately, we cannot know which of our messes will help us later or assist others in their time of challenge and difficulty. Therefore, I cringe when people say God won't bless a mess. I don't believe that. Not completely. That is a restriction we put on God. Besides, I am living proof that God can bless anybody out of messes.

We also hear that God won't put more on you than you can handle. So true! Yet, that may also have a secondary meaning. I always thought "more" referred to a challenge or heavy burden. We use it that way to stem the momentum of pity party conversations. Then, I have realized that "God won't put more on you than you can handle" may also be valid for blessings. You must be ready to be blessed, not only out of a mess but also into your purpose. Think about it. Blessing you with your life's contribution before you can handle it may lead to catastrophe. We can all look back on opportunities, such as jobs and relationships, for which we were not ready. We can also look forward to our preparing for the not-yet. So, how do you prepare for a purpose-leading blessing? As the Billie Holiday song conveys, work to have your own.

Stone 3: Self-Preservation

Some people refer to self-preservation as the first law of nature. Such a thing sounds good until we consider that ordinary Americans' cravings and tendencies favor risk for a good time usually pairs impractical choices with pure adrenaline. Caution be damned! Next, we want more. I'm no different. I could say I comply with nature's alarm and honor my sixth sense. However, as a motorcycle rider, I risk death by rolling the dice for freedom and excitement with every ride. I am risking my health and my life. So, right away, I cannot condemn another person's walk on the wild side now and then. Jumping out of planes, deep sea diving, or bull riding in Mexico, "Do your thing," your friends may say in support. Somehow, it feels worth it, even after adversity teaches its lessons.

Therefore, the apparent observation is that our fascination and appetite for danger contradict nature. For example, nature provides all animals with instinct—reactions mediated below the conscious level. So, when animals sense danger, they run. Try catching a cricket or sneaking up on a deer. Good luck!

Similarly, self-preservation prepares humans to avoid destructive attitudes, forces, and behaviors. Next, in the search for "more," our will suspends inhibitions and makes us see irrational decisions as clear options. This is similar to the guy in chapter 16, whose doctor implored him not to smoke another cigarette. Then, with his lungs filled with cancer, he lit up before reaching his car. Thus, the definition of self-preservation may work for nature, but as I've shown, not necessarily for people. Too often, we sprint toward:

- Debt and fast money like loans, theft, or lottery
- Compulsive activities like shopping, gaming, gambling, or pornography
- Self-injury, such as cutting, hairpulling, burning, or committing suicide
- Unhealthy diets, compulsive eating, and overusing substances

No less ironic is how we run toward danger in progress. I remember when my young father hurried us kids into the car and sped toward hovering helicopters or the sounds of fire trucks. I honestly hadn't a clue that we weren't innocent bystanders. Instead, we were ambulance-chasers, present to feed the rush rather than rush to intervene. Not long ago, one of my clients ended our session early so she could walk to the end of the block and watch firefighters fight a chemical blaze burning down a building. Nowadays, the adrenaline rush is to record and post online. Thus, those who took the time to travel toward danger satisfy their cravings by watching the trainwrecks of people's lives on social media. There's a lesson here. One way to self-preserve is by protecting our eyes.

Regarding self-destruction, our eyes trigger most behaviors that get us into trouble. For example, one of the most accusatory questions you can ask is, "What are you looking at?" A spirited debate often ensues when these fighting words hit their mark. This reaction is because the antagonist understands the power of messages we send and retrieve through our eyes. Everyone knows about the power of a glance. Our eyes communicate love and hate, interest and disinterest, and unlimited messages. Consider children who straighten up with only a look from their parents or how the same parents may make their children smile from closed-lip gazes. While training inexperienced models, former supermodel Tyra Banks coined "smizing," which means to smile with your eyes. Athletes can detect fear in the eyes of their opponents, and when two people attract each other, they make as much eye contact as possible. The point here is that self-preservation involves protecting what comes in and goes out through our eyes.

Stone 4: Self-Discovery

The final stone preloaded in your backpack is self-discovery, which we describe as the fuel for exploration. Carrying this stone means that the more you learn about yourself, the more you want to discover. We have so much to claim. Indeed, through experience, education, family history, or faith, we learn there is a purpose for our lives and the clues to piece it together. Remarkably, connecting piece after piece reveals, in greater detail, our reasons for being here, the contributions we will make, and how we will get there.

I could offer the seminal moment when circus elephants remember or discover their strength as an act of self-discovery for animals. If only there were something natural about being held captive and trained to adopt humiliating behaviors through violence and starvation. Perhaps scripture might offer a more apt explanation. In Lamentations 3:40 (NIV), the Bible says, "Let us examine our ways and test them, and let us return to the Lord." "Examine" describes our necessary action. First, we must inspect or look. Then, the scripture says to "test" our ways. Another word for test in this context is scrutinizing. Our "ways" include our history, culture, and behavior. You might imagine this teaching as why my elders gave historical context to my progress. You'd be right. Knowing my grandfather was never scared during a time when we'd understand if he were, encouraged me. So, I'm never scared. Likewise, my family values and my faith anchor me, and I stand when life throws a sucker punch or a knockout blow, both meant to take me out. I convert hard knocks into strength, sound decision-making, and clear vision.

Similarly, you must know that circumstances may test your thoughts and beliefs, and you must always pass—today, tomorrow, and days to come. Life is a struggle, and tomorrow you may be somewhere between fighting, testing, or standing in victory.

The apostle Paul writes in Romans 12:3 (NIV), "For by the grace given me I say to every one of you: Do not think of yourself more highly than you ought, but rather think of yourself with sober judgment, in accordance with the faith God has distributed to each of you."

This scripture inserts morality into self-discovery because humility is critical to moral development and ethical learning. The verse implores us to keep a level head while examining ourselves because we all have a measure of faith, which is evidence that we all have a purpose. It is up to us to discover, believe, and do it. The scripture doesn't say other people must believe in your assignment.

Allow me to share part of my conversation with my mother. It was May 2021, and we felt some relief from being fully vaccinated against COVID-19. Still, the deadly virus and its mutated Delta variant spread globally and locally. The news favored doom and gloom stories, and mom and I sometimes narrated in the background. In these moments of crisis, people woke up to so much. Their normal had changed, and most people found dealing with an uncertain future challenging. Violence, crime, housing costs, food prices, hate speech, mental health incidences, and gun sales quickly rose to unprecedented numbers, and so did the nation's temperature. These were the news stories and reports of widening gaps in education, politics, and income. Some people reevaluated what was important to them; others whined about how their regretful decisions walloped them. On this day, a reporter interviewed a man about his lost business and why he lost it. While recounting the unfortunate timing of his failed new venture, his voice cracked as he held back tears.

"Here we go again," I said.

Mom shook her head. I lowered the television volume and spoke over his story by brainstorming ways he could have transformed his business. I gave his hard-luck account creative, business-saving pivots. One thing led to another. And before we knew it, mom and I talked, in general terms, about people getting or not getting what they want out of life. That's just like us. Our conversations are almost always developed organically and often focus on saving the world. After making our cases for approximately thirty minutes, she hit me with what I initially thought to be a less-than-profound statement for her.

In response to those who fall short, she said, "They just didn't have enough faith."

Because this was so simplistic, I resisted. I'm good at debate; offering other points of view is a gift. This occasion may have been the first time my mother relented in all my years. When she said, "I don't know," to one of my last hypothetical questions, I had finally won. However, I didn't feel as good as I thought I might. I wasn't even sure this moment would ever come. Maybe I didn't feel the thrill of victory or that I had finally arrived because it was my mother. Perhaps it was my troubling position on the subject matter. Opposing faith as the answer to all problems felt lousy and left me contemplating further.

I felt blah walking to my car. Spiritually conflicted, I repeatedly replayed our point, counterpoint, in my head. How I led mom into a trap took skill, and incorporating enough supporting scripture took mastery. However, during the weeks following that conversation, my interpretations of her unconvincing words evolved. Her point of view left me with profound insight and feelings of guilt. If my opposition to faith could be so thorough, I may be one of the people needing more.

Just like that, she beat me again. She dropped something light that grew heavier and clearer as days turned to weeks. That conversation and my subsequent revelation were the impetus for writing this book. If anybody could make me think it was my mother. Being so profound without trying and constantly bringing new insights is how I describe my mother in conversations. The debate competition was only in my head. Mom wasn't competing; I was. Mom will know she is undefeated when she reads this chapter; I am relieved that she won.

Mom is my grandfather's daughter. Hahahahaha, duh! You know what I mean. She is the fruit of the same parents, whose blood, steeped in integrity and faith, flows through to me. Thus, studying your ancestors, celebrating traditions, embracing your culture, and understanding where you come from can open your eyes to how beautiful and unique you are. Ideally, you would get information through stories passed down through generations. But for people without complete histories or people around them to share these stories, genealogy sites, libraries, and city or county records are good places to start.

No matter where you draw information from, it only presents examples of challenges already conquered and some that may need conquering. Ultimately, each account shapes a picture of what is possible, not what you must become.

How will emerging and being you look in your life? How might you be tested, and what determines whether you pass? What will be the equivalent of Ali's round 15 in your life, and will you stand for your victory? Faith says you will! Just believe in your dreams. Only carry the stones you need in your backpack. Answer your questions of purpose. Finally, remember who you are and whose you are. Emerge. Be you!

ACKNOWLEDGMENTS

Most importantly, thank you, God, for guiding me and blessing me with the courage and strength to pursue my dreams. Your love and grace sustain me, and your presence in my life humbles me.

I am grateful to the influential men who have guided me. To my grandfather, Sultan Moore—who instilled a strong sense of values and discipline—thank you for giving me an example of manhood that pushes me to be my best. To my father, Hughes Suffren, Sr.—who showed me what true strength and resilience look like—thank you for your presence, life lessons, and support. Coaches Walter Graves and Carl Taylor, thank you for teaching me the importance of character, perseverance, and teamwork. Your mentorship and guidance have been instrumental in shaping me into the person I am today. Finally, to my brother, Adrian Suffren, thank you for always bringing common sense to complex conversations the way Granddaddy would. I feel incredibly lucky to have hit the sibling jackpot with you. You're more than a family member; you're my kindred spirit and loyal friend.

To my mother, Jacquelyn Suffren, thank you for your example of godliness and for teaching us to be a praying family of faith. To the rest of my immediate family—Viesta, Rainy, Angelica, and Valencia—as well as my close friends, thank you for your unwavering love and encouragement. Your belief in me has been a constant source of inspiration. I am forever grateful for the countless ways you have supported me. Thank you, Monique Kelly, for helping me design the cover for this book, being a sounding board, and urging me to stop editing. If not for you, I'd still be editing.

Finally, I want to express my appreciation to all the readers who have taken the time to engage with my work. Your support means the world to me, and I hope that *Emerge: Be You!* inspires you to tap into the limitless potential that lies within you.

Printed in the USA
CPSIA information can be obtained
at www.ICGtesting.com
LVHW020321150224
771724LV00016B/1008